Rome's Vestal Virgins

Rome's Vestal Virgins examines one of the most important state cults in ancient Rome and the role of the virgin priestesses in ancient Roman religion and society. It analyses the rituals these priestesses enacted, both the public rituals performed in connection with official state rites and festivals, and the private rites associated only with the order itself.

Wildfang argues that the Vestals did not participate in Rome's family structure and that this was done to ensure that the Vestals could represent Rome as a whole in the religious sphere without any risk of pollution from a family cult. She contends that the rituals the Vestals performed on behalf of the Roman state were neither fertility rites nor reflections of traditional female activities. Instead they were rites concerned with purification, storage and the preparation of harvested grain for food use, or sometimes a combination of all three areas at once.

This exploration of the function of the Vestal Virgins in the changing Roman world, exposed to new and different cultures through the expansion of the Roman Empire, provides a new and penetrating investigation of a cult which was at the very centre of ancient Roman religion.

Robin Lorsch Wildfang is Project coordinator for Studenterkurset i Sønderjylland.

Rome's Vestal Virgins

A study of Rome's Vestal priestesses
in the late Republic and early Empire

Robin Lorsch Wildfang

Routledge
Taylor & Francis Group

LONDON AND NEW YORK

First published 2006
by Routledge
2 Park Square, Milton Park, Abingdon, Oxon OX14 4RN

Simultaneously published in the USA and Canada
by Routledge
711 Third Avenue, New York, NY 10017

Routledge is an imprint of the Taylor & Francis Group, an informa business

© 2006 Robin Lorsch Wildfang

Typeset in Garamond by
Book Now Ltd

British Library Cataloguing in Publication Data
A catalogue record for this book is available from the British Library

Library of Congress Cataloging in Publication Data
Wildfang, Robin Lorsch.
Rome's vestal virgins: a study of Rome's vestal priestesses in the late
Republic and Early Empire/Robin Lorsch Wildfang.
      p. cm.
  Includes bibliographical references and index.
  1. Vestals. 2. Rome—Religion. 3. Women and religion—Rome. I. Title.

BL815.V4W55 2006
292.6'1–dc22   2006005626

ISBN10: 0–415–39795–2 (hbk)
ISBN10: 0–415–39796–0 (pbk)
ISBN10: 0–203–96838–7 (ebk)

ISBN13: 978–0–415–39795–7 (hbk)
ISBN13: 978–0–415–39796–4 (pbk)
ISBN13: 978–0–203–96838–3 (ebk)

To Leah who (almost) arrived with this book

Contents

Preface

In the last quarter of the twentieth century, scholarly interest in the history of women in antiquity has grown steadily, until now, at the beginning of the twenty-first, it encompasses countless books and articles on almost every aspect of ancient women's lives. Women's roles in marriage have been examined,[1] as have their roles in the family.[2] Women's influence on Roman politics has been discussed,[3] as has their legal position, their economic possibilities and, most recently, their place in religion.[4] Yet, surprisingly, despite this interest and the many advances in knowledge and methodology that have resulted from it, while scholars have examined various important aspects of the Vestal Virgins, the only major female Roman state priesthood, and their cult, no one has undertaken a thorough monographic examination of the ancient literary sources for these priestesses since Guizzi's well-known but largely legalistic Italian study in the 1960s.[5]

This omission is even more singular in that the Vestal order was at the heart of the Romans' state religion, and necessary to the city's continued existence. An understanding of the Vestals' rites, activities and historical roles, as portrayed in our ancient sources, ought to be of interest, not only to those studying women and gender in antiquity, but also to scholars of ancient religion and indeed to anyone interested in the Romans' views of themselves and their state.

This work is an attempt to fill this void. It focuses primarily on the Vestals and their cult in the years between the end of the Second Punic War and the end of the first century CE, the period in which most of our ancient sources for these priestesses were writing, and the period of greatest interest to students of classical literature. The rituals, privileges and restrictions which surrounded these priestesses, and made up the body of their cult, provide the framework for most of this book, but to these considerations are appended two chapters, which examine the Vestals' history as recorded by the Romans.

Within this framework, the book considers the significance of these various rituals, privileges and duties, and develops a two-pronged argument. On the one hand, it argues that the rituals the Vestals performed on behalf of the Roman state were neither fertility rites nor reflections of traditional female activities as has so often been postulated. Instead, they were rituals concerned with purification, storage and the preparation of harvested grain for food or sometimes a combination of these three activities. On the other hand, it contends that many of the most mysterious aspects of the Vestals and their cult can be explained by the theory that the Vestals were simultaneously members of the Roman women's citizen class, the *virgines*, and non-members of Rome's family structure. This dual status was important because it ensured that the Vestals could represent the Roman state as a whole on the religious level, without any risk of pollution from individual family cults.

It is hoped this book will be of interest to the general reader as well as satisfy the specialist in Roman religion, gender studies and history. In the interests of the former, English translations of the ancient sources are included in the main text and endnotes, while in the interests of the latter the original texts are included in an appendix.

Notes

1 S. Treggiari 1991.
2 J. Hallett 1984.
3 R. Bauman 1992.
4 See, for example, R. Kraemer 1992; A. Staples 1998.
5 F. Guizzi 1968. This work, while seminal in its way, obviously does not make use of the many advances in methodology which have taken place since the early 1960s, when the book was written. Also, since it concentrates largely on the Vestals' legal position and status, it leaves room for a consideration of the many other aspects of the Vestals and their cult.

   J. Saquete's Spanish work from 2000 is largely a study of the archaeological and epigraphical sources, while M. C. Martini's 2004 work is in Italian and arrived on my desk too late to appear in this book, although her two earlier articles (M. C. Martini 1997a, 1997b) on which it is based do figure frequently.

Acknowledgements

My sincere thanks are due to the Carlsbergfond of Denmark, who generously provided me with three full years of financial support for the writing of this book and to the University of Southern Denmark, who provided me with office space and many congenial and helpful colleagues during that same period. Susanne William Rasmussen and Jacob Isager read an early draft of this work and, together with my companions of the Freja study group, provided valuable oral commentaries on my ideas and work underway. The American Academy at Rome housed me on two memorable research trips to Rome and provided the photographs found within this work. Routledge's editorial and production teams ably saw this book through the production process. Thanks are also owed to my former students, at Williams College and the University of Southern Denmark, whose questions in two Roman religion courses I taught led to the idea of this book.

Finally, I wish to thank my family and friends for helping me in many ways throughout the long process of writing this book.

Abbreviations

Except where otherwise noted, abbreviations of periodical titles, ancient authors and their works are taken from *L'Année Philologique*, the *Oxford Latin Dictionary* or Liddell, H. G. and Scott, R. (1925–) *Greek–English Lexicon*.

ANRW   Temporini, H. and Haase, W. (eds) (1972–) *Aufstieg und Niedergang der römischen Welt*.

CIL   *Corpus Inscriptionum Latinarum*.

DnP   Cancik, H. and Schneider, H. (eds) (1997–2004) *Der neue Pauly*.

ILS   Dessau, H. (1892–1916) *Inscriptiones Latinae Selectae*, 3 vols.

MRR   Broughton, T. R. S. (1951–1956) *The Magistrates of the Roman Republic*, 3 vols.

OCD   *Oxford Classical Dictionary*.

OLD   *Oxford Latin Dictionary*.

PIR   Stein, A. and Petersen, L. (eds) (1952–1966) *Prosopographia Imperii Romani*.

RE   Pauly, A. *et al.* (eds) (1894–1978) *Real-Encyclopädie der klassischen Altertumswissenschaft*.

RIC   Mattingly, H. *et al.* (eds) (1923–1984) *The Roman Imperial Coinage*, 9 vols.

TLL   *Thesaurus Linguae Latinae*.

Introduction

> I shall increase and grow ever more famous, so long as the priest and the silent Virgin solemnly climb to the Capitol.
>
> (Hor. *Ode.* 3.30.8–9)

As the poet Horace emphasizes, the Vestal Virgins were synonymous with the continued existence and safety of Rome. As long as the Vestals performed their appointed religious duties, Rome, the most powerful and foremost city in the ancient world, would remain. These six priestesses, selected as children and committed to a minimum of thirty years' service, lived together in a house beside the *aedes Vestae* in the Roman Forum and were responsible for the care and preservation of the city's central hearth fire within this *aedes*, a fire whose quenching threatened the very fundament of the city's existence, the *pax deorum*. Along with this central responsibility, the Vestal Virgins performed many other unique religious tasks and duties and were marked out from other Roman women by a number of special privileges, chief among them the right to decide over their own properties and fortunes. They also risked special punishment in the form of burial alive should they fail to perform their most central duties of preserving their virginity and ensuring that the fire on the hearth of the *aedes Vestae* burned perpetually.

These priestesses were not only synonymous with the continued existence and safety of Rome, but also inseparable from the Romans' view of themselves and their state. Whatever else one says about the Vestals, these priestesses were, in the eyes of the Romans themselves, from Rome's very beginning at the heart of what it was to be Roman. Without the Vestals and their cult, Rome as we know it would not have existed. Without the Vestals and their cult, what it was to be Roman would have had a very different meaning.

Literary sources

Before we turn to an examination of the Vestal Virgins and their cult, though, a few explanatory words are necessary on a number of specific issues. The first of these is the nature of the evidence available to us, and the problems inherent in the use of this evidence. One of the major problems in any modern study of ancient Roman religion is the haphazard nature of our ancient literary sources. No ancient work exists that describes Roman religion or its rituals in an organized and detailed fashion. Instead, we are reduced to extracting titbits of relevant and semi-relevant information from the works of authors who are not primarily interested in informing their readers about Roman religious rituals and beliefs.

Our evidence for the Vestals, therefore, is drawn from a wide variety of sources. Cicero's philosophical works, the histories of Livy and Dionysius of Halicarnassus, Plutarch's biographies and Ovid's *Fasti*, all provide us with extensive accounts of the Vestals and their activities. The works of various antiquarian sources, such as Varro, Valerius Maximus, Festus and Aulus Gellius, supplement these accounts. Brief references to these priestesses and their cult can also be found in Suetonius, Tacitus and Juvenal as well as a string of other ancient authors.

This wide variety of sources presents the modern scholar with a series of related problems. The first problem inherent in the use of the ancient literary evidence as sources for the Vestals and their cult arises from these sources' varied dates. With the exception of Cicero and a few minor references to the Vestals in Varro and other early Roman antiquarians, all of our literary sources for the Vestals are from the age of Augustus or later. This means that the Vestal cult portrayed in this book is largely that described by sources writing some 700 years after the same cult's supposed founding at Rome, and may bear little resemblance to that of the early Republican or Regal period, despite our sources' implicit claims to the contrary.

Second, our sources' own interests and intentions can shape the evidence with which they present us. A poet's literary purposes, for example, can easily colour his explication of a particular religious custom, as do Ovid's in his description of the origins of the *Vestalia* in his *Fasti*. As an explanation for the role of a donkey in these rites, the poet offers a story of how Vesta narrowly escaped rape at the hands of Priapus because of a donkey's braying.[1] This story appears only in the *Fasti*, and clearly mirrors the poet's account of a similar meeting between the same god and Lotis earlier in the work.[2] This close parallelism immediately raises the suspicion that the story is nothing other than a poetic invention on Ovid's part and is included in his work for artistic reasons, but is not something that should be viewed as a general Roman explanation of the origins of the rite.[3] Even when the author in question is an historian, his evidence can also be suspect. Livy, for example, writing under the rule of Augustus, on occasion demonstrably chooses a version of the facts that supports some particular scheme of the emperor, despite the clear existence of evidence for another earlier Republican tradition.[4] Likewise, the overarching themes of his work often lead him to omit some historical events and expand on others, all depending on what he himself finds most immediately relevant or appropriate to his work. Thus, one problem with using ancient literary sources as evidence for any Roman religious practice is that they can never be accepted entirely at face value. This is no less true of those sources relating to the Vestals than of those relating to other aspects of Roman religion.

Previous scholars working on the Vestal Virgins have, with few exceptions, chosen to disregard these problems. On the one hand, they have generally accepted the information provided in our ancient sources at face value without any discussion of how these sources' intentions might colour this information. On the other, they have shown little concern with the relative dates of their sources and have instead described an order that is seemingly static and unchanging from its foundation to its dissolution. This work, however, takes a more cautious approach.

First, it should be emphasized that the Vestal order and cult described in these pages is largely that known to the Romans of the late Republic and early Empire, the period from which most of our sources stem. Whether this order and cult differ extensively from those of earlier or later periods is unknown and must remain so, without the unlikely discovery of contemporary sources for these other periods. Second, recognizing that to say anything at all about the Vestals, a scholar must assemble evidence from the wide variety of sources named above, despite the possible colouring of their literary intentions, I have generally chosen to accept ancient descriptions of actual ritual practices, duties and privileges as reflective of contemporary reality. At the same time, however, I have treated the many poetic and historical explanations of the origins and significance of these rites, duties and privileges with extreme caution. I have taken this dual approach because it seems to me that rituals, duties and privileges are factual things, which would have been known to a good many of the Romans who made up our authors' contemporary audiences, whereas explanations of the origins and significance of these same rituals, duties and privileges are more easily subject to our sources' personal whims and interpretations. Too broad a departure from reality in the case of the former would have been noticed and commented on by these audiences, while in the case of the latter, variations and vagaries would more likely be accepted as personal opinion or belief given the uncertainties of time and distance.

Other sources

Two other major sources of evidence for the Vestals and their cult exist, the archaeological remains of the *atrium* and *aedes Vestae*, and the numismatic evidence. As these sources have been well examined in José Carlos Saquete's *Las Virgines Vestales* and are outside my own particular field of expertise, I have not treated them separately in this work.[5] At the same time, since they can on occasion throw light on our literary sources' evidence, I have included references to them when they are relevant to a particular topic under discussion. The reader interested primarily in these types of evidence for the Vestals is referred to Saquete's work for a thorough consideration of their import.

Religious terminology

A few words are also necessary on the meaning of the technical terminology of religious studies frequently used by scholars in discussing the Vestals. Such a digression is particularly essential in that many, if not all, of these scholars use this terminology without defining what they mean by the various terms. Most glaringly, scholars frequently argue that the Vestals are fertility priestesses but never once define what they mean by fertility. The term 'fertility' is a relatively vague one that, particularly to a layman, has many different connotations. Is a scholar using this term in its broadest sense, as defined by Mircea Eliade, a sense which covers rites of invigoration (that is rites 'aimed at stimulating the growth of crops, the fecundity of men and beasts, and the supply of needed sunshine and rainfall throughout the year'),[6] harvest rites (that is rites which celebrate the successful completion of the agricultural year) and many things in between?[7] Alternatively, does the author mean more precisely those rites connected specifically with ensuring the reproduction of human or animal offspring and/or the growth of new crops? Or is something else entirely implied? This uncertainty and vagueness can lead to misunderstandings on the part of readers, and makes the use of this term and others like it more or less valueless.

Because of this, it is important to clarify here what is meant by the various technical terms used in this book. There are four terms in particular that must be defined, the first three narrowing the various meanings of Eliade's definition of 'fertility', the last connected solely with purification. First, 'fertility' is not used here in the broad sense of Eliade's definition. It is, to my mind, too general to be of real use to us as a tool for understanding the religious functions of the Vestals, encompassing as it does nearly every form of religious rite. Instead, the term is broken down into its constituent categories, with the term 'fertility' itself used in a more limited sense to describe only those rites connected specifically with the reproduction of people, livestock or crops, that is Eliade's 'rites of invigoration'. Rites having to do with the harvesting of crops have been separated out from the overarching term 'fertility rites' and are instead called harvest rites, while those having to do with the storage of these crops for use either as food or as seed in the following agricultural year are called storage rites. Finally, by purificatory rites is meant rites that involve the cleansing of a sacred object, place or person from all forms of pollution that would render it or them unfit to come in contact with the religious sphere.

Structure of the book

The following chapters, then, combine an examination of the ancient literary sources on the Vestals with a consideration of modern scholarly efforts on the various topics raised by this evidence and a further analysis of these topics' significance for our understanding of these priestesses' role in the religion and society of the late Roman Republic and early Empire. The first two chapters discuss the various ritual duties of the order that together suggest the order's main religious focus was on purification together with the symbolic storage and preparation of harvested grain for food. Chapter 1 examines the daily or regular religious duties that the Vestals primarily performed within the confines of the *aedes Vestae*. Included here is a consideration of these priestesses' special dress and hairstyle. Chapter 2 completes the consideration of the Vestals' religious duties by exploring those rituals the priestesses performed in public, primarily in connection with nine annual rites associated with the state cult.

The next three chapters focus on those elements of the Vestal cult that generally can be explained by and thus together demonstrate the theory that the Vestals were at the same time members of the Roman women's citizen class *virgines* and non-members of any of the individual families that together made up Rome's underlying family structure. Chapter 3 discusses the rules and rituals for initiation into the Vestal order while Chapter 4 takes up the various issues associated with the Vestals' virginity and the punishment that resulted from a Vestal's commission of the *crimen incesti*, the loss of this virginity. Chapter 5 considers the priestesses' legal and financial situation.

Finally, the last two chapters of the book investigate the various ancient historical accounts of the Vestals. Chapter 6 examines the Vestals' place in the late Republic's and early Empire's own version of Roman history, that is to say the Vestals' appearances in Roman historical accounts of the centuries between the founding of Rome and the end of the Second Punic War. Chapter 7 deals with the historical appearances of the Vestals from the end of this war to the end of the first century CE for which we have contemporary or almost contemporary sources and which are therefore more likely to be factual in nature.

Notes

1 Ov. *Fast.* 6.319–348.
2 Ov. *Fast.* 1.391–440.
3 C. Newlands 1995: 128–129. For more general discussions of Ovid's *Fasti*, see also J. Miller 1991.
4 For example, Livy's account of Cossus' *spolia opima* (Liv. 4.20.5 ff.) has been seen by many scholars as a piece of propaganda designed to support Augustus' denial of the *spolia opima* to his general Crassus after the defeat of Deldo in 27 BCE. For recent discussions of this case, see H. Flower 2000; P. Kehne 1998.
5 J. C. Saquete 2000.
6 M. Eliade 1984: 154.
7 M. Eliade 1984: 154–156.

1   Within the *aedes Vestae*

Chapters 1 and 2 consider the various ritual duties of the Vestal order and argue that taken together, these duties suggest that the order's main religious focus was on purification together with the preparation and storage of sacred flour-like substances that were meant to symbolize Rome's food stores. This chapter examines the Vestals' more regular or daily religious activities and duties performed primarily within the confines of their precinct, while Chapter 2 takes up the various annual or semi-annual public rites associated with other state cults in which the Vestals participated.

Vesta

Perhaps the best place to begin, though, is with a consideration of the goddess Vesta, whom these priestesses primarily served. All of our ancient sources are agreed on two central facts about this goddess.[1] On the one hand, she was most fundamentally associated with the domestic fire that burned on the hearth of the *aedes Vestae* and on the individual hearths of all Roman homes. On the other, she and her representative fire were essential to the preservation and continuation of the Roman state. As long as her cult continued, so would Rome. This last is a particularly important point to emphasize at the outset of our consideration of Rome's Vestal Virgins. Whatever more precise ritual functions the Vestals fulfilled, their cult was bound up with Rome itself. Without the Vestals and their cult, there would in the Romans' eyes have been no Rome.

A number of ancient sources also associate Vesta with the earth. Ovid for example writes that 'Vesta is the same as the earth' (Ov. *Fast.* 6.267–268) while Dionysius of Halicarnassus observes that 'Vesta is the earth' (D. H. 2.66.3).[2] Other ancient scholars follow suit.[3] Modern scholars joining archaeological evidence to these descriptions have argued that Vesta should also be seen as a chthonic goddess of the underworld.[4] If correct, this association could provide further evidence for the postulate that one of the Vestals' major roles was purificatory in nature. As priestesses of a chthonic goddess, the Vestals might well have had a concern with the purification and pacification of the dead.[5]

Other ancient literary sources refer to Vesta not only with the expected title *virgo* but also with the epithet *mater*,[6] and the same epithet is also used in a number of ancient epigraphic inscriptions referring to the goddess.[7] Modern scholars have seen the ancients' use of *mater* to describe Vesta as evidence for the possibility that the goddess should be seen not as a virgin goddess but as a maternal one, giving *mater* its standard translation as 'mother'.[8] Both *virgo* and *mater*, however, have other subsidiary meanings, which would not have been separated in a Roman's mind. As P. Watson has shown, the word *virgo* was used only of girls who were both virgins (in our technical sense of the word) and citizens.[9] Likewise, to a Roman the word *mater* would have meant not only 'mother' but also 'matron' or more technically 'a woman belonging to the class of married Roman citizen women'.[10] The use of both these terms in connection with Vesta can perhaps have been meant to signal not so much that she was both a virgin and a mother as that she was representative of the two major classes of Roman citizen women, the *virgines* and the *matrones.* If so, then this suggests that the goddess and her priestesses were in some way integrally bound up with Rome's women.

At the same time, however, it should also be emphasized at the outset that both ancient and modern scholars implicitly agree in excluding certain areas of Roman female life from their considerations of Vesta's significance. Therefore the argument that is often made, that the Vestals' ritual duties were meant to represent on a religious level the traditional work of women, cannot be correct. There is, for example, no evidence to suggest that Vesta was considered the goddess of weaving, marriage or childrearing, three main preoccupations of ordinary Roman women. Some of the Vestals' ritual activities may have been symbolic re-enactments of ordinary women's domestic duties,[11] but not all traditional female domestic duties were re-enacted as part of the Vestal cult. The Vestals can thus hardly be seen as simply the ritual representatives of Roman women, performing on a sacral level the regular duties of ordinary Roman women, but must instead be credited with a more nuanced and precisely defined religious role.

Purification

One possible religious role that presents itself after a close examination of the Vestals' daily ritual activities within the *aedes Vestae* is purification. Both the rites these priestesses performed in connection with Vesta's fire and their ritual use of water are purificatory in nature. So too is the symbolism of certain elements of the Vestals' dress and their special hairstyle.

That Vesta was in some way associated with fire, and that not the least of her priestesses' duties was the care of the fire that burned perpetually within the confines of the *aedes Vestae*, is impossible to doubt. As our ancient sources make clear, this fire was intimately bound up with the continued safety and success of Rome, and even its unintentional extinction was a threat to the very existence of the city and its people.[12] At the same time, however, a close examination of the Vestal rites associated with this fire demonstrates that this fire both symbolized purity and was used solely in rituals that had some sort of purificatory purpose.

Earlier modern scholars have argued that Vesta's fire represented Rome's fertility (presumably using Eliades's definition of the concept).[13] They have generally based their arguments on the frequent stories of virgins impregnated by a god on their family hearth (foremost among these is, of course, the story of Mars and the first Vestal, Rhea Silvia, the mother of Romulus and Remus), together with the supposed existence of a phallus within the *aedes Vestae*.[14] Some of these scholars have also cited one of the two ritual methods for rekindling Vesta's fire described by our ancient sources.[15] Since the early 1980s, more recent scholars have revised this theory and proposed that the Romans viewed Vesta's fire as both fertile and sterile simultaneously. M. Beard, in particular, has drawn attention to the contrast between the evidence put forward by those who view Vesta's fire as a fertility symbol and several ancient passages that suggest that the Romans viewed fire as a sterile element.[16] She concludes that this seeming contradiction symbolizes the liminality of the Vestals' ritual status.

A close analysis of the evidence, however, suggests that the Romans explicitly recognized two kinds of fire, one, simultaneously male and fertile and associated primarily with the fire god, Vulcan, and the other simultaneously female and sterile and associated only with Vesta.

First, the ancient sources, named by Beard, who describe fire as sterile, are in every instance referring explicitly to Vesta's fire. Ovid, for example, states that:

> Do not understand Vesta as anything other than a living flame;
> You see that no bodies have been born from a flame.
> Therefore, she is a virgin by right, who yields no seeds
> Nor receives them and she loves companions in virginity.
>
> (Ov. *Fast.* 6.291–294)[17]

Dionysius of Halicarnassus writes:

> Some say with reason that the guardianship of the fire is entrusted to virgins rather than to men, because fire on the one hand is unfruitful ...[18]
>
> (D. H. 2.66.2)

Plutarch believes:

> For they also ascribe to Numa the establishment of the Vestal Virgins and both the service and the honour surrounding the immortal fire, which they protect, either because fire, which offers uncontaminated and undefiled bodies, is pure and uncorrupted or because fire, which is barren and unfruitful, is like virginity.
>
> (Plu. *Num.* 9)

Other ancient authors follow suit.[19]

Second and equally telling, those ancient authors, who connect a fire with fertility, always do so in explicitly masculine terms.[20] This alone would suggest that there is a division between male and female, fertile and sterile, fires. When we add to this the fact that the Romans recognized two fire divinities, one male, Vulcan, and one female, Vesta, and that these two divinities seem clearly to have had complementary but opposite roles in the Roman pantheon, the possibility for the existence of such a division is only strengthened.[21]

The seemingly most compelling evidence used by those scholars who draw a connection between Vesta's fire and fertility are the myths involving the impregnation of a virgin by the hearth of her home. With the exception of the single story involving the Vestal Rhea Silvia, however, none of the myths named by scholars has any direct connection to Vesta. The fact that these myths take place at the house's hearth is presumably the reason that scholars draw a connection between these myths and Vesta. Since in every case, however, a male god appears from the hearth's fire and since Vesta is nowhere explicitly named, it seems just as likely that the hearth figures in these stories because that was where a well-brought-up daughter of the house was expected to be as that Vesta was in any way involved.

Some few modern scholars also use the phallic imagery inherent in the ritual method for renewing this fire as described by Festus as an argument for connecting the Vestals' cult with fertility. Festus writes:[22]

> If the fire of Vesta was ever extinguished, the virgins were beaten with whips by the pontifex. It was the custom for them to drill a board of favourable wood for a very long time, a virgin then bore the fire taken from this into the *aedes* in a bronze sieve.
>
> (Fest. p. 94 L)

While the ritual described by Festus can certainly be read as sexually symbolic, it can also be given a simpler, more pragmatic explanation and the evidence suggests that it is this explanation that would have been foremost in an ancient Roman's mind. Both Seneca the Elder and Pliny the Elder note that this method of kindling a fire was the most common method of fire starting among their ancestors and in doing so emphasize the method's antiquity.[23] It is this antiquity that would first have come to mind for a Roman considering the Vestals' method of fire starting. We should therefore see in the Vestals' use of this method of fire-starting more likely evidence of this cult's antiquity (or at least the Romans' belief in this cult's antiquity) than any connection with fertility.

If Vesta's fire is not to be connected with fertility, some other significance for its existence must be found. One likely alternative suggested by our ancient sources' coupling of their depictions of this fire as sterile with an equal emphasis on its purity, is that this fire should be seen as a purificatory medium.[24] This view is strengthened by the purpose of the various annual or semi-annual Vestal rites in which this fire played a role.

Three times a year, the Vestals prepared from scratch the ritual purificatory substance, *mola salsa*.[25] This substance was made of flour mixed with salt. Part of the preparation of the flour involved the roasting of the ears of spelt, from which it was ground, on the fire within the *aedes Vestae*.[26] The Vestals also baked the *muries* or brine used at sacrifices as another purificatory substance in this same fire.[27] Vesta's fire was used in certain purificatory rituals performed in connection with both the *Fordicidia* and the rites of the October Horse.[28] In the former, the Vestals burnt the unborn fetuses of pregnant cows in their fire while in the latter the tail of the slaughtered horse was placed upon their hearth. The ashes from both the unborn calves and the horse's tail were preserved, blended together and used as a purificatory substance in the rites of the *Parilia*. Since all of these rituals involved the use of the Vestal fire in the making of a purificatory substance, this suggests a connection between this fire and purification. More than that, though, Vesta's fire seems to have functioned exclusively in this context; at least, no other types of rites or rituals involving the use of this fire appear in our ancient sources.

Alongside their constant ritual care of the fire within the *aedes Vestae*, the Vestals also regularly performed rites involving the use of water. While these rites have occasioned less modern discussion than other Vestal rites, A. Staples has argued that the Vestals' use of water complemented their use of fire.[29] Basing her argument on the symbolism of fire and water in connection with ancient Roman marriage and exile, she claims that the Vestals' ritual usage of fire and water reflects the Roman belief that these two elements together symbolized life, and that therefore the Vestals' use of water should be seen as further evidence for their role as fertility priestesses.[30] At first glance, this suggestion can seem to have some merit but, in many ways, it is a facile one, which leaves a number of issues unaddressed.

Most importantly, Staples' argument ignores the relative importance of the two elements in the Vestals' cult. While it is evident that the Vestals made regular ritual use of water, it is nowhere evident that this water and the rituals connected with it were of the same central importance to the cult as Vesta's fire and its rituals. The Vestals' fire was a sacred object in itself, one that the Vestals constantly served and protected, while the rituals associated with water made use of this water as a sacral medium and did not focus on the water as a cult object in itself. This imbalance is manifestly not a part of the rites of marriage and exile.

As well, Staples is guilty of two further oversights, both of which have some consequence for our understanding of water's significance. First, Staples does not consider whether water by itself had some connotations of its own in Roman cult and if so, what these connotations were. Second, she does not examine the purpose of the Vestals' water rites, although this purpose obviously has some bearing on the wider symbolic meaning of these rites.

Water by itself did in fact have a special significance in Roman religion, independent of any connection with its opposite element, fire. This significance was purificatory in nature. As S. Eitrem observes, in ancient Roman religion water figured primarily as a purificatory substance in connection with sacrifices and as a purificatory libation to the dead.[31] As the significance of the Vestals' water is hardly likely to differ substantially from the normal ritual use to which this element was put, this suggests that their water too had a purificatory significance.

Our ancient sources' descriptions of the Vestals' ritual use of water reinforce this view. Although our ancient sources have differing opinions about how this water was used ritually, Ovid claiming that the Vestals used the water to wash the *sacra*,[32] Plutarch that the water was used to wash the *aedes*,[33] and Festus that this water was used in the making of *muries*,[34] they are in agreement in that all of these rituals in one way or another are rituals of purification. Ovid and Plutarch's rituals are cleansing rituals, while in Festus' account, water is used in the manufacture of a religious substance used in purificatory rites. Thus, it seems likely that any final definition of water's significance to the Vestal cult must include a purificatory element.

Such an interpretation finds added support in the various ritual prohibitions and limitations surrounding the Vestals' use of water, all of which are directed at ensuring that this water was as pure and unpolluted as possible. The water used in the Vestals' rites had to be fresh, running water that had never come in direct contact with the earth. It could be taken only from the spring of Juturna,[35] the goddess of eternally flowing streams.[36] The Vestals even had special vessels in which they carried this water, which were designed in such a way that it was impossible to set them down on the ground without spilling their contents.[37] This was done to avoid the *piaculum* (an act that had to be expiated) that would ensue should the water come in contact with the profane earth. Likewise, within the *aedes Vestae* lay a basin constructed in such a way that any liquid poured within it would immediately flow out of the basin again, thus ensuring that the water used remained constantly running.[38] The Romans believed that running water was a particularly potent purificatory agent and the emphasis on running water within the Vestal cult is further evidence that the Vestals' use of water was purificatory in nature (see Plate 1).

Finally, while not direct evidence of the Vestals' role as purificatory agents, the priestesses' dress and hairstyle do emphasize the importance of *castitas* or purity to the Vestals and their cult. At the same time, they also provide evidence for the Vestals' special liminal status as full citizen members of the Roman state but non-members of that state's family cult structure, a topic that will be taken up in greater detail in later chapters of this work.

As numerous ancient sculptures and reliefs demonstrate, the Vestals wore their hair in a special hairstyle.[39] While there are many artistic renderings of this hairstyle, only one ancient literary source refers directly to it, Festus, who notes that both Vestals and brides on their wedding day wore their hair in a style he calls the *sex crines*: 'Brides are adorned with six braids, because this was the most ancient style for them. Which indeed the Vestal Virgins also use, whose chastity for their own men -/- brides *** from others' (Fest. p. 454 L).

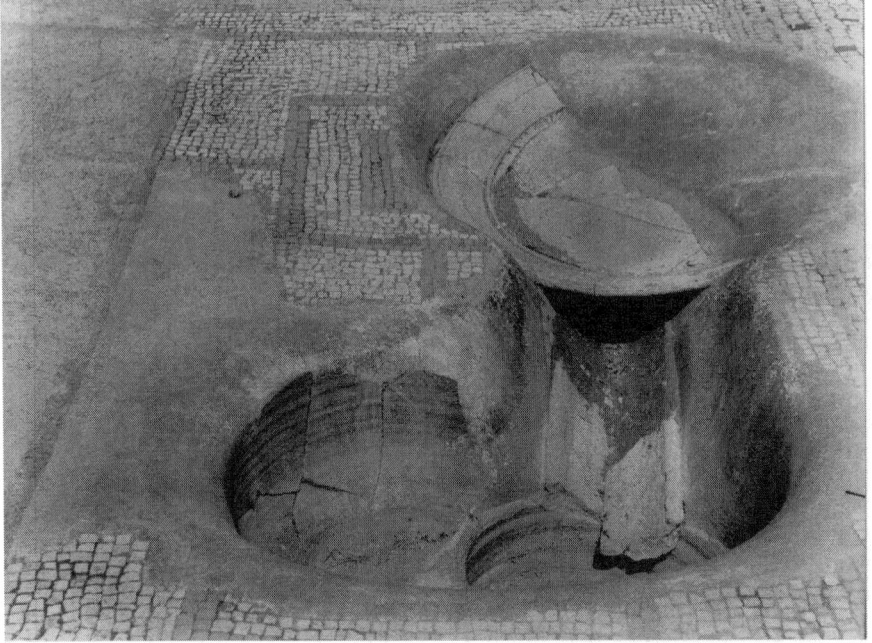

Plate 1   Basins with drain set in the floor of the *penus* of the *aedes Vestae*.
Courtesy of the American Academy at Rome.

The significance of this hairstyle has occasioned some discussion among modern scholars, most of whom have implicitly, if not explicitly, interpreted Festus' statement to mean that the Vestals' hairstyle was a deliberate replication of a bride's.[40] Festus, however, manifestly does not say that the one hairstyle is the imitation of the other. Rather he states simply that Roman brides and Vestals alike used the hairstyle called the *sex crines* and that this hairstyle was the most ancient known to the Romans. Thus, it is just as likely that the two groups used the same style because it symbolized some quality or condition common to both groups as because the one group was deliberately copying the other.[41]

One quality that is suggested by the final, and unfortunately corrupted, portion of Festus' text is *castitas* or purity. How the phrase *quarum castitatem viris suis -/- sponoe *** a ceteris* is to be translated exactly is uncertain but clearly it contains some reference to the Vestals' purity, which brides also shall demonstrate or possess. Thus, our one ancient literary source draws a connection between this hairstyle and the quality of *castitas*. As such, this hairstyle is further evidence of the central importance of this quality to the Vestals.

More than this, though, the *sex crines* hairstyle can also be explained by and thus used as evidence for another less tangible similarity between a bride and a Vestal. As we shall see, the central purpose of both the most ancient form of

Roman marriage rite that *cum manu* and the Vestal rite of *captio* involved a girl's removal from the familial cult under which she had lived from birth.[42] The marriage rite in question removed a girl from the cult of her birth family and transferred her to that of her new husband's family. The Vestal rite of *captio* removed a girl from the cult of her birth family but manifestly did not complete the transfer of a girl to the cult of any new family. Instead, the new Vestal remained in a liminal state, outside the realm of any one Roman family. In both rites, though, there existed a period of time, brief in the case of a bride and of at least thirty years' duration in the case of a Vestal, when the girl in question was no longer a member of her birth family's cult nor yet a member of a new family cult. In both cases, the girl or woman in question wore her hair in the *sex crines* style so long as the period of liminality lasted. The bride put aside her hairstyle as soon as the rites that ensured her transfer to her new family were complete. The Vestal, however, retained hers as long as she was a member of the priesthood, visibly demonstrating her peculiar liminal status and perhaps gaining protection from its existence.

It seems probable then that Vestals and brides employed the same hairstyle because they were both pure and occupied a liminal position in relation to the traditional Roman family structure. Such a solution satisfactorily avoids the traditional scholarly problem of who first made use of the *sex crines*, the bride or the Vestal. It also provides an explanation in keeping with what will be argued in later chapters of this book, namely that many of the special strictures surrounding the Vestals were connected to their liminal status as members of the Roman state, but non-members of that state's family structure.

Along with a distinct hairstyle, the Vestals seem also to have had some special form of dress.[43] Our literary sources suggest that that they regularly wore a *stola*[44] and *vittae*,[45] and when sacrificing, an *infula* and *suffibulum*.[46] The various sculptures of senior Vestal Virgins found within the *atrium Vestae* seem to bear this description out, as all are portrayed dressed in a *stola* with the *vittae* and *suffibulum* on their heads.[47] At least some of these garments were also demonstrably visual signs of the Vestals' purity and meant to serve as visual reminders to ordinary Romans of this purity (see Plates 2 and 3).

As Beard, who sees the *stola* and *vittae* as elements indicative of a general association between the Vestals and the *matronae*, observes, only two groups of women were permitted to wear the *stola* in ancient Rome, the *matronae* and the Vestals.[48] Our ancient sources add that both prostitutes and freedwomen were explicitly forbidden to wear either of these garments.[49] In other words, the *stola* was restricted to the use of certain citizen class women.

As well though, there is some evidence to suggest that a woman whose husband had divorced her on account of some adultery on her part was also forbidden to wear the *stola*.[50] Such a woman also lost her right to marry a Roman citizen and thus her status as being of citizen class herself.[51] This last suggests that the *stola* was not only the symbol of a *matrona* but also the symbol of her *castitas* or purity on which her citizen status was dependent. Should a woman be found to be unchaste, then the *stola*, as a visible sign of this purity,

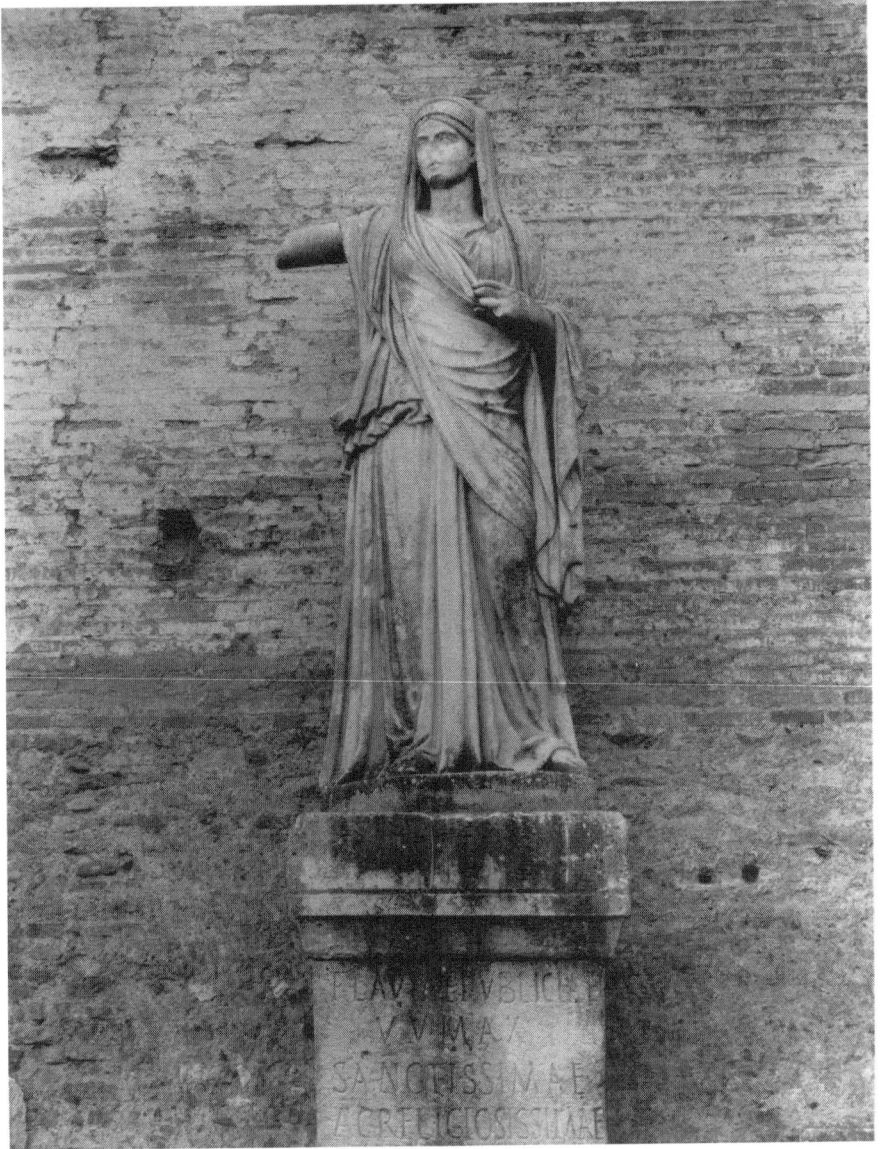

Plate 2 Statue of a Vestal from the second century CE.

Courtesy of the American Academy at Rome.

was taken from her. This raises the possibility that the Vestals wore *stolae* not only because these garments associated them with the *matronae*, but also because these garments were the visible symbols of the purity that was necessary for women to remain members of the *matronae* and thus of the citizen classes.

Plate 3 Statue of a Vestal from the second century CE.
Courtesy of the American Academy at Rome.

Such a picture finds further confirmation in the Vestals' use of *vittae*. These bands of cloth were used to tie up a woman's hair and were worn by ordinary *matronae* and brides as well as by the Vestals.[52] They also clearly had some religious significance as they were worn at sacrifices and other religious rituals together with an *infula*.[53] They were not, however, worn by freedwomen (*libertinae*), even those who were considered *casta* or pure.[54] Thus, they too were signs of their wearers' citizen status and purity. That the Vestals wore these *vittae* and *stola* can be seen as further confirmation of the importance of these two elements to their cult.

Whether or not the remaining elements of their dress had the same meaning is unclear from the ancient evidence. Certainly, they had at the least a religious significance. The *suffibulum*, according to Festus, 'was the white cloth . . . which the Vestal Virgins wore on their heads when sacrificing' (Fest. p. 74 L). The *infula* was also worn by other priests and by sacrificial victims (Fest. p. 100 L). While neither of these citations mentions purity in any form, it is not unlikely that these two items had some such symbolic connection. If so, they would serve as further evidence of the Vestals' purity. If not, then the Vestals' wearing of them on religious occasions was no doubt meant simply as a visual sign of their sacred status.

Ritual storage and manufacture of religious substances

Alongside their role as purificatory agents, the Vestals had a second and simultaneous function, the guardianship of Rome's symbolic storeroom and the ritual manufacture of certain religious substances, which, while often used in purificatory rites, seem also in some way to have been symbolic of Rome's food stores. This role is represented in their ritual preparation of *mola salsa* and *muries* and most importantly in their responsibilities for the *penus* of Rome located within the *aedes Vestae* and for its sacral contents.

Three times a year, if Servius is to be trusted, the Vestals made the ritual substance *mola salsa*:

> The three senior Vestal Virgins from 7 May to 14 May on alternate days place heads of spelt in harvest baskets, and these heads the Virgins themselves dry, crush and store when they have been crushed. From this spelt, the Virgins three times a year, at the Lupercalia, at the Vestalia and on 13 September, make *mola*, when boiled salt and hard salt have been added.[55]
>
> (Serv. *Verg. Ecl.* 8.82)

The Vestals also manufactured a type of brine called *muries*. Festus provides us with a detailed explanation of this ritual production:

> *Muries* is, as Veranius explains, that which is made out of impure (*sordidus*) salt, pounded in a pestle, and thrown into an earthenware pot, and then when it has been covered and sealed with gypsum, it is baked in an oven; to it, when it has been cut with an iron saw, and thrown into the large earthenware container (*seria*) which is within the *aedes Vestae* in the exterior *penus*, the Vestal Virgins add running water, of some sort, besides that which comes through the pipes, and this they later use in sacrifices.
>
> (Fest. p. 152 L)

In both of these rites, the Vestals prepared a ritual substance, which they then store within the *aedes Vestae* for later use in other religious rites primarily in a purificatory context.

Both of these substances, however, can also be seen as symbolic representations of Rome's most basic foodstuffs. On the one hand *mola salsa* resembles closely the flour out of which early Roman bread would have been baked, on the other, *muries* seems connected to the brine most commonly used as a preservative by the Romans.[56] The Vestals' preparation and storage of substances symbolic of these two most basic foodstuffs within the *aedes Vestae* suggests that one of their religious roles was the assurance of Rome's finished food supplies and their appropriate storage.

This role finds further support in one of the most discussed ritual duties of the Vestals within the *aedes Vestae*, their care of the *aedes' penus*, or storeroom. Although most modern scholarly discussion has focused on the supposed contents of this *penus* and the evidence these contents provide for the Vestals' role as fertility priestesses,[57] this discussion is actually of secondary importance and has obscured the primary importance of the Vestals' care of the *penus* and its contents. What mattered to the Romans was not whether or not the *fascinus* included in Plutarch's list of the contents of the *penus* was a symbol of fertility but that all of the contents of this *penus* were both secret and Rome's most holy *sacra*. Plutarch himself as much as says this in his description of these contents:

> And the most common opinion was that the Trojan Palladion was kept there, because Aeneas had brought it to Italy. Yet, there are those who say that the Samothracian statues also are kept there, and they tell the story that Dardanus brought them to Troy, and that after he had built the city, he celebrated the rites and dedicated those statues, and that Aeneas, after Troy's destruction, took them and kept them safe until he reached Italy. Still others, believing that they know more of the matter, say that there are two medium sized wine jars, one of which is open and empty, while the other full and sealed up. The sacred virgins alone see both of these.
>
> (Plu. *Cam.* 20)[58]

Even the ancients themselves were uncertain of what was hidden within the *aedes Vestae*. As such, a single ancient notation that the *fascinus*, which may or may not have had a connection to fertility, was included among these *sacra* should not be taken as weighty evidence of the Vestals' role as fertility priestesses.

What should be emphasized instead is the Vestals' role as guardians of Rome's symbolic storehouse. These priestesses were, as Plutarch observes, the only Romans allowed within the *penus*, and they alone knew the exact nature of the objects preserved within this storeroom. What was important was not so much the precise contents of the *penus* as the fact that the Vestals alone had responsibility for these contents and that these contents, whatever they were, were integral to the continued existence of Rome.[59] The Vestals were in charge of Rome's symbolic storeroom and its contents and the proper fulfilment of this duty ensured the continued existence of Rome.

Conclusion

The rites performed by the Vestals within the confines of their *aedes Vestae* suggest a two-pronged role for these priestesses in the construct that was Roman religion as a whole. On the one hand, they had a purificatory role. Our ancient sources' emphasis on the purity of the Vestals, their goddess and her fire all point in this direction as does much of the symbolism inherent in the Vestals' costume and hairstyle together with a close consideration of the rituals of water and fire these priestesses performed. On the other, they were concerned with the ritual protection of Rome's symbolic storeroom and the manufacture of religious substances that were kept within it, as is demonstrated by the use to which they put Vesta's fire as well as most importantly their guardianship of Rome's symbolic *penus* or storehouse within the *aedes Vestae.*

Notes

1 For modern discussions of this goddess, see R. Wright 1995; R. Bodeüs1983; G. Wissowa 1971: 32–38; K. R. Prowse 1967; A. Brelich 1949; P. Lambrechts 1946: 322–329 and for a brief overview *DnP* 12² 130–131.
2 For a brief discussion of other ancient references to this relationship, see F. Bömer 1957–1958: 2.357.
3 Arn. *Adv. nat.* 3.32; Aug. *C. D.* 7.16; Cic. *Dom.* 57. 144; Fest. p. 230 L; Plu. *Num.* 11; Sen. *Con.* 4.2.1; Serv. *A.* 1.292.5; Serv. *A.* 2.296.1; Serv. *A.* 3.281.6.
4 See, for example, R. Wright 1995; K. R. Prowse 1967: 178; P. Lambrechts 1946: 322–329.
5 This possibility finds some support in the fact that the late antique (*c.* 354 CE) calendar of Philocalus notes that on 2 February, the Vestals performed rites in honour of the dead.
6 For example, Cic. *Dom.* 144; Cic. *Har.* 12; Ov. *Fast.* 4.828; Sen. *Con.* 4.2.1; Verg. *G.* 1.498; *ILS* 2492, 4930, 4937, 5035, 5047, 5048.
7 *CIL* 10. 1125; *ILS* 2942, 4930, 4937, 5035, 5047 and 5048.
8 See, for example, R. Wright 1995.
9 P. Watson 1983.
10 *TLL* 8¹. 435–447, especially 439–441, which gives examples of just this use of *mater. DnP* 7. 998.
11 Indeed, at least one ancient source, Plut. *Quaest. Rom.* 85, notes that married women were not allowed to cook at Rome. See M. Beard 1980: 15 and n.22 for a discussion of this problem.
12 See, for example, Cic. *Catil.* 4.18.11; Cic. *Leg.* 2.20; Liv. 5.52.7; Liv. 5.54.7; Liv. 28.11.6; Sil. 4.411; Vell. 2.131.1.3.
13 See, for example, A. Staples 1998: 149; M. Beard 1980: 19; H. Hommel 1972: 407. For general discussions of fire in antiquity, see D. Zhuravlev 2002; M. Paschalis 2001; *DnP* 4. 498–501, especially 501, which discusses the uses of fire in Roman religion; M. Roussel 1982; G. Nagy 1974; G. Wissowa 1971: 159–160.
14 See, for example, J. Hallett 1984: 84; H. Hommel 1972: 406–16; K. R. Prowse 1967: 181–183; L. Euing 1933: 20–40.
15 See, for example, M. Beard 1980: 19; H. Hommel 1972: 406–416.

16 M. Beard 1980: 24, n.99.
17 See F. Bömer 1957–1958: 360; J. Frazer 1931: 216.
18 On Dionysius as a source for ancient roman religion, see G. Capdeville 1993b.
19 See, for example, Cic. *Leg.* 2.12.29; Ov. *Fast.* 6.283.
20 Cic. *Leg.* 2.12.29; D. H.2.66; Ov. *Fast.* 6.283; Plu. *Num.* 9.5; Var. *L.* 5.61.
21 On Vulcan, see *DnP* 12². 296–297; C. Pailler 1997; E. Simon 1990: 248–255; M. York 1986: 87–90; G. Wissowa 1971: 231.
22 See, for example, H. Hommel 1972: 406–416. A second method is described by Plutarch in his *Life of Numa* 9:

> If by some chance [the fire] goes out,... they say that it could not be kindled from another fire, but had to be made new and afresh by lighting it from a pure and unpolluted ray of the Sun. They place a bowl, which is hollow having been made from one side of a right-angled, isosceles triangle, and it converges into a single point from the edge. Therefore they place the part opposite the handle in the Sun, so that the rays being driven back from every side are concentrated and collected about the center, and here it dissolves the air becoming light and the lightest and driest of things being placed at the point light up according to the resistance, when the ray takes the body and force of fire.

23 See, for example, Plin. *Nat.* 16.208; Sen. *Nat.* 2.22.1.
24 For examples of this coupling, see D. H. 2.66.2; Ov. *Fast.* 6.291–294; Plu. *Num.* 9.
25 For discussions of *mola salsa* itself, see A. L. Prosdocimi 1991 together with *DnP* 8.235; G. Wissowa 1971: 159; C. Koch 1932.
26 Serv. *A.* 4.57; Serv. *Verg. Ecl.* 8.82. A. Staples 1998: 154 suggests that *mola salsa*'s 'function was to make every sacrifice, however exclusive in other respects, nevertheless representative of the collectivity'. The ancient evidence in no way supports this interpretation.
27 Fest. p. 152 L; Ov. *Fast.* 3.11; Plu. *Num.* 13; Prop. 4.4.15. See also *DnP* 8. 498; R. Curtis 1991; A. Hug 1933.
28 For the *Fordicidia*, see Ov. *Fast.* 4.629–640. For the October Horse, see Fest. p. 190 L. For a more in-depth discussion of these rites and a full bibliography, see Chapter 2.
29 A. Staples 1998: 149–150. M. C. Martini 1997b: 499–500 also describes the Vestals' use of water. She does not, however, attempt to define its ritual significance.
30 A. Staples 1998: 150.
31 S. Eitrem 1915: 76–197.
32 Ov. *Fast.* 3.11–14.
33 Plu. *Num.* 13.4.
34 Fest. p. 152 L.
35 Serv. *A.* 7.150 suggests instead the river Numicius. For Juturna, see *DnP* 6. 109–110.
36 W. Roscher 1965: vol. 2.1, pp. 762–764. The simplest and perhaps earliest explanation for the priestesses' use of this spring is that it was the source of water closest to them. Archaeological evidence in fact suggests that in the earliest period the shrine of Juturna was part of the precinct of Vesta. A. Staples 1998: 150 argues that the Vestals made use of the water from the spring of Juturna because it was located in the area where the *ancile* – a shield symbolic of Rome's power – was found. Another possible explanation can be found in the Romans' belief that this spring was particularly health giving.
37 Both literary and archaeological sources are evidence for this fact. See Prop. 4.4.15–16; Serv. *A.* 339. Remains of jugs similar to those described by Servius have been found within the *aedes Vestae* by archaeologists. See, for example, A. Bartoli 1959; H. Jordan 1886; J. H. Middleton 1886.

38 See Plate 1.
39 See M. Lindner 1995 for a general discussion of the Vestal statues found within the *atrium Vestae*. See also H. Jordan 1886. For discussions of the *seni crines*, see A. V. Siebert 1995; L. LaFollette 1994; L. LaFollette and R. Wallace 1993; G. Giannecchini 1980–1981.
40 See, for example, L. LaFollette 1994; L. LaFollette and R. Wallace 1993; M. Beard 1980: 16. A. Staples 1998: 146, however, maintains that the priestesses' use of this hairstyle was meant simply as a visible sign of their membership in the Vestal order.
41 It is perhaps telling that while literary scholars and historians talk about the *sex crines* as primarily a bridal hairstyle, archaeologists regularly describe it as the 'Vestal hairstyle'. Special thanks are due to Lektor Birte Poulsen, Aarhus University, who first brought this anomaly to my attention.
42 See Chapter 4.
43 For earlier discussions of this dress, see L. LaFollette 1994; H. Dragendorff 1896.
44 Plin. *Ep.* 4.11.
45 Juv. 4.9; Juv. 6.50; Ov. *Fast.* 3.30; Ov. *Fast.* 6.457; Virg. *A.* 7.418.
46 Fest. p. 100 L; Fest. p. 474 L; Prudent. *c. symm.* 11.1085 and Prudent. *c. symm.* 11.1094.
47 See M. Lindner 1995; E. Van Deman 1908, who question the value of these statues as evidence for the Vestals' dress. See also Plates 2 and 3.
48 L. LaFollette 1994; M. Beard 1980: 16. Other theories include: F. Guizzi 1968: 11–12; H. Jordan 1886: 43–56, who both argue that the Vestals' dress shared significant elements with that of a bride. C. Koch 1958: 1743 argues simply that the Vestals' whole costume marked them out from all other Roman women. For the use of the *stola* exclusively by married women, see Fest. p. 122 L and Plin. *Nat.* 33.40. For a discussion of the *stola* itself, see H. Blanck 1997; P. Grimal 1985. For further bibliography, see also *DnP* 11. 1018–1019.
49 Mart. 1.36.8; Tib. 1.6.67; Tib. 4.10.3.
50 Mart. 2.39; Mart. 6.64.4; Schol. *ad. Hor. l.c.*
51 Since women could not vote, the real measure of their membership in Rome's citizen body was their ability to marry a Roman citizen and have Roman citizen children.
52 *DnP* 12^2. 270 together with A. Siebert 1995: 77–92.
53 *TLL* 7^{1}1498–1500; *DnP* 5: 998.
54 Tib. 1.6.67.
55 See also Plin. *Nat.* 18.7. For a list of the other modern discussions of this substance, see above note 25.
56 G. Wissowa 1971: 260; F. Guizzi 1968: 109.
57 In particular, the observation of Plin. *Nat.* 28.7. 39 that: 'and the *fascinus*, the protector not only of infants, but also of *imperatores*, which deity the Vestals guard among the Roman sacred items, and as a cure for jealousy protects the chariots of triumphators, hanging under them'. See also Var. *L.* 5.157. The *fascinus* was a magical amulet, shaped like a phallus and used to protect its wearer from possible harm. Using this single reference to such an item as evidence for the claim that the Vestals were fertility priestesses, modern scholars have enlarged the import of this single statement out of all proportion to its actual contents. What Pliny the Elder actually writes is that this *fascinus* was among the *sacra Romana* protected by the Vestals. From this statement, it is just as easy to make the case that this *fascinus* was kept by the Vestals because of its role as one of Rome's *sacra* as because of any direct connection between the Vestals and fertility.
58 For another ancient description of the *penus*, see Fest. p. 296 L.
59 Cic. *Phil.* 11.24 describes the *palladium*, one of the items most generally accepted as part of the contents of the Vestals' *penus*, 'as that statue which fell down from heaven

and is kept in the custody of Vesta, and whose safety means we also shall be safe'. He makes a similar observation in his *Scaur.* 48.3. Flor. *Epit.* 1.1.105 offers a similar picture of the *palladium*'s importance, describing 'the shields [of the Salii] and the Palladium, [as] the secret emblems of *imperium*'. For further discussion of the *palladium* and a full list of ancient sources who discuss this relic, see *DnP* 9. 192–193 together with K. Prowse 1967: 186; R. Siekveking 1924.

2   The Vestals in public

Alongside their religious duties within the precincts of the *aedes Vestae*, the Vestal Virgins also participated more publicly in at least nine annual state rites.[1] These rites spanned almost the entire calendar year, beginning with the traditional New Year's rites on 1 March and ending with the rites of *Bona Dea* in December. The Vestals' roles in them varied from a brief appearance at the side of the Pontifices at the *Consualia* to a more central position as the religious officials primarily responsible for tossing straw figures into the river Tiber at the rites of the Argei. Despite this seemingly broad range of rites and ritual activities, the same common motifs of purification and storage that we have seen in Chapter 1 appear here as well, suggesting once again that it was these ritual areas that were of special concern to the Vestals.

Purification

Of these nine rites, six clearly involved the Vestals in purificatory activities. The New Year's rites of 1 March and the rites of the *Vestalia* find the Vestals performing cleansing rituals within the *aedes Vestae*, while in the rites of the *Fordicidia* and the October Horse, the priestesses prepared purificatory substances which were later distributed and used at the rites of the *Parilia*. Finally, the rites of the *Argei* also seem to have had purificatory overtones.

The first set of annual rites, in which the Vestals participated, and for which we have contemporary sources, took place on 1 March but were actually New Year's rites according to the original Roman calendar. Ovid's *Fasti* contains a detailed account of this day and its rites, and provides us with some insight into the Vestals' ritual duties on this occasion:

> So that Vesta may also shine shaded with new leaf,
> The white laurel departs from the Trojan hearth.
> Add, that new fire is said to be lit within the secret shrine
> And the renewed flame gains strength.
> (Ov. *Fast.* 3.141–144)

On this traditional first day of the New Year, the priestesses replaced the previous year's decoration of laurel branches on the *aedes Vestae* with new ones and kindled a new fire on the *focus* in place of the old one.[2]

While to some extent because of their timing, both of these rituals are connected with the renewal of the year, it should also be recognized that the Vestals' duties on this occasion primarily involved the cleansing of the *aedes Vestae* and the hearth within it. As such they suggest a second, more exact purpose for these priestesses' activities, a purpose that is in keeping with what we have discovered in our examination of the Vestals' daily rites, that is the purification of the Vestals' shrine by the removal of the old year's debris in preparation for the beginning of the new.

The Vestals also performed cleansing rituals in connection with the *Vestalia*, which itself took place on 9 June.[3] These rituals were even more clearly purificatory than those that took place on 1 March. Ovid notes in his account of the religious events that took place on 6 June that:

> For the Dialis' holy wife said to me:
> 'Until the placid Tiber's yellow waters carry
> Trojan Vesta's sweepings to the sea,
> I am not allowed to comb my hair with clipped
> boxwood or trim my nails with iron,
> or touch my husband, although he is Jupiter's priest
> and given to me by perpetual law.
> You, too, should not hurry. Your daughter will wed better,
> when blazing Vesta shines with a clean floor.'
> (Ov. *Fast.* 6.226–234)[4]

Under 15 June, he again refers to the disposal of these 'sweepings'.

> This is that day on which you carry Vesta's sweepings
> to the sea, Tiber, through the Etruscan waters.
> (Ov. *Fast.* 6.713–714)

Two other ancient sources also name this ritual, Festus writing:

> Q.S.D.F. [The day named] 'When it is permitted to carry out the muck', this day is noted in the same way in the Fasti as that on which the [*aedes Vestae* is purged] and the dirt *in alvum ca. ... cum id factum sit ... ta.*
> (Fest. p. 310 L)

and Varro:

> The day that is called 'when it is permitted to carry out the muck' is called this because on that day the dirt from the *aedes Vestae* is swept out and is carried through the *Capitolium Clivum* into a certain place.
> (Var. *L.* 6.32)

Whatever else the *Vestalia* involved,[5] one aspect of this period was purificatory, with the Vestals cleaning out their shrine and disposing of its dirt in the purificatory element of running water.

The next three rites to be discussed form a related complex with the first two rites, the *Fordicidia* and the rites of the October Horse, involving purificatory activities leading up to and in preparation for the third, the *Parilia*. The first of these, the *Fordicidia*, took place in April. Ovid, the most detailed of our sources for this rite and the only one who explicitly mentions the Vestals in this connection, writes of these rites:[6]

> When the third dawn after the Ides of Venus rises,
> Pontifices, sacrifice a pregnant cow.
> A 'pregnant' cow is in calf and is called 'fruitful' from 'bearing' (*ferendo*):
> From this they think the name 'fetus' is taken.
> The herd is now pregnant; the fields are also impregnated with seed:
> A full victim is given to full Tellus.
> Part of the sacrifice falls at the citadel of Jupiter, thirty *curia* accept
>   a cow and drip with blood spattered widely.
> But when the assistants have dragged the calves from the wombs
> and given the cut-up entrails to the smoky hearths,
> whoever is the oldest Vestal by birth burns the calves in a fire,
> so that that ash may purify the people by the light of Pales.
>
>   (Ov. *Fast.* 4.629–640)

On 15 April, the Pontifices sacrificed a pregnant cow at the citadel of Jupiter while in each of the thirty *curiae* other pregnant cows were also sacrificed. After these cows were slaughtered, their calves were torn from their wombs by the priests' assistants and then burned in a fire by the senior Vestal Virgin. The ashes from the calves were then preserved for use at the later purificatory ritual of the *Parilia*.[7]

The main purpose of the *Fordicidia* as a whole is unambiguous. At *Fasti* 4.633–634, Ovid writes: 'The herd is now pregnant; the fields are also impregnated with seed: / A full victim is given to full Tellus'. The *Fordicidia* were fertility rites meant to ensure the success of the coming year's crops and herds.[8] Scholars have generally assumed that the Vestals' activities in connection with these rites were sacrificial in nature and had the same general purpose as the rites as a whole. Yet, the Vestals' actions were separate from and subsequent to the main event of the rites, the sacrifice of the thirty cows, and the result of their actions was a sacred substance used in a later purificatory rite. This suggests first that there is a subtle difference between the purpose of the Vestals' participation in these rites and the purpose of the rites as a whole, and second that the purpose of the Vestals' activities was purificatory.

While the actions performed by the Vestals on this occasion at first glance might seem to be sacrificial in nature, a closer examination of Ovid's description reveals certain elements in them that set them off from ordinary sacrificial practice and thus from the main rites of the *Fordicidia*. First, the whole calf was burned on the altar, and not just the entrails and blood as was traditional Roman sacrificial practice.[9] Second, as part of his description of the *Fordicidia*, Ovid states, 'But when the assistants have dragged the calves from the wombs / and given the cut up entrails to the smoky hearths, / whoever is the oldest Vestal by birth burns the calves in a fire, / so that that ash may purify the people by the light of Pales' (Ov. *Fast.* 4.637–639). The burning of the calves was performed only after the cows' entrails had been placed on the altar. As this disposal of the entrails was traditionally the last step of performing a sacrifice, it seems clear that the burning of the calves was at the very least set off and separated from the main sacrifice. Ovid also notes that the calves were all burned by the senior Vestal Virgin, something which suggests that the calves from the thirty curia were brought from the individual curia to a central location, perhaps the *aedes Vestae*, where the senior Vestal received them. The senior Vestal could not have simultaneously been present at all the various *curiae*'s sacrifices and thus her part of the rites was spatially removed from the sacrifice as well. Finally, her collecting and preserving of the ashes does not have, as far as we know, any counterpart in ordinary sacrificial procedure. Thus, rather than classifying the Vestal's burning of the calves as a sacrificial action meant to enhance Rome's fertility, it must be defined in some other way. Since the substance manufactured by the Vestals on this occasion was stored for later use in the purificatory rituals associated with the *Parilia*, it seems likely that the Vestals' actions in connection with the *Fordicidia* should be seen as being primarily purificatory in nature.

The same is also true of the Vestals' participation in the rites of the October Horse, which took place on 15 October.[10] We have two main sources for the existence of a connection between the Vestals and these rites, Ovid and Festus, and while neither of them describes the Vestals' actual activities in any detail, together they make it clear that these activities were also directed primarily to purificatory goals. Festus, the more detailed of the two, writes:

> The October Horse is the name for the right-hand horse of the span that is victorious on the Field of Mars and which is sacrificed in the month of October every year to Mars ... the tail of this horse is with the greatest speed carried into the *regia* so that its blood can be poured on the hearth.
>
> (Fest. p. 190 L)

Ovid states briefly as part of his description of the *Parilia*, 'the blood of the horse will be the purificatory substance' (Ov. *Fast.* 4.733), a reference, which since it is generally accepted as referring to the blood collected at the rites of the October Horse, can mean only that the Vestals' activities here are connected with purification.[11]

The culmination of this complex of rites was the *Parilia*, which occurred a week after the *Fordicidia* in April.[12] Ovid, describing these rites, writes:

Night has gone, and dawn comes. The *Parilia* call me.
I am not called in vain, if gentle Pales is favourable.
Gentle Pales, may you favour me singing of the pastoral rites,
if I honour your holy days with my service.
Certainly I have often carried in my full hands ash from a calf
and bean stalks, burned sources of purification.
Certainly I have jumped the flames placed in a triple row
and shaken water drops from the damp laurel.
The goddess is moved and favours my work. The ship
leaves the dock, my sails now have their winds.
Go people; seek the fumigant from the virginal altar;
Vesta will give it; you will be made pure by the gift of Vesta.
The blood of the horse and the ash of a calf will be the fumigant;
The third part will be a hard bean's empty stalk.

(Ov. Fast. 4.721–734)

While Ovid does not explicitly mention the Vestals, it seems clear from his use of the description 'virginal altar' and his references to Vesta in his statement 'Go people; seek the fumigant from the virginal altar: / Vesta will give it, you will be made pure by the gift of Vesta' (Ov. *Fast.* 4.731–732) that the goddess' priestesses were in some measure involved in these rites.[13]

Like the *Fordicidia*, the *Parilia* seem to have had some fertility and some purificatory aspects.[14] Unlike the rites of the previous week, however, these rites' immediate purpose seems to have been purificatory and only in a very general sense might they be considered fertility rites. In describing the *Parilia*, Ovid, devotes by far the greatest part of this passage to prayers for purification, making only a few brief references that hint at a connection between the rites and a concern with the continued fertility of the crops and herds.[15] He begins his account with a description of the ashes, beans and blood to be sought, calling them 'pure fumigants'.[16] He then continues with a command to the people to seek the means of purification from the altar of Vesta, explicitly saying that they will be made pure through Vesta. After this, he turns to a description of rural *Parilia* rites and gives an account of a prayer offered by a shepherd, most of which is taken up with requests to be forgiven for possible sins.[17] The only time that we find anything to suggest that these rites were fertility rites in the narrower sense is in this prayer and this is limited to a few lines whose content is closely entwined with the farmer's plea for purification. The bulk of Ovid's account of the *Parilia* is taken up with what are clearly purificatory measures. This overwhelming concern with purification and the minimal references to fertility suggest strongly that these rites were meant primarily as purificatory measures and were concerned with fertility only in as much as many ancient agricultural rites were to some extent fertility-related by their very nature.

Even if this were not the case, Ovid makes it clear that, as with their role in the *Fordicidia*, the purpose of the Vestals' activities in connection with these rites was twofold. On the one hand, the Vestals are clearly participating in these rites in their role as guardians of Rome's stores, doling out a sacred substance that has been preserved within their precincts. On the other, the substance they dole out is purificatory in nature. When Ovid speaks of Vesta (and hence presumably of the Vestals), he speaks of her (and so of them) as the keeper and provider of the means of purification – the ashes of the calves and the blood of the horse, which together make up the *suffimen*.[18] Furthermore, he explicitly tells his audience that they 'will be made pure by the gift of Vesta' (Ov. *Fast.* 4.732). Other than this, he makes no statement that could be construed as connecting the Vestals with participation in these rites. Indeed, his whole account intimates that the other rituals associated with these rites were carried out by private individuals, for he speaks of himself as performing the actual rituals on occasion and credits a nameless shepherd with carrying out the rural version of these rites. This limited nature of the Vestals' participation has the effect of suggesting again that one of their primary religious concerns was purification.

The last of the six annual rites that involved the Vestals in purificatory activities is that of the *Argei*. Dionysius of Halicarnassus offers the most complete description of the general ritual involved in these rites, but he has little to say about the Vestals' role in them, except to note that they were present along with a number of other Roman priests and dignitaries:[19]

> . . . a little after the spring equinox, in the month of May, on what they call the Ides (the day they consider to be the middle of the month); on this day after offering the preliminary sacrifices according to the laws, the Pontifices, as the most important of the priests are called, and with them the virgins who guard the immortal fire, the Praetors, and whatever other citizens as may lawfully be present at the rites, throw from the sacred bridge into the river Tiber thirty effigies made in the likeness of men, which they call Argei.
>
> (D. H. 1.38.3)

Fortunately, two other ancient sources' briefer references to these rites provide us with a more detailed picture of the Vestals' ritual duties in this connection. The first of these two sources, Ovid, writes of the rites, 'Today also the Virgin hurls the straw dummies / of earlier men from the oaken bridge' (Ov. *Fast.* 5.621–622),[20] while the second, Festus, adds: 'Argeos is what they used to call the effigies of reeds, which were thrown by the Vestal Virgins each year into the Tiber' (Fest. p. 14 L). Taken together, these accounts suggest that the Vestals' ritual duties were central to this occasion and consisted first in taking part in a procession, which also included the Pontifices, the Praetors, and other citizens who were legally allowed to participate (whoever they may have been), from some undetermined point in Rome to the *pons sublicus*, and second in throwing somewhere between twenty-four and thirty human figures made of rush off this bridge into the river Tiber.[21]

Since the Vestals' ritual duties formed the centrepiece of these rites, it seems likely that their purpose and that of the rites as a whole is the same. While it is not entirely certain what the purpose of these rites was, D. Harmon posits that these rites were primarily purificatory ones, meant to symbolically dispose of the ghosts and spirits thought to be present at Rome during the *Lemuria*, the period immediately preceding the rites of the *Argei*.[22] Harmon further argues that the Vestals' actions represented some sort of purification of the city, suggesting that whatever the precise significance of the rush figures, the Vestals' action in throwing them off the bridge into the Tiber was likely to have been a purificatory act.[23] His theory finds support in other instances of which we know (some of them involving the Vestals) where unclean objects were thrown into the Tiber in order to avoid the pollution of the land or the city: at the *Vestalia*, for example, the *purgamenta* of the *aedes Vestae* were thrown into the Tiber, as were the bodies of criminals and anything seen as a *prodigium*.[24] Following Harmon's theory, we have a final piece of evidence supporting the contention that one of the major aspects of the Vestals' religious position was purificatory in nature.

Ritual storage and manufacture of religious substances

Not only does the Vestals' participation in these nine annual rites focus on purification, but also their ritual activities in connection with many of these rites show a concern with the storage and manufacture of holy substances that can be seen as symbolic of the preparation of grain to flour. Of the nine rites under discussion, again six of them provide evidence of this type of task. The *Fordicidia* and the rites of the October Horse involved the manufacture of a flour-like substance that was stored for subsequent use in the *Parilia*. The *Vestalia* were in some way connected with bakers and the milling of grain, while the *Consualia* and *Opsconsivia* both honoured deities of storage. The fact that of these six rites four also had a purificatory element suggests as well that these two Vestal duties were inextricably linked in the minds of the Romans.

From 7 to 15 June, the *aedes* of Vesta was opened to the women of Rome. In the midst of this period, on 9 June, Vesta's own special festival, the *Vestalia*, took place. Ovid devotes a relatively long section of his work to this day, offering a detailed description of its mythical origins, but providing only hints of the actual rites that might have been carried out by the Vestals. Nevertheless these hints are enough to at least demonstrate a connection between their goddess and the manufacture of grain into flour and bread.[25]

> There survives to this time a piece of ancient custom:
> A pure platter brings Vesta offered food.
> Look, bread hangs from garlanded donkeys,
> and chains of flowers veil rough millstones.
> Farmers used to roast only spelt in ovens
> (these are the rites of the Goddess, Fornax).

The hearth itself baked the bread covered in its ash;
after a chipped tile had been placed on the warm floor.
Hence the baker serves the hearth and the mistress of the hearths
And the donkey who turns the pumice millstones.

(Ov. *Fast.* 6.309–318)[26]

When we add to these lines Servius' discussion of the Vestals' making of *mola salsa*, this connection is broadened to include the Vestals as well: 'From this spelt, the virgins made *mola* three times a year, at the *Lupercalia*, at the *Vestalia* and on 13 September, when boiled salt and rough salt had been added' (Serv. *Verg. Ecl.* 8.82).[27]

Some modern scholars have wished to see these rites as related to the fertility of the crops,[28] but this seems dubious in light of Ovid's comparison of Vesta to a sterile flame and his description of her as one who 'is a virgin, giving and taking / no seed, and [who] loves companions in virginity' (Ov. *Fast.* 6.291– 294). It is difficult to see how rites celebrated in honour of a goddess described in such a fashion could be seen as fertility ones. In Ovid's account of the myth behind these rites, however, Jupiter commands Vesta to see to the drying of the grain and the baking of bread.[29] This seems to offer a clue to a more likely significance for these rites, suggesting that they celebrated Vesta's provenance as the manufacturer and provider of food through fire, her special element. Ovid's remarks about the significance of the festival to bakers as well as his description of bread as a suitable offering to Vesta lend further support to this possibility.[30] So too does Servius' linking of the Vestals' manufacture of *mola salsa* to this day. Thus on the balance, the evidence suggests that these rites were meant as a celebration of the power of the hearth-fire and particularly its ability to ensure the successful transformation of raw grain into a finished, edible product. This fits well with the concern with the manufacture (again through the use of fire), storage and distribution of various substances, some of which clearly symbolize Rome's food supplies, which we have already demonstrated in Chapter 1, and perhaps explains where this aspect originated.

With the *Vestalia* we reach the end of our best source for annual Roman religious festivals, Ovid's *Fasti*, and instead must depend on passing references in other authors' works for information about the year's remaining rites. Unfortunately, this means that our knowledge of the Vestals' role in the rites of the second half of the year is weaker than it is for the first half. Two rites to which ancient sources do connect the Vestals though, the *Consualia* and the *Opsconsivia*, give further evidence of their concern with Rome's stores.

The early Christian author Tertullian observes of the first:

And now the altar to Consus is buried under the earth in the circus at the first turning posts with an inscription of this sort: *CONSUS CONSILIO MARS DUELLO LARES COILLO POTENTES*. The public priests sacrifice at this altar on 7 July, and on 21 August the Flamen Quirinalis and the virgins.[31]

(Tert. *Spect.* 5.7)

Although some few ancient sources seem to have believed that Consus was the god of counsel (based on the etymology of the god's name), the bulk of scholars, both ancient and modern, have chosen to see him instead as the god of stores.[32] This combined with the timing of the festival, in August at the time of the traditional Roman harvest, suggests that the *Consualia* were rites meant to ensure the protection and successful storage of the newly gathered harvest.[33] The Vestals' participation in these rites connects them once again with the preservation of Rome's stores.

Roughly one week later, on 25 August, the *Opsconsivia* were held. Although very little is known about these rites, Varro makes a rather cryptic statement that suggests the Vestals might have had some role in them. Writing of this festival and of the goddess, Ops, he notes: 'The day *Opsconsivia* takes its name from the goddess Ops Consiva, whose shrine is in the Regia, so that no one besides the Vestal virgins and the public priest may enter it' (Var. *L.*6.21).[34] While Varro does not explicitly state that the Vestals participated in the *Opsconsivia*, it seems likely that, since the Vestals together with the *sacerdos publicus* (presumably the Pontifex Maximus) were the only ones allowed in the shrine of Ops, they were in some way involved in her rites.[35]

Festus suggests that Ops was the goddess of plenty, a manifestation of the Earth herself with all her wealth, and our other ancient sources are in accord with this.[36] Modern scholars, following the ancients' descriptions, have therefore seen Ops as a harvest goddess closely connected with Consus, and have suggested that the *Opsconsivia* were rites connected in some fashion to a symbolic storehouse of Rome.[37] If so, we once again have evidence that connects the Vestals to the rites of a deity whose main provenance was the protection of the stores and of the harvest.

Finally, the rites of the *Fordicidia* and the October Horse, already discussed, not only had purificatory overtones, but also simultaneously involved the Vestal manufacture of ritual substances, which were stored and subsequently distributed at the *Parilia*. During the *Fordicidia* the Vestals burned the calves torn from the thirty cows on their fire while during the rites of the October Horse, the priestesses burned the blood from the tail of the horse. In both cases the resulting ashes were then stored for use at the later purificatory ritual of the *Parilia*.

All of the above rituals in one way or another involve the Vestals' manufacture of some flour-like substance using Vesta's fire, and in most cases also include the subsequent storage of these substances. As such, these ritual activities closely replicate the ordinary Roman procedure for transforming the harvested grain into flour. As such they serve as further evidence that one aspect of the Vestals' religious position was a 'storage function', that is a concern with the symbolic manufacture and successful protection of Rome's stores, whether religious or otherwise.

The December rites of *Bona Dea*

Only one annual rite in which the Vestals participated does not immediately fit the patterns established above. This is the December rite of *Bona Dea*.[38] As a women's mystery rite, it might be expected to present a special challenge to us, since our male sources are unlikely to have known the details of rites to which they were not admitted. Surprisingly, this is not the case, for we are provided with some fairly detailed and seemingly accurate descriptions of the rituals performed in connection with these rites. H. H. J. Brouwer, summarizing these various ancient descriptions in his book on *Bona Dea*, writes:

> On the eve of the feast all the men, both members of the family and of the staff, leave the house of the magistrate where that year the rites are to be performed. The mistress of the house together with the female servants (?), decorates the festive hall with plants and flowers, and bowers are arranged, covered with vine – though this must have been somewhat problematic in December. The cult statue, borrowed for the occasion from the temple (?), is set up in the festive hall and in front of the statue the *pulvinar* and a small table with the sacred vessels from which the goddess is thought to eat and drink. Next a young sow (Juvenal) or a pregnant sow (if Macrobius' remark also relates to this feast) is sacrificed and a libation is poured by the mistress of the house. Then the participants, the noble women of Rome and the Vestal Virgins, make merry, drinking wine and being enlivened by music performed by female harpers and flautists.[39]

The wording of Brouwer's description, however, unfortunately masks one major problem inherent in our sources: the question of who sacrificed the pig, the Vestals or 'the mistress of the house'. Our ancient sources themselves are divided on this issue, with some of them claiming the former, others the latter, still others making no comment. Cicero in his *De Haruspicum Responso* credits the Vestals with the explicit performance of a sacrifice, writing, 'what is done by the Vestal Virgins is done for the Roman people' (Cic. *Har.* 17.37). He is supported in this by Asconius, who writes that 'the Virgins made a sacrifice for the Roman people' (Asc. *Mil.* 43). Against this evidence must be placed Plutarch, who claims that the matron of the house performed the sacrifice.[40] On the balance, Cicero, as a native Roman with close connections to participants in these rites (his wife Terentia after all was the 'mistress of the house' in question on one occasion) and supported by Asconius, seems the more reliable source in this instance, so it is likely that the Vestals themselves performed this sacrifice.

If we are right in seeing the Vestals as the sacrificants, then we have here clear evidence that they had full sacrificial capacities.[41] At the same time, it must be remembered that this sacrifice took place in the context of women's rites and that as such it falls into a special category, for women's rites often turn traditional religious practices on their heads and permit to women a latitude of action that is not regularly allowed them. This means that the Vestals' full sacrificial capacity may well have been an anomaly permitted only in the context of a women's rite and that at other times their capacity may have been more limited. When we add to this the fact that in every one of the other instances of possible Vestal sacrifice the exact extent of their participation is ambiguous, we are left with the very real possibility that their sacrificial capacity was limited. Unfortunately, no definitive conclusions can be reached on this issue, but the possibility should at least be raised.

If we are right in seeing the Vestals rather than 'the mistress of the house' as the sacrificant(s), then we are almost certainly justified in seeing the purpose of their actions as being the same as the general purpose of the rites. Here, however, we run into problems, for where the rites already discussed all fall into more or less clearly definable categories – purification and/or storage rites – the purpose of these rites is much less apparent. The fact that these rites were mystery rites, open only to women, has suggested to some scholars that their purpose may originally have had some connection to fertility (on an analogy with the Greek, Eleusinian mystery rites and presumably meant in the broadest sense of the term).[42] Yet our ancient sources, most notably Cicero, say only that these rites were celebrated 'for the safety of the Roman people' (Cic. *Har.* 17.37), a statement which is only vaguely related to fertility. Thus, we are also left with some uncertainties here. Probably, the best solution is that of Brouwer, who suggests that these rites were originally women's fertility rites that over time took on a broader application and came to be considered rites meant to ensure the general safety of the Roman people.[43]

The Vestals' participation in these rites does not fit neatly into either of our previous categories. This seeming discrepancy can, however, be explained both by the fact that these rites were women's rites and the Vestals' participation in them due to this fact and by the fact that these rites were, as Cicero states, celebrated 'for the safety of the Roman people', a purpose which was in the end at the heart of all the Vestals' rituals, whatever their primary roles might otherwise be.

Other public ritual appearances

As well as publicly participating in these nine rites, ancient sources note that the Vestals also made public appearances sitting in special seats at the gladiatorial games.[44] Cicero, for example, writes in his defence of Murena, 'what if a vestal virgin, my client's close relation, gave up her place at the games in his favour' (Cic. *Mur.* 73). The seating arrangements referred to here by Cicero are likely to have had their roots in the need for the Vestals' participation in various rites connected with some, if not all, of the gladiatorial games they attended. Public theatrical performances and gladiatorial games in Rome were as much religious rites meant to honour various divinities, as they were sources of public entertainment. At the beginning of each performance, offerings were made to the deity or deities in whose honour the games were being held. The priests who performed these rites also had special seats at the games, from which they could oversee the spectacle performed in honour of their god.[45] While we have no firm evidence that the Vestals played an official role at every games, we do know that they had a religious role to play in at least some of them. Twice a year together with the pontiffs, the priestesses participated in rites honouring Consus, which were held within the Circus before the performance of games in his honour.[46] As well, a number of the other festivals, which involved the performance of public games, were ones in which we know the Vestals had a ritual responsibility. For example, both the *Parilia* and *Cerialia* in April seem to have involved some form of public performance, as did the *Vestalia* and the *Lupercalia*.[47] In all of these rites, the Vestals took, if not the central role, an important one. One reason for the Vestals' special seating at the front of the circus, therefore, seems likely to have been the requirements of their ritual duties in connection with each of these public spectacles. At the same time, it should not be overlooked that the special seating arrangements kept the Vestals separate from the profane crowds and served as a visual reminder of their special status.

Conclusion

Our examination of the Vestals' religious activities in connection with various public, state rites reveals a definite pattern. First and foremost, the combination of the fact that the largest group of the Vestals' ritual duties falls under the rubric 'purification' and the fact that four of the nine annual rites, in which they participated, were mainly purificatory in nature suggest that one major aspect of the Vestals' religious position was purificatory. This supposition is further strengthened when we take into account the fact that even in some of the rites directed towards other purposes, most notably the fertility rites of 1 March and the *Fordicidia*, the Vestals' participation is primarily limited to purificatory actions. Next, the fact that a second substantial group of ritual duties revolves around the manufacture, preservation and distribution of religious stores and the fact that three of the nine rites, those I have termed 'harvest rites', are also concerned with similar activities suggest that a second aspect of the Vestals' religious position was a concern with the protection of Rome's stores, that is a storage function.

It is noteworthy that this pattern repeats the one already discovered in connection with the rituals the Vestals performed within the *aedes Vestae*. In other words, the Vestals' ritual activities in both the public and private sphere follow the same pattern. The priestesses cleaned and purified *sacra*; they prepared and stored religious substances, and performed rites associated with the city's hearth fire. The reiteration of this pattern in both annual and daily cult duties emphasizes this pattern's centrality to any clear understanding of the Vestals' religious role. However we define this role in the end, this definition must include some reference to these sorts of activities.

Notes

1 By public, annual, state rites, I mean religious rites which were open to at least some substantial portion of the general public and which were performed every year on behalf of the Roman state and Roman people as a whole.

   The Vestals' participation in a tenth annual rite, the *Parentalia*, is also mentioned in the fourth century CE calendar of Philocalus. Because this source is outside the general time period of this book, a detailed discussion of this rite and the Vestals' role in it is not included here. Nothing in the Vestals' participation in this rite, though, is out of keeping with my findings here. Those interested in the Vestals' role in the *Parentalia* are referred to R. Wildfang 2001.

2 In both instances, although Ovid never explicitly states that the Vestals performed these tasks, it seems safe to assume that this was the case, as both the *aedes Vestae* and the flame within it were one of their order's primary responsibilities, and only they and the Pontifex Maximus were permitted entry into the shrine. Macr. 1.12.6 writes of a related rite, 'on the first day of this month, they lighted a new fire on the altar of Vesta, so that when the year began the care of preserving a renewed fire began again', although Macrobius' statement does leave unclear whether he was describing the fire on the central hearth of Vesta or that within a private house. Possibly he was speaking about a ritual performed in every Roman household on this day.

   See also J. Frazer 1931: 38–41 for a longer and somewhat dated discussion of the many supposed parallels between the annual renewal of Vesta's fire and similar renewals of fire in other cultures, and F. Bömer 1957–1958: 153 for a briefer discussion of these rites. See also G. Radke (1993) for a general discussion of these rites.

3 M. Torelli 1995; H. Scullard 1981: 148–150; G. Wissowa 1971: 158–160. For a discussion of Ovid's portrayal of these rites, see G. Williams 1991.

4 For commentators' discussions of this passage and these rites, see F. Bömer 1957–1958: 351–352; J. Frazer 1927: 166–168.

5 See pages 28–29.

6 References to the *Fordicidia*, which do not explicitly mention the Vestals, include: *CIL* 1^2 p. 315; Fest. p. 91 L; Lyd. *Mens.* 4. 72 p. 124 W; Var. *L.* 2.5.6. Although our ancient sources differ on some minor details relating to these rites, most noticeably the spelling and pronunciation of *forda* versus *horda*, they are agreed on the basic aspects of the rituals involved and, most important for our purposes, none contradict Ovid's view of the Vestals' part in them. For discussions of these rites, see D. Porte 2003; *DnP* 4. 589; H. Scullard 1981: 102; G: Wissowa 1971: 192; H. Le Bonniec 1958: 66–67.

7 F. Bömer 1957–1958: 263 discusses this description at some length and makes a similar point about the grammatical construction of this passage, without drawing any conclusions regarding the possible significance of this construction for our understanding of the Vestals' roles in this rite.

8 H. Le Bonniec 1958: 66–67. See also E. Fantham 1998: 212; F. Bömer 1957: 264; J. Frazer 1931: 316–317.

9 H. Scullard 1981: 24; G. Wissowa 1971: 409 ff.

10 For general discussions of these rites, see M. York 1986: 178–179; C. B. Pascal 1981; J. Vanggaard 1979.

11 For detailed discussions of this passage, none of which contradicts this connection, see E. Fantham 1998: 230; F. Bömer 1957–1958: 274; J. Frazer 1931: 344.

12 For general discussions of these rites, see F. Graf 1992; M. Beard 1987, 1988a; J. Vanggaard 1971; G. Wissowa 1971: 199–201.

13 So all commentators on Ovid. E. Fantham 1998: 230; F. Bömer 1957–1958: 274; J. Frazer 1931: 344.

14 Ov. *Fast.* 4.767–776.

15 Our other ancient sources, Ath. 8.361; Cic. *Div.* 2.98; D. H. 1.88.3; Plu. *Rom.* 12.1; Prop. 4.4.73–78; Tib. 2.5.89 ff.; Var. *L.* 6.15; Vell. 1.8.4, all offer even less detail than Ovid and are thus of little help to us. For a discussion of the passage in Propertius, see J. L. Butrica 2000.

16 Ov. *Fast.* 4.726.

17 Ov. *Fast.* 4.747–755.

18 The term *suffimen* appears only here and seems to be a poetic diminution of the word *suffimentum* used by Cicero and Pliny the Elder. In all of the instances it is used, it is used to describe 'a substance meant to fumigate' (*OLD* 1861). See also E. Fantham 1998: 274; F. Bömer 1957–1958: 274, who both discuss Ovid's *suffimen*.

19 Authors who refer to the Argei, but do not mention the Vestals, include: Cic. *S. Rosc.* 100; Gel. 10.15.30; Macr. 1.11.46; Plu. *Quaes.Rom.* 32.86; Var. *L.* 7.44. For modern discussions of these rites, see F. Graf 2000; W. Pötscher 1998–1999; A. Ziolkowski 1998–1999; A. Storchi Marino 1991–1994; G. Radke 1993; B. Nagy 1985.

20 F. Bömer 1957–1958: 327–330 discusses this passage at some length. So too does J. Frazer 1931: 74–109, who discusses the various theories of the origins and significance of this rite in even greater detail. In the end, Frazer decides in favour of the possibility that these rites were purification rites, arguing convincingly against the theory that they were 'vegetation rites' (p. 86).

21 Again our sources vary concerning the precise number of the figures and the significance of that number: Dionysius suggests thirty, while Varro suggests either twenty-four or twenty-seven. For modern discussions of this issue, see F. Graf 2000; H. Scullard 1981: 120.

22 D. Harmon 1978: 1454–1459. A third theory, that of L. Holland 1961, which posits that this ceremony was part of a series of rites, all performed by the Vestals and all meant as fertility rites, should be noted here because it is so closely based on the Vestals' participation, but it meets with two particular problems raised by Harmon. First, the theory does not adequately explain why human figurines were disposed of on this occasion. Second, and more convincingly, it is difficult to reconcile the theory that this ceremony was the culmination of a series of harvest/fertility rituals, in which case we would expect the figures to be made of straw, with our ancient sources' belief that the figures were made of rush (*scirpeas*). See also *DnP* 1. 1057–1059; F. Graf 2000; A. Ziolkowski 1998–1999; B. Nagy 1985.

23 D. Harmon 1978: 1455.

24 Liv. 27.35.5; Liv. 36.37.2; Obs. 25. For a modern discussion of this practice, see: C. O. Thulin 1906: 117 ff.

25 There is in fact nothing in Ovid's account, other than the name of the festival itself, to suggest that the Vestals participated in the rituals he describes. It in fact seems quite likely that the rites described by the poet were mainly celebrated by private individuals. Nonetheless the name of the rite together with Servius' observations on the Vestals' manufacture of *mola salsa* on this day suggest that the Vestals had some part to play in these rites.

26 Prop. 4.1.21–22 also mentions the decoration of donkeys in connection with Vesta. Again see F. Bömer 1957–1958: 359–361; J. Frazer 1931: 230–231.

27 H. Scullard 1981: 149–150 suggests that the year's supply of *mole salsa* was prepared on this occasion, following the gathering of ears of spelt on 7, 9 and 11 May, but it is unclear what evidence he uses as a basis for this claim.

28 H. Versnel 1993: 167 discusses this issue.

29 Ov. *Fast.* 6.381–383.

30 Ov. *Fast.* 6.317–318.

31 For other descriptions of the rites, see D. H. 1.33.2; 2.31.3; Plu. *Quaest. Rom.* 48; Var. *L.* 6.20. In none of these passages, though, do our authors mention the

presence or participation of the Vestals. See also F. Bernstein 1997; G. Capdeville 1993b; U. Scholz 1993.

32 H. Scullard 1981: 163; A. Piganiol 1973: 175–177; G. Wissowa 1971: 201–204; P. Stehouwer 1956.

33 *DnP* 3: 148–149; G. Wissowa 1971: 202; K. Latte 1960: 72.

34 On *Ops*, see P. Pouthier 1981; P. G. Stehouwer 1956.

35 Our other ancient sources for the *Opsconsivia*, Fest. p. 292 L; Fest. p. 202 L and Liv. 39.22.4, do not mention the Vestals' participation, but because they are so imprecise, this should not be taken as negative evidence.

36 Fest. p. 202 L.

37 See B. Liou-Gille 2002; P. Pouthier 1981. H. Scullard 1981: 181, beginning from Livy's (39.22.4) statement that Ops had a shrine in the Regia, posits that this shrine may have originally been connected to the storehouse of the king.

38 Modern discussions of these rites are extensive. See, among others, H. Versnel 1992, 1993; H. Brouwer 1989; G. Wissowa 1971: 216–219.

39 H. Brouwer 1989: 369.

40 Plu. *Cic.* 19.

41 O. De Cazanove 1987, for example, has argued that of all Roman women, only the Vestals were allowed to sacrifice and that this capacity should be seen as evidence of the Vestals' male aspect.

42 H. Brouwer 1989: 387. For a slightly revised view of the significance of this festival, see also H. Versnel 1992.

43 H. Brouwer 1989: 396–397.

44 Cic. *Mur.* 35.73 is our earliest source for this privilege, which was seemingly expanded over time. See Chapter 6 for more details on this expansion.

45 See, for example, D. Bomgardner's 2000: 18–19 discussion of the Arval brothers' seating at the Circus Maximus.

46 See pages 29–30 for a discussion of the Vestals' participation in these rites.

47 See G. Capdeville 1993a for a general discussion of this practice.

3 Vestal initiation – the rite of *captio*

When a girl became a Vestal Virgin, she underwent a religious ritual whose procedure can hardly have reassured a nervous, young Vestal candidate.[1] Seated on her father's lap,[2] she awaited the approach of the Pontifex Maximus, who seized her by the hand and took her away 'as if', Aulus Gellius remarks, 'she had been captured in war'.[3] At the same time as he took charge of her, the Pontifex solemnly recited:

> I take you thus, Amata, as a Vestal priestess, who will perform the rites, which it is right that a Vestal priestess perform on behalf of the Roman people, on the same terms as she who was a Vestal on the best terms.
>
> (Gell. 1.12.14)

This chapter examines Aulus Gellius' account of this so-called rite of *captio*,[4] together with his description of the process for selecting a Vestal candidate and his accompanying list of requirements and exemptions that had to be met before a girl could be considered an eligible Vestal candidate. It argues that the rite of *captio* primarily aimed at ensuring that the Vestals remained full members of the Roman civic body (i.e. the female equivalent of citizens), while becoming non-members of any of the individual families that together made up Rome's underlying family structure. This theory is reinforced in Chapters 4 and 5, which consider other aspects of the Vestals' cult and daily life, in particular the most central requirement of the order, these priestesses' continual virginity, and their special legal and financial status.

The ritual of *captio*

Ever since I. Santinelli at the beginning of the twentieth century drew a comparison between the Vestal rite of *captio* and a Roman marriage ceremony,[5] modern scholarly discussion of this rite has focused on the question of whether or not his comparison was correct. Scholars have argued for or against this comparison in turn, seemingly according to where they stand on the question of whether the Vestals symbolically represented the wives or the daughters of the archaic Roman kings.[6] Those scholars who favour the view that the Vestals embodied the wife of the king argue that the rite of *captio* symbolized the marriage rites of the king and queen (with the Pontifex Maximus taking the role of king and the Vestal candidate that of queen).[7] Those who, on the contrary, believe that the Vestals represented the daughters of the king, claim equally fervently that the rite of *captio* manifestly did not symbolize this marriage ceremony.[8] What it did symbolize, though, they leave largely unexplained.

This discussion has perhaps been so enduring because both sides have some merit to their argument. As Santinelli and others have observed, the rite of *captio* does indeed resemble a Roman marriage ceremony in some respects.[9] In both rites, the girl is removed from the embrace of one of her parents, and both rites seem to have had some war imagery. Aulus Gellius, for example, observes that in the rite of *captio*, the removal of a girl from her father's lap was done as if in war, while Festus notes that the bride's hair was parted with a spear.[10]

At the same time, however, as other scholars have also observed, there are some marked differences between the two rites. The Vestal candidate was taken not from her mother's lap, as a bride was, but from her father's, and the war imagery described is not directly parallel. In the marriage rite *cum manu*, a bride's hair was parted with a spear; in the rite of *captio*, the Vestal candidate was treated as a captive of war. Neither do the remaining rituals of *captio* parallel the remaining rituals of a Roman marriage ceremony. The Vestal candidate was not accompanied to her 'symbolic' husband's house by a torch-lit procession, nor were any other rites reminiscent of the Roman wedding ceremony performed in connection with her induction into the Vestal order. Thus, to say that the rite of *captio* was merely a symbolic marriage ceremony is to oversimplify. At the same time, however, to claim that the two rites are wholly unrelated goes too far in the other direction. Instead, some middle ground must be found, one that can simultaneously explain the two rites' similarities and clarify their differences.

One possible explanation that accounts for both the similarities and differences between these two rites is that, while their main purposes may have been different, they had a common subsidiary purpose. The main purpose of the rite of *captio* was, of course, to induct a girl into the Vestal order and make her a priestess. As part of this process, however, Aulus Gellius notes:

> Moreover, a Vestal Virgin, as soon as she has been taken and led into the atrium of Vesta and handed over to the Pontifices, immediately at that moment she leaves her father's *potestas* without emancipation and without the diminution of her rights and obtains the right of making a will.
>
> (Gell. 1.12.9)

Thus, the rite of *captio* not only aimed at making a girl a Vestal but also simultaneously resulted in her removal from her father's *potestas* and her becoming in effect *sui iuris*.[11] Likewise, while the main goal of a wedding ceremony was the marriage of the bride and groom, it too, in its most formal and ancient incarnation – that of a marriage *cum manu* – resulted in the removal of the bride from her father's *potestas*. In this latter case, however, the transfer of the bride into the *potestas* of her new husband or his family completed this removal.[12] Both rites then had as one of their purposes the transfer of a girl out of her father's *potestas*. In the marriage rite, the establishment of the bride within her new family's *potestas* completed this transfer. In the rite of *captio*, this transfer was never completed, the Vestal instead becoming *sui iuris*. The two rites involved similar actions because they both had as one of their intended results the removal of a girl from her father's *potestas*, not because one was the symbolic re-enactment of the other. At the same time, both rituals also had some differences because their main goals – marriage on the one hand and induction into the Vestal order on the other – were different.[13]

It remains to be explained why the correct transfer of a Vestal candidate out of her father's *potestas* seems to have played such a major role in her induction into the order. The answer is to be found in the religious facets of *potestas*, which are often overshadowed in modern considerations of the topic by examinations of the relationship between *potestas* and a woman's financial and legal position.[14] A woman's transfer from her father's *potestas* to her husband's not only meant a transfer from her birth family's financial and legal sphere to that of her husband's family, but also meant a transfer from her birth family's religious sphere to her husband's, since a woman who married *cum manu* ceased to be able to participate in her birth family's religious rites and instead took part in those of her husband's family.[15]

The rite of *captio* involved a similar transfer from one religious sphere to another for the new Vestal but, with one important difference, in her case the transfer was from her birth family's cult to a state one. It is the contrasting nature of these two religious spheres, one private and familial, and the other public and official, that lies behind the rite of *captio*'s focus on a girl's removal from her father's *potestas*. As a state cult, the cult of Vesta did not belong to a single Roman family but to all of them together, collectively. If either the cult itself or its priestesses had come under the *potestas* of a single family, both it and they could not have continued to represent the state as a whole but would instead have become entangled in the domestic rites of the family in question. The Vestals could neither remain under the *potestas* of their fathers nor enter under the *potestas* of a new man and for this reason, the rite of *captio* developed as it did.

The similarity in the rituals involved in the rite of *captio* and those of a marriage ceremony *cum manu*, then, can be explained by the fact that the two rites had a similar result, the transfer of a girl out of her birth family's cult. At the same time, their differences can be explained by the fact that in the one case (the marriage ceremony) the transfer was completed, while in the other (the rite of *captio*) it remained uncompleted. Such a theory serves to explain the more puzzling features of Aulus Gellius' account of the rituals involved in *captio*. As well, it highlights an important facet of the Vestals' religious and societal role – their ability as the only people in Rome to represent religiously the state as a whole and not just one family.

The formula

At the same time that he took a Vestal candidate from the lap of her father, the Pontifex Maximus recited:

> I take you thus, Amata, as a Vestal priestess, who will perform the rites, which it is right that a Vestal priestess perform on behalf of the Roman people, on the same terms as she who was a Vestal on the best terms.
>
> (Gell. 1.12.14)

Like all ritual formulae and prayers which accompany a religious rite, this formula has as its main purpose the verbal definition of the significance or meaning of the rite it accompanies. The rite of *captio*, as this formula states, made a girl a Vestal Virgin. At the same time, however, the formula's wording suggests that the rite had a more complex purpose, ensuring that every priestess inducted into the Vestal order was inducted on precisely the same terms as the first Vestal chosen.

Most scholars embarking on a study of this formula have focused exclusively on the significance of the single word *amata* that the Pontifex used in addressing the new Vestal. Ignoring or dismissing Aulus Gellius' own explanation – *Amata* was the name of the first Vestal[16] – these scholars have over the years put forward various suggestions as to the meaning and significance of this word, which they have then used as the basis for constructing a theory as to the significance of the formula as a whole. G. Wissowa, taking the most direct approach, argues that *amata* should be translated as 'beloved' from the perfect passive participle of 'amare' (to love).[17] G. Dumézil believed that it was connected with a Vedic term meaning 'youngest'.[18] Other scholars have seen *amata* as the Latinization of the Greek ἀδμῆτα, which translates as 'unmastered' or 'virgin',[19] or as a variant of the Latin perfect passive participle 'emeta', meaning 'acquired' from the verb 'emere'.[20] None of these theories, however, has proved particularly convincing.

A single scholar, A. Brouwer, begins his examination of the formula with a discussion of its other puzzling phrase, 'on the same terms as her who was a Vestal on the best terms (*optima lege*)'.[21] He explains this phrase by referring to Festus' definition of the phrase *optima lege*.[22] Festus writes that laws governing the appointment of a *dictator* included this phrase as a rider meant to ensure that whoever was so appointed had all the original rights and privileges pertaining to this position, no matter how much they might have been limited or curtailed in later laws. Brouwer suggests that the '*optima lege*' used in the Vestal formula should be taken as having a similar meaning, that 'une Vestale *optima lege* est une Vestale complète qui jouit de tous les droits, de toutes les prérogatives des Vestales'.[23] In other words, this phrase's inclusion in the formula suggests that a subsidiary purpose of this formula was to ensure that the last and most recent Vestal had exactly the same status as the first and earliest Vestal, no matter what limitations were placed on her and her position intentionally or unintentionally by later laws.

When seen in light of this explanation, Aulus Gellius' explanation that *Amata* was the name of the first Vestal takes on an added significance. While it should not perhaps be taken as the literal truth, the fact that Aulus Gellius' explanation focuses on the name of the first Vestal and thus emphasizes her importance in this connection implies, if nothing else, that the Romans of his period were aware that this formula in some way referred back to the earliest Vestals and their status.

Because of this, it seems possible to argue that the central purpose of the formula as a whole was to ensure that later Vestals were 'taken' into the order on the same terms and conditions as the earliest Vestal had been. Such a theory provides a single explanation for the two parts of the formula that have given rise to modern scholarly puzzlement – the word *Amata* and the phrase *optima lege* – and gives greater coherence and meaning to the formula as a whole. As such, it also emphasizes how strongly the Romans felt about ensuring that no change in a religious rite or ritual, whether intentional or unintentional, interfered with or altered the Vestals' original status. This, as we shall see, is an important aspect of many of the rites and regulations surrounding and attached to this priesthood.

Qualifications for selection

Before Aulus Gellius describes the actual rite of *captio*, he offers a long list of criteria that a girl had to meet in order to be considered as a suitable Vestal candidate:

> Those who have written about the taking of a Virgin, of whom Labeo Antistius wrote most diligently, deny that it is permitted to take a girl who is less than six years in age or greater than ten; or to take one whose father or mother is not living; or one who has been shown to be lacking in speech or hearing or has some other bodily fault. Nor is it permitted to take one whose father has been emancipated or one who has been emancipated herself, even if her father is living and she is in the *potestas* of her grandfather, nor one whose parents, either one, have been slaves or engaged in a low occupation. But they also say that she, whose sister has been chosen for this priesthood, deserves to be excused, as does a girl whose father is a flamen or an augur or a quindecimvirum sacris faciundis or a septemvirum epulonum or a Salius. Also it is customary to give an exemption from the rites of the priesthood to the fiancée of a Pontifex and the daughter of a tubicinius. Moreover, Capito Ateius has left an account that the daughter of a man who did not have a home in Italy might not be chosen, and that the daughter of one who had three children must also be excused.
>
> (Gell. 1.12.1–8)

Many of these criteria can be shown to be concerned with ensuring that the lines of *potestas* relating to a candidate and thus that candidate's familial cult status were pure and that all question of her possible pollution through an incorrect transfer from one domestic religious sphere to another was avoided. The existence of these requirements and their implicit emphasis on the importance of a Vestal candidate's familial cult purity further reinforce the connection between the rite of *captio* and this purity already delineated. They thus serve as further evidence that this issue was of central importance in the selection and induction of a new Vestal.

Aulus Gellius writes that neither a Vestal candidate nor her father could ever have been emancipated from the *potestas* of the head of their family, even if, in the case of the girl, she was in the power of her grandfather and her father was still living. As well, a candidate could not have undergone any form of *emancipatio*, a ritualistic form of sale designed to free one person from another's *potestas*. Finally, while at first glance Aulus Gellius' notation that a Vestal candidate's parents must never have been slaves also has at its root a similar concern with ensuring that there was no doubt about whose *potestas* a Vestal candidate had been under since birth, since when a slave was freed he or she underwent a form of *emancipatio* similar to that which was used when a child was freed from his father's *potestas*.[24] In other words, the *potestas* under which a girl had been since birth must in no way have been disturbed or changed, if she was to be eligible to become a Vestal.

Aulus Gellius' notation that a prospective Vestal could not be more than ten years of age when she was chosen also reveals a concern with issues of domestic cult purity. Scholars have generally argued that this age limit was established to ensure that a girl did not enter puberty before she was inducted into the Vestal order.[25] One of the primary duties of a Vestal was, of course, the preservation of her virginity and without a doubt this upper age limit was meant to ensure that this virginity and the powers associated with it would not have been secretly polluted before it was confined within the limits of the Vestal order and dedicated to its purposes. At the same time, however, because this upper age limit ensured that a girl had not yet reached sexual maturity at the time of her entry into the order, it also ensured that she was unlikely to have partaken in any illicit sexual activity.[26] Such activity would by definition have polluted the girl's family's cult and rendered her as the agent of such pollution unfit to enter the Vestal order. In other words, this age limit may have ensured a Vestal's virginity but this virginity in turn ensured that a Vestal candidate was likely to be in the same pure and unaltered state with regards to her family cult that she had been in since birth.

Aulus Gellius also notes that girls with two or more siblings could not be chosen as Vestals. Reference to the issues of *potestas* and domestic cult purity, which, as we have seen, were of such concern in connection with the choice of an appropriate Vestal candidate, again helps to explain this condition. This time, however, the status of a girl's mother lies behind this clause, not that of her father. In 18 BCE, Augustus gave the *ius trium liberorum* to all citizen class women who had borne three children and to all freed women who had borne four. This right freed them from male tutelage and thus affected the *potestas* their father or husband held over them.[27] If, as seems likely, this condition was a later addition to the traditional list of conditions, one made at the time of or shortly after Augustus' *ius trium liberorum* was passed, then it can be seen as yet another restatement of the rule that if a girl or her parent had been emancipated at any time, the girl was ineligible to be chosen as a Vestal Virgin. The fact that the Romans found it necessary to restate this condition yet again emphasizes just how central were issues of *potestas* in the selection of a Vestal candidate. At the same time, it demonstrates again the concern with ensuring that later Vestals had exactly the same status as earlier ones which we have seen expressed earlier in the oral formula attached to the ritual of *captio*.

One final criterion named by Aulus Gellius also seems to have its roots in concerns with a Vestal candidate's cultic purity. In order to be acceptable as a Vestal candidate, a girl had to have parents who had never engaged in a business considered by the Romans to be *sordidum*. This term has a variety of meanings ranging from simply filthy or dirty to common or of low origin to dishonourable.[28] If, as seems likely, it is the last that was meant by Aulus Gellius, then the reasons for this qualification rest both on the absolute necessity for a Vestal candidate's purity and on the necessity for her to have citizen status. In the ancient Romans' eyes, people who were engaged in a *sordidum negotium* ran the very real risk of becoming religiously polluted. Indeed, some ancient evidence even suggests that engaging in a *sordidum negotium* was enough to remove a person from the ranks of Roman citizens because engagement in this sort of business resulted almost certainly in the person's religious pollution. In the Romans' minds, if a parent was religiously polluted, his or her child could also be contaminated and such a risk must at all costs be avoided when choosing a Vestal candidate, hence the inclusion of this requirement.

Not surprisingly with any religious institution as complex as the Vestals and their cult, there remain some criteria on Aulus Gellius' list that do not fit neatly into any one category. These requirements and exemptions owe their existence to a variety of concerns and issues, most of them being practical in nature. A number of them, though, show a concern with guaranteeing that a Vestal candidate was physically perfect and pure in other ways as well.

A Vestal candidate, Aulus Gellius writes, could have no speech or hearing impediment or any other bodily imperfection. In this, Fronto supports him.[29] Such physical requirements were necessary for obvious reasons. A Vestal who could not hear or speak properly would not have been able to offer prayers to the goddess on behalf of the Roman people. Roman prayers were spoken aloud and one of the basic tenets of Roman religion held that one mispronounced or misspoken word in a prayer endangered the *pax deorum* (the balance of power between men and gods).[30] It would, thus, of course, have endangered Rome's very existence, if a Vestal had had a speech impediment or hearing defect. Likewise, the requirement that a Vestal candidate must be physically perfect can be traced to the dangers inherent in an improperly performed ritual. A girl who limped or had a withered arm could not bear the heavy vessels of water that were part of the Vestals' daily ritual nor perform the other ritual tasks associated with Vesta's cult without risk of failure. Such a failure, like the omission of a word in a prayer, would endanger Rome. As well, the Romans believed generally that anything dedicated to the gods or entering the sacred sphere had to be physically perfect.[31] The requirement that the Vestals be physically perfect was also assuredly due to this belief as well.

The lower age limit for a Vestal candidate may well be due to the simple fact that a child younger than six was thought to be too young to be taken from her mother or incapable of performing the ritual duties required by the order. It can, however, also be ascribed to the same concerns with physical perfection expressed in the requirements just considered. Physical defects, such as those proscribed by Aulus Gellius, are often first fully revealed some time after a child's birth (for example after he or she has reached the age at which children customarily learn to speak and walk). Therefore, by waiting until a girl had passed her sixth birthday, the greatest risk of her having some hidden physical defect or blemish yet to be revealed was removed. As well, this lower age limit ensured that a girl had survived the most dangerous years of her childhood.[32] Roughly, 50 per cent of Roman girls died before they reached their sixth birthday, while those that lived to that age had a correspondingly greater chance of surviving to adulthood.[33] While it is impossible to know how many of those who survived to adulthood suffered some disfiguring illness in their early years, the figures are likely to be somewhat similar. Thus, the age limit of six ensured that the worst risk of a girl developing some physical defect not visible at birth or caused by an early childhood illness was avoided.

A Vestal candidate had to be *patrima et matrima* at the time she was chosen. That is to say, both of her parents had to be alive.[34] This requirement, as far as we know, was shared with only one other religious group within the Roman community, the Salii, the priests of Mars who, clad in archaic military dress, twice a year ritually danced through the streets of Rome. Wissowa suggests that in the case of these latter priests this demand was in effect a hidden age limit meant to ensure that the priests would be of relatively young age when chosen.[35] Following a similar line of reasoning in the case of the Vestals would suggest that such a qualification in their case was simply a rewording of the upper age limit of ten years noted by Aulus Gellius. The demand that both parents be living could, however, also be based on a desire to ensure that a Vestal candidate was in as perfect a state as possible with respect to her family circumstances. In an age with a high mortality rate due to the dangers of childbirth and disease, relatively few children could expect to reach adulthood with both parents living.[36] Those who did were considered especially fortunate and favoured by the gods.[37] Under such circumstances, the fact that both of a girl's parents were alive was a sign that the Vestal candidate was favoured by and thus acceptable to the gods.

A girl was exempt from being taken as a Vestal Virgin, if her sister had already been chosen. The reasons for this condition are likely to be practical and rooted in the political and social realities of the Roman upper classes. J. Hallett argues that the Vestal order provided a welcome opportunity for relief to those fathers of several daughters who could not afford to find dowries for all of them.[38] Following her line of reasoning, one of the reasons for this exemption may have been a desire to ensure that as many families as possible had access to this opportunity. The reverse of her theory is equally true however. A family's daughters were often valuable playing pieces in the chess game of shifting political alliances that might be strengthened through two families' inter-marriage. This exemption protected a family from the necessity of giving up more than one of its marriageable and perhaps politically valuable daughters to the order. Finally, this condition also protected the order and Rome by preventing a family from gaining too great a share of the order's power and influence (an influence which could at times be great).[39]

The significance of a second ground for exemption noted by Aulus Gellius poses a more complex and seemingly insoluble problem. According to the ancient author, the daughters of a long list of priesthoods (the Flamines, the Augurs, the Quindecimviri, the Septemviri, the Salii and the Priests of the Tubilustrium) were exempt from being 'taken' as a Vestal Virgin, as was any girl betrothed to a Pontifex. Missing from the first category is one major group of state priests, the Pontifices; at the same time, this group is the only one to appear in the latter category. Clearly there is some essential similarity between the status of the daughters of the priests in the first category and the fiancées of the Pontifices in the second. Because in every instance the men concerned are priests, it seems equally clear that this similarity has a religious basis. Unfortunately, the precise nature of this significance is unclear. At a guess, it would seem to have something to do once again with the religious aspects of the *potestas*, which was an integral part of any father–daughter or husband–wife relationship in ancient Rome, and which, as we have seen, played a central role in determining who was, and who was not a suitable Vestal candidate. This, however, is just a guess. In this instance, we simply lack the necessary infor-mation to make any real steps forward in understanding this condition's purpose and significance.

The final ground for the exemption of a girl was that her father did not have an Italian residence. This is a deceptively simple sounding condition that actu-ally relates to one of the most fundamental aspects of the goddess Vesta. Vesta was believed by the Romans to be in some way synonymous with the Earth itself and with the particular location in which she was worshipped.[40] Roman Vesta remained Roman only so long as she (or her temporal representative, the hearth fire in the temple of Vesta) remained in Rome on Roman earth. Had she, or her fire, been moved to another city or location, she would still have been Vesta but no longer Roman Vesta. Instead, she would have become Vesta of the new location. In such circumstances, it is not hard to imagine that the Romans would have thought it at least religiously unsuitable and probably even reli-giously dangerous for a goddess so inextricably connected with the Earth and with one particular location on that earth to be served by priestesses who themselves were not innately connected to the same location.

That the version of this requirement given by Aulus Gellius stipulates all

Italy and not just Rome itself is no real barrier to this explanation. From a relatively early date, the Romans accepted most of the inhabitants of the Italian peninsula as quasi-Romans in a way that differed notably from their attitudes towards those living in Gaul, Spain or the other provinces. By the late Republic, there was no real discernible difference between a man such as Cicero from an Italian provincial family and a man born in Rome itself. For all practical intents and purposes, the two groups had the same rights and duties. This was not the case, though, for those born outside of Italy. Although some Gauls were also granted citizenship as early as Julius Caesar's time, they remained outsiders with limited access to the privileged institutions of Rome. This was particularly true of the state religious sphere where generally only Italian and Roman residents filled the traditional state priesthoods in this period (although nowhere else is an explicit requirement of an Italian home similar to that for the Vestals recorded). The limitation of Vestal candidates to girls from Italian families and not just Roman ones is thus very much in keeping with Roman practices and beliefs in the historic period under consideration.

Selection process

Having set out the various positive and negative criteria that had to be met before a girl could be considered for entry into the Vestal order, Aulus Gellius turns his attention to the actual selection process that had to be undergone before the religious rite of *captio* itself could be performed:

> Concerning the custom and ritual of taking a Vestal Virgin, no ancient accounts exist, except that the first one was taken by King Numa. But we have found the *lex papia*, by which it is advised, that twenty virgins be selected from the populace through the judgement of the Pontifex Maximus and that from this number one be selected by lot in an assembly, and her the Pontifex Maximus takes as sacred to Vesta. This selection by lot, according to the *lex papia*, however, is rarely needed today. For if someone of respectable birth approaches the Pontifex Maximus and offers his daughter, as long as it is possible in keeping with the religious observations, an exemption from the *lex papia* is given.
>
> (Gell. 1.12.10–12)

This selection process, he notes, could take place in one of two ways. First, the Pontifex Maximus himself, following the Papian law, could select twenty girls, from whom one was chosen by lot. Second, a man of 'respectable birth' could offer his daughter of his own accord and if the senate approved the offer, and as Aulus Gellius explicitly states, if all of the religious aspects were in order, she might be accepted without taking all the steps decreed by the Papian law.

While the first method may not be the earliest means of choosing a final Vestal candidate (if Plutarch is to be believed, originally the king himself chose the Vestals),[41] by Aulus Gellius' own account it is the older of the two methods known to him. The first step of the process is similar to that used in choosing other special members of the Pontifical College (the Rex Sacrorum and the various Flamines) in that a list of acceptable candidates was first presented and then a final candidate chosen.[42] It differs, however, in that the Pontifex Maximus himself alone chose the candidates for the Vestal order while in the case of the other priesthoods the Pontifices as a whole made the choice.

The Pontifex Maximus' absolute authority in this process can be taken as yet further evidence of the Romans' overwhelming concern with ensuring that there was no uncertainty about the *potestas* under which a Vestal candidate belonged. The Pontifex Maximus was consulted in all matters connected with the transfer of an individual from one family's *potestas* to another's (adoptions, marriages *cum manu*, etc.). This consultation took place because of the dangers of religious pollution that an improper transfer from one family's domestic cult to another carried with it. The Pontifex Maximus' central role in the selection of a Vestal candidate can be traced to a similar concern, and thus, it highlights once again just how important familial cult purity was in the case of a Vestal candidate.

The second steps of both the selection processes described by Aulus Gellius in any case support the view that at least general cultic purity was of central concern in the choice of a Vestal.[43] In the case of the Rex Sacrorum and the Flamines, a list of candidates was presented to the Pontifex Maximus, who then made the final choice. In the case of the Vestals, one girl was chosen by lot from those on the list. We know from other occasions in antiquity that such lottery systems were frequently used when a choice was to be left up to the gods, and it is not hard to see the process here as having a similar purpose. The Pontifex Maximus might make the first selection but Vesta herself must make the final choice. Because this is the only time a final candidate for a Roman priesthood is chosen in this manner, this method suggests again that extra care was taken to ensure that all religious concerns were in order and that a Vestal candidate met with the approval of the goddess she was to serve.

If there remained any doubt that issues of religious purity played a role of paramount importance in the final choice of a Vestal candidate, this doubt is removed by Aulus Gellius' description of the alternative method that could be used for choosing a new Vestal. If a man of respectable birth offered his daughter for the priesthood, the Pontifex Maximus could decide to accept her without going through the full process of selecting twenty candidates, provided that the religious observations were in order and that the senate exempted the man making the offer from the Papian law. Unfortunately, Aulus Gellius does not say what form these religious observations took, but it does not seem too extreme to suggest that they, like the lottery used in the first method, were meant to ascertain that the goddess approved of the girl in question.

Both methods, then, express the same concern for ensuring that the religious proprieties were observed and that, in effect, the goddess herself was allowed the final say in the choice of her new priestess. In the first instance, the Pontifex Maximus may have made a preliminary selection but the final choice was left to the goddess herself through the use of a lottery. In the second instance, while a girl's father might voluntarily offer her, it is clear that some religious proprieties had to be observed. While it is unclear what these proprieties were, it seems likely that they were designed to address the same concerns as the first method did. Thus, in this part of the process too, we see the thread of religious purity that runs throughout Aulus Gellius' description. For the Vestals, more than for any other priesthood, this religious purity was of paramount importance.

Conclusion

The rite of *captio* itself and many of the requirements, which a girl had to fulfil before she could be chosen as a Vestal, suggest that issues of *potestas* and familial cult purity are fundamental to an understanding of the order and its place in Roman religion. Aulus Gellius' qualification that neither a girl nor her father could ever have been emancipated from the head of their family's *potestas*, no matter what the circumstances, raises this issue explicitly for the first time. Variants on the same theme appear again in later conditions, making this one of two specific areas that are repeatedly identified as being of concern to those selecting a Vestal. The actual rite of *captio* itself also suggests a concern with the same topic, in that it seems designed to facilitate the transfer of a girl out of her father's *potestas* and thus out of her family's cult.

As well as a specific concern with *potestas* and domestic cult purity, Aulus Gellius' description of the rite and its requirements also reveals a more general concern with the overall purity of a Vestal candidate. This purity is to be expected in a community that often set such demands on performers of religious rituals but it should be noted that this concern extends much further and covers a wider range of areas than does a similar concern for any other priesthood. This in turn suggests, not surprisingly, that purity was also a major concern for members of the Vestal order.

Notes

1 Gell. 1.12. Although Aulus Gellius is our single source for these details and is of relatively late date, his text's usefulness as evidence for our period should not be dismissed out of hand. The author names many of his sources for the information he provides, and these sources all stem from the period under discussion.
2 The Latin text actually reads 'the lap of that parent who has *potestas* over the Vestal candidate'. This can only be the girl's father or perhaps grandfather. The fact that Gellius emphasizes this connection only strengthens my argument concerning the relationship between the rite of *captio* and *potestas*.
3 Gell. 1.12.
4 It should be noted at the outset that the use of the term *captio* in the sense of a Vestal ritual is itself a modern invention, which does not appear in any of our ancient sources. As such the term itself is of dubious value except as an illustration of how modern research into the Vestals and their cult has overlooked the importance of our original sources or in this case their lack. See *TLL* 1907: 3.3645 for a discussion

of the more usual ancient uses of the word *captio.*

5 I. Santinelli 1904: 63.

6 The only noteworthy exception to this is H. Cancik-Lindemaier 1990: 14, who draws the conclusion that *captio* marked the abandonment of the regular Roman world for the religious sphere.

7 See, for example, K. Mustakallio 1992: 74; M. C. Martini 1997a: 257–258.

8 See, for example, H. J. Rose 1926: 445; G. Wissowa 1958 *RE*, vol. 8A.2: 1774.

9 Earlier scholars simply compare the Vestal rite of *captio* to a Roman marriage ceremony without specifying which form of marriage ceremony they mean. Since the religious rites described by Festus were used only in the most formal type of marriage, that transferring the bride from one *potestas* to another, it can in fact be only these rites that are meant. For a discussion of the differences between the various types of Roman marriage rites, see S. Treggiari 1991: 21–24.

10 Fest. p. 364/5 L.

11 That is to say independent and able to make her own financial decisions without having to seek the consent of a male guardian.

12 R. S. Kraemer 1992: 50–51; B. Rawson 1986: 19.

13 The fact that the two rites had different final results, with the Vestal entering a public religious sphere and the bride a new family's domestic sphere, can also be used to explain the difference in the main similarity between the two rites, the removal of the girl from the lap of her father in the one rite and the lap of her mother in the other. A marriage ceremony *cum manu* transferred the bride from her birth family's cult to that of her new husband's family. This transfer involved movement from one private religious sphere to another and took place as the result of a private agreement between two families. The Vestal rite of *captio*, however, transferred the Vestal candidate out of her family's cult into the Vestal order. Such a transfer was very much an official, state concern, involving as it did the transfer of a girl from the private sphere of her birth family to the public sphere of the Vestal order. It has become a scholarly truism that women in antiquity generally symbolized the private, domestic sphere while men symbolized the public. This truism, however, does offer an obvious explanation for why a girl's mother played the central role in one rite and her father in the other. A marriage rite, which accomplished the transfer of a girl from one domestic sphere to another, was a private one and thus the mother of the family took the central role. The rite of *captio*, which accomplished a transfer from the private sphere of the family to the public sphere of the state, was a public one and thus the father of the family played a central part.

14 See, for example, W. K. Lacey 1992; R. Saller 1986; J. Crook 1967a, 1967b; A. Guarino 1967.

15 See, for example, R. S. Kraemer 1992: 50–51; S. Treggiari 1991: 29; S. Dixon 1988: 45.

16 Gell. 1.12.19.

17 G. Wissowa 1971: 510 n.4.

18 G. Dumézil 1963: 89–91. For further possibilities, see F. Guizzi 1968: 130–137.

19 A. von Blumenthal 1938: 268–269.

20 G. May 1905: 14–15.

21 A. Brouwers 1933: 1080 ff. M. Jehne 1989 also discusses the use of this term but primarily in relation to the laws governing the appointing of a *dictator.*

22 Fest. p. 216 L.

23 A. Brouwers 1933: 1081.

24 See *TLL* 5² 441 for the Latin usage of the term. See T. Mommsen 1952: 3.59ff and *RE* 5.296 for a discussion of the legal implications.

25 See, for example, M. Beard 1980: 19.

26 For a good introductory discussion to adultery and its consequences in Rome, see A. Richlin 1981.

27 For a man it meant that the waiting periods between his standing for the various political offices of the *cursus honorum* was shortened by one year for every child.

28 *OLD* 1794.

29 Fro. *Amic.* 149N. See also M. G. Morgan 1974.

30 H. H. Scullard 1981: 25–26. For a more detailed discussion of prayers and praying in ancient Rome, see F. Hickson 1991.

31 A cow, for example, that was to be sacrificed to the gods had to be perfectly formed and coloured without any visible blemishes. After it was sacrificed, its entrails were closely examined to ensure that no unseen inner blemishes existed either. If they did, the offering was declared null and void and a new expiatory one had to be performed.

32 R. Saller 1994: 24.

33 For a discussion of these statistics, see R. Saller 1994: 22–24.

34 It should be noted, however, that Gaius *Inst.* 1.31 suggests that the phrase *patrimi et matrimi* refers to children whose parents were married by the ancient marriage ceremony of *confarreatio*. While this raises the possibility that a suitable Vestal candidate had to have parents married by such a rite, this possibility is weakened by the fact that while in the late first century BCE, certain flaminates went unfilled because of a lack of boys whose parents were married in this way, this does not seem to have been the case with the Vestals. See also *TLL* 8.1. 481 and *TLL* 10.1.5. 756.

35 *RE* 1A.2. 1882.

36 R. Saller 1994: 12–25.

37 S. Dixon 1991: 99–113.

38 For further discussion of possible Roman attitudes to handing their daughters over to the Vestal order, see J. Hallett 1984: 85–87.

39 See Chapter 6.

40 See pages 6–7. See also W. K. Lacey 1996: 125–127.

41 Plu. *Num.* 10.2.

42 M. Beard and J. North 1990: 22.

43 The first step of the second process, involving simply, as it did, a father's volunteering of his daughter, requires little further comment, although it should be noted that one reason for this arrangement was perhaps the very real possibility that twenty acceptable candidates were not available at a single given time. See, however, M. C. Martini 1997a: 1.254 for a brief discussion of this matter.

4 The Vestals' virginity

The historian Livy writes of Numa's founding of the Vestal order:

> [Numa] also appointed the Vestal virgins. This priesthood originated in Alba and was not at all foreign to the founder's people. He established for them a public stipend so that the temple might have constant priests, and he made them sacred and venerable by virginity and other religious ceremonies.
>
> (Liv. 1.20)[1]

Virginity was at the very centre of the Vestals' religious cult. Whatever else these priestesses were and whatever else they did, they were virgins, and their cult had as one of its central aspects the preservation of this virginity.[2]

This chapter considers the various facets of this virginity and its antithesis, the *crimen incesti* (the loss of this virginity). It argues first that there was more than one reason for this virginity, and second that one of these reasons was that it enabled the Vestals to remain in the liminal position in which the rite of *captio* had established them as full members of the Roman state's civic structure but non-members of the same state's family structure.

Virginity

The Vestals were required to retain their virginity throughout their period of service to their goddess.[3] This period of service was not necessarily a lifelong one, although most priestesses chose to make it so, but instead was of a minimum of thirty years' duration. Thus, the Vestals' virginity was also not necessarily a lifelong commitment but one that might last no more than thirty years. A loss of virginity during a Vestal's period of service, however, led to charges of *incestum*, a crime viewed as a particularly dire threat to the Roman state, and punished by burial alive.

Studies by H. Guizzi and others have advanced many different theories on the significance of this virginity over the years. It has been argued, for example, that the Vestals' virginity was rooted in a univirate Roman matron's chastity or that it was meant to separate the Vestals from the profane world of ordinary women and give them a special sacred status.[4] Others have contended that the Vestals' virginity prevented the order from becoming too closely connected to a single Roman family,[5] or that this virginity represented a stored-up power, the suppression of which gave the Vestals a special status.[6] While each of these theories has something to recommend it, no single one in the end has proved more convincing than others.

The scholars behind these theories, however, have overlooked another explanation of Vestal virginity, already recognized by Cicero, who in his *de legibus* observed: 'virgins should be present to worship her, so that the care and custody of the fire may be more easily accomplished, and women may perceive that feminine nature is capable of complete purity (*castitas*)' (Cic. *Leg.* 2.29). In other words, as the ancient author explicitly states, the priestesses' virginity had more than one explanation. Since all of the above theories have been proved feasible, we should perhaps take Cicero's quote as our example and recognize that the Vestals' virginity had several explanations. That is to say, that what is necessary for a full understanding of the Vestals' virginity is a theory that recognizes the possibility that this virginity functioned on a variety of levels and had a variety of meanings.

Such a theory without a doubt should include the four theories delineated above. At the same time, it must include an additional argument. At least part of the explanation of Vestal virginity can be found in the need to ensure for religious reasons (not just social ones as H. Cancik-Lindemaier suggests) that after becoming a priestess, a Vestal could not become a member of an individual Roman family, while at the same time she retained her citizen status as a member of the Roman state.[7] Such a liminal status was necessary in the eyes of the Romans in order for these priestesses to be able to represent their state as a whole.

The Vestal initiation rite of *captio* removed a Vestal candidate from the *potestas* of her family and thus from its religious control.[8] This removal was completed not by a girl's transfer into another Roman family, as happened when a bride married *cum manu* or a child was officially adopted into a new family, but instead by her placement in a sort of no-man's land, where she remained a member of the Roman state's civic structure but not its individual family one. A Vestal's virginity ensured that the separation from the individual families of Rome brought about by the rite of *captio* continued throughout her priestly tenure.

As long as a Vestal had to remain a virgin, she could not marry. As long as she could not marry, she could not participate in, nor had she any means by which she could return to, the ordinary family and domestic cult structure of Rome, outside of which the rite of *captio* had placed her. Such a status, unique at Rome, would have made the Vestals the only Romans capable of devoting all of their religious energy to the state cult without also having to fulfil a role in, or risk being polluted by, the private cult of an individual family.

At the same time as their virginity kept the Vestals outside the Roman state's domestic cult structure, it also served to keep them securely within

Rome's citizen body. Before we turn to a more detailed discussion of this topic, however, it is necessary to outline briefly the semi-official Roman classification system of citizen women, which functioned especially in the religious sphere, since this classification system serves as a basis for much of what follows.

In ancient Rome, all citizen women were considered members of one or the other of two semi-officially recognized classes, the *matronae* and the *virgines*.[9] Each of these classes had definite criteria that a woman had to meet in order to be considered a member. To be a *matrona*, a woman had to be the respectable wife or widow of a Roman citizen.[10] To be a *virgo*, a woman had to be the morally pure, respectable, sexually intact (as we define the English word virgin) marriageable daughter of a Roman citizen.[11] Women who did not qualify as either *matronae* or *virgines* were effectively non-members of the Roman state and of its cult, banned, with a few specific exceptions, from participating (except perhaps as spectators along a parade route) in many of Rome's most central religious rites.

When one considers these classifications and various aspects of the Vestals' virginity closely, it becomes apparent that at least one of the purposes of the Vestals' prolonged virginity must have been ensuring their eligibility to remain members of the *virgines*. Not least, the regular use of *virgo* in all forms of the Vestals' Latin titles points to some connection between the groups. As well, an affiliation with one of the two groups just named seems, in light of the legalistic nature of Roman religion, both fitting and perhaps even necessary for a group of women who functioned at the centre of the Roman state cult. Finally, and most concretely, many aspects of the Vestals' virginity seem emphatically calculated (if one may use so intentional a word) to ensure that these priestesses met the qualifications necessary for inclusion in the *virgines*.

The most obvious criterion for inclusion among the *virgines* was the requirement that a woman be a sexual virgin. This is so self-evidently met in the Vestals' case as to require almost no further comment. Not a single one of our ancient sources even hints at anything to the contrary, and it is clear from the many references to the crime of *incestum* that, whatever the less tangible aspects of this crime were, its physical basis was the loss of this sexual virginity.

The second criterion, that a woman be morally pure and respectable, is also clearly met by these priestesses. Repeatedly in the ancient sources, we find forms of the word complex *castus/castitas* (translated as 'morally pure, chaste') used in connection with these priestesses.[12] Cicero, as we have seen, writes:

> And since Vesta, who takes her name from the Greek language (for we use almost the same word as the Greek, instead of translating it), protects the city hearth, virgins should be present to worship her, so that the care and custody of the fire may be more easily accomplished, and women may perceive that the feminine nature is capable of complete purity (*castitas*).[13]
>
> (Cic. *Leg.* 2.29)

Valerius Maximus, describing how the Vestal Tuccia proved herself innocent of *incestum*, uses *castitas* as a synonym for her virginity:

> With the same sort of help the purity (*castitas*) of the Vestal virgin Tuccia, who had been accused of *incestum* was cleansed of the cloud of ill repute by which it had been obscured.
>
> (V. Max. 8.1.abs5)

Festus writes:

> Brides wear the six braids, because this was the most ancient style for them. Which indeed the Vestal Virgins also use, whose purity (*castitas*). . . .
>
> (Fest. p. 454 L)

The poets also regularly used the adjective *casta* to describe the priestesses and their goddess.[14] Finally, the name given to the Vestals' most terrible crime, the loss of their virginity, is *incestum*, an older form of *in-castum*, the negation and antonym of *castum*.[15] Such a connection cannot but add weight to the view that one of the aspects of Vestal virginity was a concern with *castitas* or moral purity.

To be a *virgo* a woman had to be eligible for marriage. This is the most difficult criterion to prove in relationship to the Vestals, since their long-term virginity might well seem to make this impossible. The Vestals' virginity, however, was not perpetual but instead had a minimum limit of thirty years. This limit has puzzled modern scholars, who seek to explain it in a variety of ways, most commonly connecting it with the period of a woman's greatest fertility.[16] Such an explanation is plausible and should not be dismissed out of hand. Yet, alongside it and simultaneously, there exists another possibility. By setting this time limit, the Romans left open the possibility that the Vestals could eventually marry if they wished. This measure may seem like a legal nicety but it does satisfactorily explain why this limit existed. Such a clause nominally preserved the fiction that after thirty years' service, the Vestals could choose to marry. Thus, they remained marriageable, and this fiction allowed the priestesses to retain the right to be recognized as members of the *virgines*.

A *virgo* also had to be the daughter of a Roman citizen. As Aulus Gellius makes clear in his description of the rite of *captio*, one of the requirements for a suitable Vestal candidate held that neither of a Vestal's parents could ever have been slaves or 'held lowly occupations'.[17] This in effect meant that a girl had to be the child of Roman citizen parents since both freedmen and those with sordid occupations were shut out from Roman citizenship. Thus, a Vestal also fulfilled this last criterion.

The question then is, if part of the reason for the Vestals' virginity was a need to ensure that these priestesses remained members of the *virgines*, why was it so important that they remain so. One obvious answer is that it was necessary for the Vestals to retain their citizen status if they were to represent Rome on a religious plane. The only way they could do so according to the legalistic Roman mindset was to remain qualified for membership in one of the two 'female citizen classes' regularly allowed to participate in the Roman state's cults. Their virginity, which was necessary if they were to remain outside the family structure at Rome, locked them out of the *matronae* (even if in other aspects, they show some relation to this class). Thus, the only option open was the *virgines*. (As noted earlier, women who did not fulfil the qualifications of either the *matronae* or the *virgines* were viewed as non-members of the Roman state for religious purposes and banned from participating in almost all state rites.)

The Vestals were virgins then because this virginity enabled them to remain members of the Roman state's civic structure while at the same time placing them outside the state's family cult structure. This peculiar status enabled them to represent the Roman state as a whole. At the same time, their virginity kept the Vestals pure and enabled them both to approach the gods in an appropriate state and to set an example to other Roman women. This virginity also ensured that the Vestals did not become members of an individual Roman family, and thus prevented them from favouring one Roman family over others. Finally, this virginity set them off from the profane, made them sacred and thus gave them a special power as interceders for the Roman people.

Crimen incesti

The Vestal virgins alone of all Romans had a peculiar status as members of the Roman state's civic structure yet non-members of the same state's underlying family structure. The necessities engendered by this peculiar status can be used to explain some of the most mysterious aspects of this priesthood and its cult. This is also true of the single most discussed aspect of all those associated with the Vestals and their cult, the *crimen incesti*, that is the loss of their virginity during their period of priestly service.[18]

According to ancient sources, when a Vestal Virgin was accused of *incestum*, she was ordered by the Pontifical College to refrain from the sacred rites and from selling her slaves.[19] She was then tried, originally by a court made up of the Pontifices, later by a quaestorial tribunal.[20] If she was found guilty, she was dressed in funereal garments, and then carried, bound hand and foot in a closed litter, accompanied by her family and friends as if at a funeral, to the *campus sceleratus* near the Colline Gate.[21] Here she was taken by the Pontifex Maximus and sent down a ladder into an underground chamber furnished with a bed, blankets, a lighted lamp, water, bread, milk and oil. As soon as she was placed upon the ladder, the Pontifex Maximus and the other priests accompanying him turned away. After the priestess had descended the ladder, it was removed and the hole through which she had entered the room filled in until no trace of its existence remained. Her lover was bound to a *furca* and beaten to death.[22]

Judicial process

It has often been remarked that the original judicial method used to try the Vestals for the *crimen incesti* was anomalous in both Roman religion and law. Of all Roman officials, only a Vestal was suspended from her duties on the slightest suspicion of wrongdoing, and only she faced a judicial inquiry by the full Pontifical College. Of all Roman women accused of sexual misdeeds, only a Vestal faced such a court or such public proceedings. Of all Romans, only a Vestal seemingly faced a trial with so little possibility of defending herself.

These anomalies have, over the years, quite naturally met with a number of scholarly attempts to explain them. Many scholars, following G. Wissowa's original explanation, have concluded that this judicial procedure should be seen as an examination of a possible *prodigium* (an evil omen).[23] This conclusion, however, does not fit the general pattern associated with these *prodigia*.[24] A *prodigium* was a warning that the *pax deorum* had been broken by some human action not the human action itself.[25] In every instance where a Vestal was accused of *incestum*, this accusation was brought on by the occurrence of another, often mysterious event (the sudden and unexplained extinguishing of the fire in the *aedes Vestae* was the most common one). This other event was the *prodigium*, while the Vestal's crime was the act that the *prodigium* announced.[26]

Recognizing this and taking his cue from the name given to the Vestals' crime, *incestum*, C. Koch has argued that a Vestal who lost her virginity was in some way guilty of incest (in the modern English sense of the word) and that her trial and punishment were a version of the normal treatment meted out to perpetrators of such a crime.[27] There is, however, no clear evidence to suggest that *incestum* originally meant incest (sexual relations with a close family member). Rather it seems likely that this meaning came later, and that early on in Roman history, when presumably a Vestal's loss of virginity was dubbed *incestum*, the word meant simply *in-castum*, not-pure. Under these circumstances, it is unlikely that the Vestals' *crimen incesti*, which seemingly pre-existed the definition of the word *incestum* as incest, should be seen as simply a special type of this incest.

T. J. Cornell was clearly well aware of these problems when he argued that the whole procedure's existence rested upon the Pontifex Maximus' traditional role as chief discipliner of the Roman priestly colleges as the stand-in for and replacement of the earlier kings.[28] His argument too, however, meets with certain obstacles. Not least of these is the fact that there is no definite evidence to suggest that the Pontifices exercised any disciplinary powers over any priests other than the Vestals. Even the Flamines, who as official members of the Pontifical College ought to have come under the disciplinary powers of the Pontifices, if any priests should have, show no signs of having done so.

A. Staples suggests that a Vestal was tried in this way because she 'transcended the status of *civis* as long as she was a Vestal'.[29] This slightly cryptic statement comes perhaps closest to the argument that the Vestals remained virgins because their virginity allowed them to be members of the Roman state's civic structure without being members of its familial one. There is, however, a clearer explanation for this judicial procedure that is more in keeping with the Romans' legalistic and religious mindset.

One of the Pontifices' major responsibilities was the overseeing of any marriage ceremony that involved the transfer of *manus* from the bride's father to her new husband. Another was the supervision of any official adoption. The Pontifices were in both cases involved in order to ensure that the transfers from one family cult to another that accompanied both an adoption and a marriage *cum manu* were properly carried out so that all risk of the pollution of one cult or the other was avoided. They were also, as Koch has noted, the judges in any case concerning incest involving ordinary citizens.[30] The Pontifices acted as judges in this last case precisely because one effect of incest was the pollution of the involved family's cult. Thus, while it is going too far to claim, as Koch does, that the Vestals' *crimen incesti* was simply a special version of ordinary incest, it is not going too far to say that the Pontifices were involved in judging a *crimen incesti* for the same reasons that they were involved in judging ordinary cases of incest, as both these crimes affected the domestic religious status of the individuals involved and led to a risk of a break in the *pax deorum*.

Burial alive

The especially dangerous nature of the Vestals' crime, which carried with it the risk of a break in the *pax deorum*, might seem by itself to be enough to explain why a convicted Vestal was buried alive. As Cornell points out, however, the actions of other priests could on occasion lead to a similar break in the *pax deorum*.[31] If, for example, a priest sacrificed a bull to Juno or a heifer to Jupiter instead of the reverse, then he put the *pax deorum* equally at risk. So did a general who called on the wrong deity before a battle. Although to modern eyes such offences can seem less serious than the Vestals', this was patently not the case for the Romans. All of them, as far as the Romans were concerned, carried with them an equal risk of endangering the city and its people. Therefore, there must be more behind the burial alive of a Vestal than simply the serious nature of her crime.

Cornell suggests that the real reason for the Vestal's death sentence was the voluntary nature of the *crimen incesti*.[32] Other priests presumably did not deliberately intend to flout the rules of their order when they sacrificed a bull to Juno instead of a heifer or used the wrong words in a prayer. Rather they did so by mistake. Those Vestals convicted of the *crimen incesti*, however, had presumably chosen to break their vows when they committed this crime, thus deliberately jeopardizing the *pax deorum*. It is because of this voluntary aspect of her crime that a Vestal faced death, Cornell argues, just as an ordinary Roman guilty of betraying his city faced it. This argument is accurate enough as far as it goes.

Yet, there is perhaps more to the choice of burial alive for a Vestal convicted of the *crimen incesti* than just this. For this crime shares another characteristic with other crimes that among the Romans led to a death sentence of some form (for example, the crimes of parricide or ordinary incest). All of these crimes have in common not only that they were voluntary in nature – in the case of incest for example, if a couple or a woman could plead ignorance, a lighter sentence was passed – but also that they were especially repugnant to the Romans because they polluted the ordinary religious connections that existed between family members, and damaged them in a way that was serious enough to threaten not just the individual family involved but also the state. The similarity the Romans saw between these crimes' impact and that of the Vestals' *crimen incesti* argues that alongside the voluntary nature of this crime should be placed the danger it posed because of the pollution that it caused in normal family religious connections.

Although this explains the serious and final nature of the Vestals' punishment, it still does not explain why the precise form of burial alive was chosen as the appropriate sentence nor the many odd ritual features that accompanied this burial. Why, for instance, were the Vestals buried rather than thrown into the sea, as was usually done with religiously impure creatures and objects? Why did the chamber, in which they were buried, contain a bed, blankets, a lighted lamp, water, bread, milk and oil? Why did the rites accompanying a Vestal's punishment resemble those of an ordinary funeral in certain aspects, but not in others? What is the significance of Pliny's remark that a *carnifex* or executioner was present at the scene?[33]

A Vestal who was convicted of the *crimen incesti* was buried alive in an underground chamber outside the Colline Gate in the *campus sceleratus*. Scholars have generally argued that a Vestal's burial in this underground chamber together with the necessities of life (water, bread, milk, etc.) was due to the Romans' desire to avoid the blame for physically putting to death a priestess dedicated to the goddess.[34] This possibility is plausible but it overlooks the fact that the same argument could technically be made of the most common means by which the Romans disposed of other religiously impure creatures, the throwing of the creature in question still living into running water. Hermaphrodites, for example, were sent out to sea while patricides were sewn into a sack with a monkey, a chicken and a dog and thrown into the Tiber. In both cases, the humans were still alive when they were thrown into the water. Thus, these forms of disposal could also have been used to preserve the fiction that it was not humans who put the victim to death but the gods.

A better explanation for this particular form of punishment is perhaps to be found in Vesta's position as an earth goddess, combined with the Romans' concern that the right offering reach the right deity as expeditiously as possible.[35] This latter concern is reflected both in the exact lists of the appropriate offerings to be made to each deity, which the Pontifices kept, and the wording of Roman prayers, which traditionally began with a list of all the various names a particular deity was known by, ending with the escape clause 'or by whatever name he or she wishes to be known'.[36] It is also apparent in the different methods used to make offerings to various deities. Offerings to the gods who dwelt in the sky (Jupiter, for example) were burnt on an altar so that the smoke from the fire would carry them up to the heavens. The image of the god, Robigor (Rust), however, was smeared with oil, his appropriate offering, while drink offerings to the gods and spirits of the underworld were most often poured directly on the ground, presumably in the belief that the liquid would pass directly down to the deities and spirits for whom it was meant.

Ensuring that the right offering reached the right deity was especially important in cases of expiatory offerings. If such an offering did not reach the right god, then the *pax deorum* remained broken and Rome at risk. The Romans, therefore, made special efforts to ensure that such offerings reached the deity for whom they were intended. If earlier scholars are right in seeing Vesta as fundamentally a goddess of the Earth and the underworld as well as of the hearth,[37] then this principle offers another explanation for the burial alive of an unchaste Vestal. Such a Vestal was buried in order to ensure that Vesta received the appropriate expiatory offering as quickly and directly as possible.

Alongside the central question of why a Vestal was buried alive lies the question of the precise significance of certain other ritual elements of this punishment, specifically the presence of water, bread, milk and oil in the Vestal's burial chamber. The traditional explanation for the inclusion of these items has always been that this inclusion was a further attempt on the part of the Romans to avoid the blame for killing a priestess dedicated to a goddess.[38] By providing her with water, bread, milk and oil, the theory goes, the Romans left the guilty Vestal with the means to keep herself alive, thus preserving the fiction that it was the goddess' decision that she should die rather than a mortal's. While there is no denying that this theory is a plausible one, it lacks an explanation of why these particular items and not others were buried with a Vestal. Since the provisions included in this list are actually an odd combination, this explanation is in fact of some significance.

Of the items buried with the Vestals, the beverages especially ought to have alerted earlier scholars to the essentially odd nature of this list. Not least, the inclusion of not one but two liquids in a Vestal's burial chamber seems excessive if the sole purpose of these items was the providing of nourishment for the Vestal in question. More specifically, the milk itself is an unusual item to see included on such a list, as in the historical Rome of our period and earlier, milk was not an ordinary drink but was consumed regularly only by small children and invalids. So too is the oil, unless it was included as replenishment for the lamp named in the same list.

Because of these oddities, it is surely worthwhile to consider further the significance of these four provisions. One possible explanation is that they represent the traditional foodstuffs of the agricultural society of the early Romans. Such a theory would explain nicely the presence of both the milk, which was, according to authors of Cicero's period and later, drunk regularly by the farmers who primarily made up the citizenry of early Rome, and the water, which the Romans also believed that their ancestors had drunk before the use of wine became known. In this case, however, we might expect pease porridge, which the Romans believed to be their ancestors' most common form of sustenance, to have been included in place of bread.[39]

A second possibility is suggested by the fact that all of the liquids placed within the chamber were used as purificatory substances in Roman religious cult. Milk was used in the rites of the *Lupercalia* as a means of purification.[40] Water fulfilled the same role in a number of other Roman rites.[41] So too did oil.[42] The possibility that these offerings were included because of their purificatory use is particularly appealing in that a desire to purify Rome of the Vestal's misdeeds was surely part of the reasoning behind this whole burial. It has the failing, however, that here too the bread cannot be fitted into such a scenario.

Two other possibilities are more promising. One possibility suggested by the presence of the milk is purely speculative and can never be proved because of a lack of ancient evidence. It does have, however, the advantage of relating specifically to the Vestals' cult. Modern readers seeing milk included in a list think immediately of cows' milk, the type of milk we most commonly drink today. The Romans, however, used more than one kind of milk. Milk from sheep, from goats and also from donkeys was used.[43] This last raises an interesting possibility. Donkeys played a central but mysterious role in Vesta's own festival, the *Vestalia*. If the milk buried with a Vestal was donkeys' milk, this throws a new light on the remaining substances. Both water and fire figure prominently in Vesta's cult. So too do grain and products made from grain (*mola salsa*, for example). At the *Vestalia*, for example, donkeys were decorated with loaves of bread.[44] If the milk in question was donkeys' milk, then it is possible to draw parallels between all the substances buried with the Vestals and the substances especially associated with the cult of Vesta. The water would be equivalent to the water used in the daily rituals within the *aedes Vestae.* The lighted lamp (and the oil to refill it) would represent the eternal fire of the *focum Vestae*, the bread the substances of grain prepared by the Vestals. Finally, the milk would be related to the mysterious ass that appears in the rites of the *Vestalia*. Such a theory at least has the advantage of explaining why these particular and peculiar substances were included.

The second possibility is that all of the items left within the Vestal's chamber were left there because they were the standard offerings made to the dead.[45] The inclusion of these particular provisions might suggest an attempt to appease the shade of the Vestal in question. While Dio's statement that the Vestals received no funeral memorial, rites or offerings may seem to preclude this interpretation, it is possible that the historian misunderstood the significance of these items' inclusion in the underground chamber.

Certainly the argument that the Romans viewed many of the rituals surrounding a Vestal's burial alive as equivalent to ordinary funeral rites and thus her burial alive as equivalent with her death fits well with what the remaining ancient evidence on this crime suggests. Both Dionysius and Plutarch describe the series of actions that led up to a Vestal's being placed on the ladder leading down into the underground chamber in such a way as to suggest that the

Romans viewed these rites as funereal in nature. Both authors describe how the convicted Vestal, dressed in funereal garments, was placed upon a bier and carried through Rome to the Colline Gate, accompanied by her family and friends lamenting as at a funeral. Most intriguingly of all, Pliny in his letter describing the ritual burial of the Vestal Cornelia mentions the presence of a *carnifex*. The presence of a *carnifex* at this rite suggests more clearly than anything else could that the rite must be viewed as an execution and thus a death ritual, or why else would the *carnifex* have been present?

Conclusion

The concept of Vestal virginity is a complicated one, operating on many levels and admitting of many different, but perhaps equally valid explanations. On one level, this virginity kept the priestesses pure and enabled them both to approach the gods in an appropriate state and to set an example to other Roman women. On another, this virginity set them off from the profane world of ordinary Rome, made them sacred and thus gave them a special power as interceders for the Roman people. This virginity ensured that the Vestals did not become members of an individual Roman family, both for social and religious purposes. At the same time, it ensured that the Vestals remained securely within the Roman civic order, thus creating for them a special status that allowed them to represent Rome as a whole. This last goes a long way to explaining the danger inherent in a Vestal's commission of the *crimen incesti*, in that by doing so a Vestal took an action that reattached her to the ordinary world of the Romans, and broke the links that held her outside the individual families of Rome and their cults.

Notes

1 For a discussion of this passage, see R. M. Ogilvie 1970: 97–98.
2 This chapter had its origins in an article published in *Hommages à Carl Deroux* (*Collection Latomus*) and is a much revised version of that work: Wildfang 2003. The reader interested in a more in-depth discussion of the impact of various scholarly schools of thought on research into the Vestals' virginity is referred to that work. See also H. N. Parker 2004, who independently arrived at much the same conclusions (and much the same title) a year later. See also S. Boldrini 1995.
3 Gel. 7.7.2.
4 K. Mustakallio 1992: 62; F. Guizzi 1968: 102–108. See also H. Rose 1926: 442–443. In many ancient cults, not just Roman ones, Rose points out, a person who had recently engaged in sexual intercourse could not take part in that cult's worship. Because the Vestals were constantly required to come in contact with their goddess, sexual intercourse became an impossibility. For other views of this virginity, see G. Wissowa 1924: 264; A. Brelich 1949: 57–67.
5 H. Cancik-Lindemaier 1990: 14.
6 A. Staples 1998: 147. See also M. C. Martini 1997a: 247.
7 By 'citizen' I mean those women who fulfilled certain criteria generally accepted by their male-counterparts (i.e. they were eligible to marry, were married to or were the widows of Roman male citizens).

8 See Chapter 3 for a full discussion of this rite.

9 For a full discussion of this topic, see J. Gagé 1963.

10 For a brief discussion of this class as it pertains to women's religious roles, see R. Kraemer 1992: 51–52. See also *TLL* 8.1.486–487, where examples of *matrona* used in this sense are given, together with *DnP* 7. 1030–1131; M. E. Assis de Rojo 1998; B. Feichtinger 1993; P. Grimal 1985; B. Holtheide 1980; R. Schmittlein 1965; J. Gagé 1963.

11 P. Watson 1983. See also G. Sissa 1990; K. Haastrup 1978.

12 See *TLL* 3.564–571 for a list of the many ancient uses of this adjective in this sense, and *TLL* 3.538–541 for similar usage of the related noun, *castitas*.

13 Italics are mine.

14 See, among others, Ov. *Fast.* 3.417; Prop. 3.4.11; Sil. 7.184.

15 *TLL* 7[1]. 893–896.

16 See, for example, M. Beard 1980: 14.

17 Gel. 1.12.

18 For earlier scholarly discussions devoted solely to aspects of this topic, see S. Boldrini 1995; K. Mustakallio 1992; A. Fraschetti 1984; D. Porte 1984; F. Hampl 1983; A. Fraschetti 1981; T. J. Cornell 1981.

19 Liv. 8.15. See also D. H. 2.66 and Plu. *Num.* 10.

20 Cic. *Har.* 13.3. R. G. Lewis 2001:142 argues, however, that this court was a one time affair established at the time of the accusations of the Vestals Marcia, Aemilia and Licinia in 114/113 BCE. See Chapter 7 for a discussion of these accusations.

21 See Fest. p. 333 L for the *campus sceleratus*.

22 Fest. p. 277 L.

23 For more recent discussions based on this viewpoint, see K. Mustakallio 1992; A. Fraschetti 1984. For a list of earlier scholars of similar opinion, see Nock and Stewart 1972: 1.254 with notes.

24 S. P. Oakley 1998: 2. 578–579.

25 On *prodigia* in general, see B. MacBain 1982.

26 For further discussion of this issue, see T. J. Cornell 1981: 31.

27 C. Koch 1960: 67.

28 T. J. Cornell 1981: 36. For a detailed discussion on the Pontifices' role in the judgement of cases of *incestum*, see C. Lovisi 1998.

29 A. Staples 1998: 152.

30 C. Koch 1960: 70.

31 T. J. Cornell 1981: 33.

32 T. J. Cornell 1981: 35.

33 Plin. *Ep.* 4.11. On the translation of the word *carnifex*, see *TLL* 3. 478–479. See also A. N. Sherwin-White 1966: 282–283.

34 Most recently, A. Staples 1998: 151.

35 See Chapter 4.

36 See, for example, Cato *Agr.* 15.9; Liv. 7.26.3; Serv. *A.* 11.251. For a modern discussion of this topic, see M. Morani 1981.

37 For a discussion of this connection, see R. Wright 1995; K. R. Prowse 1967: 178; P. Lambrechts 1946: 322–329.

38 See, for example, K. Mustakallio 1992; A. Fraschetti 1984.

39 For discussions of the Romans' customary drinking and eating habits, see N. Purcell 2003; T. Braun 1995; G. Baudy 1995; A. Cubberly 1995; K. D. White 1995; P. E. McGovern *et al.* 1995; K. Flint-Hamilton 1999; L. Foxhall and H. Forbes 1982; D. R. Brothwell and P. Brothwell 1969.

40 Plu. *Rom.* 21.5. For a discussion of the *lupercalia*, see D. Harmon 1978: 1441–1446.

41 S. Eitrem 1915: 176–197.
42 I. Nielsen and H. Sigismund Nielsen 1998.
43 *RE* 15.2 1569–1580.
44 Ov. *Fast.* 3.611.
45 For discussions of Roman funerary practices and rites, see K. Hopkins 1983: 217–226; J. M. C. Toynbee 1971: 42–64.

5 The Vestals' legal and financial position

The Vestals had an unusual legal status at Rome, one that was shared by no other Roman, male or female, religious official or otherwise. Their financial position was also in many respects anomalous, especially when compared to that of other Roman women. These two topics are closely related, if for no other reason than that the Vestals' legal freedom from tutelage had direct consequences for their ability to manage their own private fortunes, many of which seem to have been considerable. The first of these topics has been a popular one among modern scholars and is well examined. Surprisingly, however, the second has been largely unconsidered by these same scholars. This chapter, therefore, will of necessity take two different approaches to these two separate but related areas. In examining the Vestals' legal status, it will consider the ancient evidence but focus primarily on various modern scholars' interpretations of it. In considering the priestesses' financial situation, it will concentrate primarily upon the various types of ancient evidence available to us today rather than the discussions of modern scholars, which are largely non-existent. In both instances, though, it will argue that the anomalies found in these areas are due to and can be explained by the Vestals' peculiar liminal position as members of Rome's citizen group but non-members of its family structure that has been delineated in Chapters 3 and 4.

Tutelage and inheritance

According to Gaius' *Institutes*, a girl who entered the Vestal order automatically and immediately became free of *tutela* (that is to say tutelage or male guardianship).[1] This meant in effect that she was able to make her own financial decisions, buying and selling property, freeing slaves or accepting an inheritance without having to consult or secure the consent of a male guardian. She also gained the right to write her own will and to leave her property to whomever she herself wished.[2] Two noteworthy limitations accompanied these freedoms, however. First, if a Vestal did not write a will and died intestate, the Roman state inherited her property; second, she ceased to inherit property automatically from her birth family.

A Vestal's freedom from tutelage and the accompanying ability to write her own will have occasioned much discussion among modern scholars. In recent years, two main schools of thought on these topics have emerged. One, following the work of M. Beard, who argued in her first article on these priestesses that their freedom from tutelage was evidence of their male aspect, either accepts this view or takes it one step further and uses the Vestals' legal freedom to argue that the Vestals belonged only to the 'male category' and should in fact be seen as the complete antitheses of the Roman *matrones*.[3] As Beard herself observes in a second article, however, this argument is based on some dated theoretical premises that have led to a 'more or less dazzling dead end' and which show little concern with how the Romans themselves would have defined the Vestals' status.[4] The second school argues more accurately that a Vestal's release from tutelage occurred because she no longer had rights to her family's estate nor her family to hers.[5] A woman's tutor was there, J. Gardner, the main proponent of this theory argues, to protect the rights of the family and not those of the individual. Because a Vestal's *familia* no longer had rights to her estate, there was no need for a tutor to protect this estate and ensure that it returned intact to the *familia*.

What Gardner fails to consider, however, is the reason for this loss of reciprocal rights. A Vestal and her family no longer had automatic rights to each other's estates. Why, however, did they no longer have these rights? This question has not been adequately investigated despite the fact that it should be a central one in any discussion of this aspect of the Vestals' legal status. The answer to it is to be found in what we have already seen regarding other aspects of the Vestals and their cult. The Vestals and their families no longer had rights to each other's estates because the Vestals were no longer considered members of their families. Roman law held that only the agnate members of a deceased person's family might inherit automatically if the deceased had died intestate.[6] All other heirs had to be named in a will, including children who had been previously emancipated. The Vestals had to name their heirs in a will because they had no family to inherit their estates automatically. Likewise, they had to be named in the wills of their family members, if they were to inherit, because as non-members of their families, they did not inherit automatically. Therefore, by a somewhat circular argument they were by definition no longer members of these families.[7]

At the same time that the Vestals were freed from tutelage, they also received the ability to write their own wills. This ability is further evidence of the same special familial status. Since the Vestals were not members of a Roman family, inheritance of the Vestals' property was not covered by any of the ordinary laws concerning the inheritance of a woman's property. Their property could not automatically devolve on their next of kin since legally they did not have any kin. Instead, they, like all other Roman citizens without family of their own, had themselves to determine who should inherit their often extensive properties.

Not all Vestals, however, seemingly managed to write a will before they died. The property of those who did not went to the state, according to Labeo, who commenting on this legal provision is said to have noted, 'it is uncertain what legal principle is here involved' (Gel. 1.12).

Modern scholars interested in this provision have focused primarily on explaining what it was that so puzzled Labeo, namely the legal principle in question. Two explanations have been proposed. On the one hand, the legal scholar J. B. Moyle argues that there was no specific legal principle behind this provision but instead a simple, logical equation.[8] An intestate Vestal's estate went to the state for sacrificial purposes, his reasoning runs, because her life had been dedicated to the gods to whom these future sacrifices would be made. It was only logical, he claims, that the property of a priestess, whose life had been dedicated to the gods, went to the state for the further service of these same gods. On the other hand, scholars such as Gardner and Guizzi conclude that Labeo was simply expressing puzzlement at finding so early an example of what later became the standard procedure for the disposal of the property of someone who died intestate.[9]

Both of these views have a kernel of truth in them. Yet, both ignore certain problems that in the end make them inadequate. Without argument, the Vestals did devote their lives to the service of the goddess Vesta. On occasion, they did indeed participate in rites performed on behalf of other Roman gods. Nothing in our ancient sources, however, suggests that the Vestals dedicated their lives to the service of all the Roman state gods. Nor does anything in these same ancient sources suggest that an intestate Vestal's estate was to be used by the state for sacrificial, or even more general religious, purposes.[10] The lack of evidence for both halves of this theory's equation seriously weakens its supposed logic.

The second theory, that of Gardner and Guizzi, while offering a credible explanation for Labeo's surprise, in the end does little to explain why an intestate Vestal's property went to the state. If, as these two scholars suggest, Labeo was surprised to discover a provision of this sort already in existence at so early a period,[11] then it follows that this provision came before the more general rule regarding all intestates' property. As such, it cannot be explained simply as a case of standard legal practice. Some other solution must therefore be found.

One possible explanation can be found in the theory developed in the preceding chapters. The Vestals' peculiar status as members of the Roman state but non-members of this state's underlying family structure left them in a vacuum, when it came to matters of inheritance. Before the legal codification to which Gardner in particular refers,[12] the estate of an ordinary Roman who died intestate went to his nearest agnate family members, if any existed. As we have seen, many of the rites and duties with which the Vestals were bound were devised with one purpose in mind. This was to ensure that the Vestals no longer had any official connection to these family members. As we have also already seen, in other instances the Roman state functioned in the role of family for the Vestals, when such a function was necessary. The same is likely to be true here as well. The state inherited the estate of an intestate Vestal, because it stepped into the vacuum created by the necessities of the Vestals' peculiar status and fulfilled the function of *familia* for the Vestals.[13] Thus, the same principle that operated when an ordinary individual died intestate also operated here. The state functioned in *locus familiae* for the Vestals, inheriting their estates, if they died intestate.

Juridical status

The Vestals' legal position embraced other peculiarities as well. Alongside their special status in relation to matters of tutelage and inheritance, the Vestals also seem to have had a unique position in the judicial sphere.[14] Three ancient authors testify that either some or all of the Vestals alone among Roman women gave evidence orally in open court.[15]

Plutarch writes: 'Now Tarquinia was a sacred virgin, one of the Vestals, and received great honours for her act, among which was this, that of all women her testimony alone be accepted' (Plu. *Publ.* 8.4). Aulus Gellius offers somewhat the same story but calls the Vestal in question, Taracia:

> And the *lex horatia* witnesses also that Taracia was a Vestal Virgin, whom this same law raised above the people. She received many honours from this law, among which was included the right of giving evidence, and she alone of all women received this [right]. This is a direct citation of the *lex horatia*; on the other hand in the twelve tables is written: 'let an inferior person be unable to witness'.
>
> (Gel. 7.7.2)

Tacitus offers a somewhat broader interpretation:

> But Urgulania's power was too great for the state so that when as a witness in a certain case, which was being tried before the senate, she refused to appear, a praetor was sent to interrogate her at home, although it was an ancient custom that the Vestal virgins be heard in the Forum and in the court, whenever they were required to give testimony.
>
> (Tac. *Ann.* 2.34)

Quite possibly, though, the Vestal referred to by both Plutarch and Aulus Gellius was the first Vestal to receive a right that subsequently came to be standard practice for all Vestals.

Although both Aulus Gellius and Plutarch unequivocally state that alone of all women a single Vestal was given the privilege of testifying in open court, modern scholars have drawn attention to three ancient texts that seemingly contradict this picture and have argued that there must be some misunderstanding on the part of our sources on the Vestals.[16] A close examination of these three ancient texts, however, reveals that the women to whom they refer may have appeared in open court but if they did so, they did so as mute witnesses, whose testimony was read aloud by others.

The first passage is found in the first of Cicero's *Verrines*, where the orator asks the defendant:

> Why do you force your friend's wife, your friend's mother-in-law, in short, your dead friend's whole family, to hear evidence against you? Why do you force most modest and commendable women to come against our customs and against their desires into so large a gathering of men? Recite the evidence of them all.
>
> (Cic. *Ver.* 1.37.94)

This passage has been taken to mean that Verres' female relatives both appeared and spoke in open court. Cicero, however, does not necessarily say that these women spoke in open court, only that they appeared (*prodire*) in it. While Cicero does use the phrase *testimonium dicere*, which translates literally as 'speak the evidence', this phrase has more properly a less literal translation. It is, in fact, the standard Latin idiom for the English phrase 'give evidence'. Ancient authors employed it both of situations where witnesses themselves delivered their evidence in person before an open court and of instances where witnesses' testimony had clearly been taken down beforehand in private and was simply to be read aloud in court. Quintilian, describing Roman juridical procedures, even notes explicitly, 'testimony may be given (*testimonium dicere*) in writing or by those present in court'.[17]

The rest of Cicero's passage supports such a conclusion. Cicero's second question is: 'Why do you compel most modest and admirable women to come against their wont and against their will into so great an assembly of men?' The Latin verb Cicero chooses to employ here, *prodire*, can be translated as 'appear, enter or show oneself'.[18] It cannot mean 'speak'. Thus, this question can at most be taken as evidence for the women's presence in the court and not for their speaking there. Most telling, though, is the Latin command with which Cicero ends this passage, 'read aloud' (*recita*). This passage, therefore, cannot, and should not, be taken as evidence that ordinary women directly addressed the open court. Instead, it portrays the mother and grandmother of Verres appearing in a more limited role as a mute presence in the open court.

The other two passages commonly cited as problematic in this context in no way contradict this picture. Twice, in his *Vita Claudii*, the biographer Suetonius mentions women who had roles in court cases: 'When a woman refused to recognize her son, and the evidence on both sides was conflicting, [Claudius] forced her to admit the truth by ordering her to marry the young man' (Suet. *Cl.* 15.2) and

> Once when a witness had been brought before the senate, [Claudius] said: "This woman was my mother's freedwoman and maid, but she always regarded me as her patron; I mention this because there are still some in my household now who do not look on me as patron."
>
> (Suet. *Cl.* 40.2)

In the first passage, a woman is clearly the defendant but nothing in the text suggests that she herself spoke in her own defence. Instead, Suetonius states only that the case was directed against her. The second passage as well notes only that a freedwoman was led into court as a witness. It does not say that she, any more than Verres' female relatives, spoke to the court directly.[19] Nothing in any of these three passages suggests that the women in question themselves spoke in open court. Rather everything implies that if a woman had evidence to give in a court case, this evidence was taken down as a written deposition earlier in private and then read aloud to the court, with the women appearing only as mute witnesses of their own testimony.[20]

This impression is strengthened by a passage in Valerius Maximus' work, *Factorum et Dictorum Memorabilium Libri Novem.* Valerius Maximus observes that while women could bring suit in civil court on their own behalf, it was rare, if not unheard of, for them to actually appear before the court.[21] Thus, the ancient evidence actually demonstrates that, while ordinary Roman women might appear in court, if they did so, they did so mutely. What testimony they had to offer on a specific legal matter was given ahead of time privately and then read aloud from a deposition in court. Since this is the case then, it seems that our sources on the Vestals are correct. The Vestals alone of all Roman women actually spoke in open court.

This special status is evidence once again of the Vestals' liminal position within the Roman civic and familial structure. As we have just seen, when ordinary Roman women were required to give testimony in a court case, their evidence was taken down privately ahead of time and then read aloud in the open court. Although no ancient evidence explicitly states this, it seems likely that one reason for this practice was to ensure that this deposition would be taken under the supervision of a woman's guardian.[22] The Vestals, however, not being under anyone's tutelage, would have had no one to represent or supervise them in such instances. Because the Vestal had no such person to apply to, she had to act for herself, hence her ability to speak in open court and by extension to act as witness.

One further twist to this whole issue, however, appears in another passage of Aulus Gellius, where the author notes: 'I have written down the words of the praetor from the *edicta perpetua* about the Flamen Dialis and the priest: "I may not compel the Flamen Dialis or the Vestal priestess to swear an oath on anything in my jurisdiction"' (Gel. 10.15.31). Asconius also comments on this special status.[23]

Whether this special status was limited only to a praetor's court or not (and which praetor's court it was) cannot be known. The existence of these two passages, however, does strengthen the claim that the Vestals appeared as witnesses in court. It also suggests one final refinement to our understanding of the Vestals' legal status within the judicial sphere. Unlike other Romans, the Vestals and the Flamen Dialis could not be compelled to swear an oath. These two priesthoods shared other noteworthy characteristics. Candidates for both were 'taken' into their respective priesthoods; members of both were permitted to ride through Rome on priestly business, and members of both were also bound by more restrictions than other Roman priesthoods.[24] These similarities suggest first that we should see a religious significance to this prohibition and second that this religious significance is related to a special status shared by these two priesthoods. J. Vanggaard has argued convincingly that the many prohibitions which surrounded the Flamen Dialis were meant to give him a special sacred status and were in part due to his special role as Jupiter's human representative.[25] The many similarities between the Vestals and Flamen Dialis make it possible and indeed likely that the same argument applies here. The Vestals could not be bound by oath because they had in some way been made sacred, and this sacrality would have been polluted by human bonds.

Financial position

Related to the discussion of the Vestals' release from tutelage and the accompanying ability to choose their own heirs is the question of how they acquired the fortunes, which they seemingly had to leave. Related to this question in turn is the question of how the Vestals' finances functioned in general. This topic is a complex one that has remained largely unconsidered to this day, probably because the particularly haphazard nature of our evidence makes it a particularly difficult one. For some aspects of this topic, most notably the question of the Vestals' expenses, almost no evidence or indeed no evidence at all exists. For other aspects, most notably the sources of funding available to the Vestals and their order, evidence does exist, but must still be treated with caution as it offers only tantalizing glimpses into this issue's complexities. Despite these drawbacks, the topic is both an important and a neglected one that needs to be considered. For it is in fact possible, using not only literary but also archaeological and epigraphical sources, to come to at least a partial understanding of the Vestals' financial situation and thus of their status in Roman society.

In the first book of his history, Livy describes Numa's foundation of the Vestal order, writing among other things, 'For these [priestesses], he established a public stipend so that they might be constant guardians of the temple' (Liv. 1.20.3). While Livy's claim that Numa established this *stipendium* is not necessarily accurate, his statement that the Vestals received a *stipendium* no doubt reflects the reality of his own era and probably of those immediately preceding. This means that by the late Republic, if not before, the Vestals did in fact receive some sort of regular state *stipendium*.

The type of funds Livy is describing when he uses the word *stipendium* is less certain than is apparent from the works of those modern scholars who touch upon this topic. The majority of these have generally assumed that this *stipendium* was a lump sum paid once to each Vestal at the beginning of her tenure. In assuming this, they seemingly combine Livy's statement with a remark of Tacitus, who, discussing the emperor Tiberius' generosity, notes that the Vestal Cornelia received two million sesterces upon her entry into the order.[26] Tacitus, however, wrote a century after Livy, at a time when many imperial policies, which were new or nonexistent in Livy's time, had become well established. Thus, what Tacitus describes was not necessarily in existence during Livy's time, and indeed seems a special instance out of the ordinary since Tacitus chooses to comment on it. As well, Livy's use of the word *stipendium* – traditionally used of the pay a soldier received at the end of each annual campaign – implies that the sum involved was an amount of money given annually rather than a one-time sum.[27] A very few scholars recognizing these facts and differentiating between Livy's remark and that of Tacitus have argued that each Vestal received an annual payment. This argument comes closer to the truth than the first but even it meets with some difficulties.

It is not immediately clear from Livy's choice of vocabulary and use of the plural and singular forms whether each individual Vestal received her own *stipendium* or the order as a whole received one single large one. Livy uses the singular form of *stipendium* to refer to the payment received by the Vestals and the plural *his* to refer to the Vestals themselves. One way to translate this statement certainly is to say that Livy is using the singular *stipendium* as a collective singular noun meant to refer to a group of stipends. It is this option that most modern scholars have presumably followed. It is equally possible, however, that *stipendium* should be translated literally as a single sum of money and *his* as a plural representing the Vestals as a single group. In other words, Livy could just as well be saying that the order as a whole received an annual payment from the state to cover its expenses as that each individual Vestal received the equivalent of a dowry upon entry into the order.

If this interpretation is correct and the order as a whole received a yearly stipend, then neither Mommsen's claim that this *stipendium* should be seen as a sort of dowry,[28] nor Gardner's argument that it was a *peculium* can be correct.[29] Both of these payments were one-time, lump sum gifts made to an individual, the one made at the time of a girl's marriage, the other at the time of one person's release from another's *potestas*. A *stipendium*, however, was an annual payment rather than a one-time gift, which both a dowry and a *peculium* were. As well, as we have just argued, the Vestals' *stipendium* was likely to have been a collective payment made to the order as a whole. Both of these facts militate against either of these suggestions as accurate explanations for why the Vestals received such a payment.

A more likely explanation for this payment is to be found in the Romans' careful separation of the Vestals from their birth families. A Vestal had no legal claim on or official connection to her family after she became a Vestal. Her family's continued financial support in these circumstances could not have been expected and would have punctured the carefully created image of the Vestals as independent women with no further relationship to their birth families. Yet the Vestals still had to eat and clothe themselves as well as feed and clothe their servants. Someone had to pay for such necessities, as well as the order's other expenses (for example, the upkeep of their house, their ritual supplies, the wood for the fire within the *aedes Vestae*). Therefore, it was necessary for someone else to step in and provide financial support. This some-one else was the same state that in other connections also functioned in *locus familiae* to the Vestals.

Besides the funding provided by the *stipendium*, however we define it in the end, literary evidence also suggests that the Vestal order as a whole had a substantial rental income. Hyginus, describing various categories of land, observes: 'From antiquity, they learn this, so that they also use the ancient names, such as the rented (*vectigalis*) land of the Vestal Virgins, and altars, temples, tombs and the like' (Hyg. *agrim.* p. 82).[30] His use of the adjective *vectigalis* to describe these lands implies that the lands were rented out.[31] This premise is further strengthened by Hyginus' later notation that although on occasion land of this type was leased annually, most frequently it was rented out on a five-year contract.[32] How extensive the Vestals' lands were is unknown. Quite clearly, however, they would have brought in some rental income, which might well have been fairly substantial. Presumably, the rental income from these lands was freely available for the order's use.

As well as this land outside the city boundaries, archaeological evidence suggests that at least during the Republic and early Empire, the Vestals also had rental property within the city proper. Along the northern and eastern side of the Republican *atrium* are the remains of two rows of shops facing onto the *via sacra* and the *via nova*. Although some of these shops gradually disappeared as their space was incorporated into the *atrium* proper, others remained in existence throughout the Vestals' tenancy of the *atrium*.[33] These shops must have been rented out, and again it is not too much to assume that at least some of their rent went to support the Vestals, the inhabitants of the house to which these shops were attached.[34]

Finally, archaeological, epigraphical and numismatic evidence attests that the Vestals and their order frequently received generous, and often financially advantageous, gifts from wealthy individual patrons, and in particular during the imperial period from the emperors and members of the imperial family. The *atrium Vestae* was rebuilt five times during the course of the imperial period, each time more elaborately than before. Inscriptions associated with two of these rebuildings name the generosity of particular emperors. Hadrian, for example, took credit for the addition of a shrine outside the main door of the *atrium*,[35] while Julia Domna did the same for a later addition and the restoration that took place after the fire of Commodus.[36] Coinage offers further evidence that various emperors and their families wished to be known as benefactors of the goddess and her cult. Lucilla, the daughter of Antoninus, had coins cut with her image on one side and that of Vesta's temple on the other.[37] Frequent representations of the goddess and her temple also appear on coins from the reigns of Vespasian, Hadrian and Nero, suggesting that these emperors too wished to celebrate on coinage their close connection to the goddess and her order.[38]

The second century CE statues of senior Vestal Virgins and their pedestals, found in the *atrium*'s courtyard, flesh out this picture.[39] Many of these bases bear dedicatory inscriptions from private individuals, thanking the Vestal in question for her patronage and support. Their existence and that of the statues indicate that not only emperors but also private individuals were in this period willing to spend money to 'beautify' the Vestals' home.

So far, we have been primarily concerned with the finances of the Vestal order as a whole. Ancient literary evidence, however, shows that individual Vestals also had money and property of their own. Plutarch writes that the Vestal Licinia was accused of *incestum*, because she had been closeted privately in a room with a man.[40] She was able to refute the charge, however, by arguing that the man, Crassus, was her cousin and that they were discussing the purchase or sale of some of her property. Such an explanation was evidently realistic enough to be believable or Licinia would not have escaped with her life. This suggests that it was normal or, at the very least, not unusual for a Vestal to have business interests and a fortune of her own. Such a view is supported for the imperial period as well by the passage of Tacitus, quoted above. Finally, the various ancient references to one or another Vestal's personal slaves also suggest that these priestesses had substantial private property of their own.[41] Thus, while by my reading the literary evidence suggests that the order as a whole received the stipendium mentioned by Livy, individual Vestals also clearly had access to funds of their own.

Unfortunately, we do not know much about how the Vestal order and the individual Vestals used the funds to which they had access. Beyond, the knowledge provided by Plutarch, mentioned above, that individual Vestals bought and sold property, no real evidence for this side of the Vestals' financial picture exists. We have no records of the Vestals' yearly expenditures. We do not know whether the state *stipendium* was meant to cover both ritual and daily expenses or only one or the other. We do not know how the Vestals acquired the grain they needed to make *mola salsa*, the cloth for their clothing or the wood for their fire. Were these and other items donated and delivered by the state or by private individuals? Or was a slave sent to the nearby market with a basket and money in hand to return with what was needed? It seems likely, given the existence of the *stipendium*, that the Vestals were expected to administer and pay for their own expenses themselves, but we have no concrete proof of this. In the end, all that can be said of this aspect of Vestal finances is that there can be no definitive answer to our questions without the unlikely discovery of further ancient evidence.

Conclusion

The Vestals' legal and financial situation further flesh out the picture we have seen developing in Chapters 3 and 4. Here too there is evidence that the Vestals had a special status unique to them among all Romans, one that ensured that they remained securely within the Roman citizen body while at the same time avoiding all possible ties to an individual Roman family. This special status guaranteed that these priestesses were able to represent Rome as a whole on a religious level without owing any allegiance to or risking being polluted by a domestic cult. A study of the Vestals' legal and financial positions sheds some light on a subsidiary issue, the question of how the order was financed and paid for.

Notes

1 Gaius *Inst.* 1,145. While Gaius' work is from the second half of the second century CE, other evidence suggests that at least some central aspects of this freedom were of an early date, and therefore it is likely that this freedom also was. See below on Labeo.

2 Cic. *Rep.* 3.10.17 mentions this ability also.

3 M. Beard 1980: 17; O. De Cazanove 1987: 169; K. Mustakallio 1992: 75.

4 M. Beard 1995: 168.

5 J. Gardner 1986: 24. As always, many different scholarly views have been advanced on the significance of this freedom and its accompanying ability. As we have already seen, J. B. Moyle 1912 has argued that the Vestals were released from human tutelage, because they were placed under that of the gods. Beard 1980 claimed that both the Vestals' ability to make their own wills and their freedom from tutelage should be seen as signs of a partially masculine status. Although each of these theories in its own way reflects some element of truth concerning the Vestals' peculiar legal status as a whole, only the last of them even begins to approach a complete and accurate explanation of this status and its significance. We have already considered the first of these theories above. The second suggestion – that the Vestals' freedom from tutelage and their right to write their own wills was a sign of their partially masculine status – accurately highlights the Vestals' liminal position but does not accurately reflect the facts of a man's emancipation. A Vestal was similar to an emancipated man in that she did not have automatic rights to her birth family's property. Unlike an emancipated man, however, a Vestal did not automatically become head of a new family, which was, after all, the main point of a Roman man's emancipation.

6 For a discussion of an ordinary woman's role in matters of inheritance, see J. Gardner 1986: 190–200. For a general discussion of Roman inheritance laws, see U. Manthe 2002; J. Hillner 2003; E. Craik 1984. On intestacy in ancient Rome, see J. Crook 1973.

7 See also A. Staples 1998: 143, who from a somewhat different perspective argues the same point, concluding that this legal freedom resulted from the Vestals' placement outside 'the kinship system based on the institution of *patria potestas*'.

8 J. B. Moyle 1912: 183: '[a Vestal's] life having been devoted to [the gods'] service, it was only consistent that, on her dying without disposing of her property by will, it should go to the treasury for sacrificial purposes'.

9 J. Gardner 1986: 23.

10 And while an argument from *absentia* is always risky (perhaps the appropriate source simply did not survive), in this instance the legal texts with which we are dealing make it natural to expect such a clause, should this be the purpose.

11 J. Gardner 1986: 23–24. Despite the relatively late date of our ancient source, F. Guizzi 1968: 166–167 has conclusively argued that the Vestals' legal privileges were established at a very early date, probably codified at the time of the twelve tables. Carefully analysing Gaius' usage of the term, *veteres*, Guizzi shows that in the *Inst.* it appears only in connection with the very oldest Roman laws, those dating from the pre-republican period. Thus, its use in connection with this privilege argues for an early date.

12 J. Gardner 1986: 23.
13 See A. Staples 1998: 143 also.
14 For a general discussion of women's role in the Roman civil law courts, see A. Marshall 1989.
15 Gellius' text says that one Vestal Virgin, Taracia, was given this right. Vestal scholars, no doubt basing their supposition on the further evidence of Tacitus, however, have traditionally taken this text to mean that all Vestal Virgins after Taracia had this right. Whether this is the right interpretation is something to be considered below.
16 For example, M. Beard 1980: 17.
17 Quint. *Inst.* 5.7.1. This notation of Quintilian provides the key for solving the seeming contradiction between Cicero's evidence and that of Aulus Gellius and Plutarch. Where the former is clearly using *testimonium dicere* in the sense of *per tabulas*, the latter are using it in the sense *a praesentibus*.
18 *TLL* 10.2.X. 1596. The other meanings of this word given here in no way contradict this interpretation.
19 As well, as a freedwoman, it is not certain that the same rules would have applied to her as applied to Roman citizen women.
20 Something which resembles a common ploy used by the defendant in raising sympathy for his case
21 V. Max. 8.3.
22 J. Gardner 1986: 261–263 has demonstrated that ordinary women who wished to bring a legal suit did so through their closest male relative (father, husband, brother or son) or guardian. It seems likely that something similar was the case when they were required to give testimony in court cases.
23 Asc. *Mil.* 43.
24 For a discussion of those binding the *flamen*, see J. Vanggaard 1988.
25 J. Vanggaard 1988: 101.
26 Tac. *Ann.* 4.16.6. R. M. Ogilvie 1970: 97–98 draws this connection but does not otherwise discuss the use of the word *stipendium*.
27 H. C. Boren 1983 discusses the military *stipendium*.
28 T. Mommsen 1952: 2, 64.
29 J. Gardner 1986: 24.
30 For the land in Lanuvium, see B. Campbell 2000: 184, who notes that this may be a confusion with Lavinium from which he believes the Vestal cult originally came.
31 B. Campbell 2000: 360, n.20, discusses this term and its significance.
32 Hyg. *agrim.* 84. See also Hyg. *agrim.* 131.
33 The shops to the east of the building disappeared first under the renovations undertaken by the Flavians. Those on the eastern half of the northern side disappeared under Hadrian. Their gradual disappearance might be taken to suggest that the Vestals no longer had need for the income supplied by their rental, although this supposition is improvable. For discussions of the *atrium* and *aedes Vestae*, see G. Carettoni 1978–1980; E. Van Deman 1909; H. Auer 1888; H. Jordan 1886; J. H. Middleton 1886. The recent excavations of the site by R. Scott have not yet been fully published.
34 Whether the state or the Vestal order owned the *atrium Vestae* is unknown.
35 The shrine outside the main entrance to the *atrium* bears the text (CIL 6.31578).
36 S. Platner and T. Ashby 1929: 69.
37 RIC 788 sear5 #5493.
38 E. Van Deman 1909.
39 For a full discussion of these statues, see M. Lindner 1995.
40 Plu. *Crass.* 1.2.
41 B. Scardigli 1997 discusses this issue and provides a detailed account of the slaves in question.

6 The Vestals in the Romans' history

Although many of our ancient sources for the Vestals focus on these priestesses' religious rituals and cult activities, others concern themselves with specific historical events. Chapters 6 and 7 examine these references both for what they can tell us about the Vestals' place in the Romans' view of their own history and for what they can tell us about the priestesses' actual role in Rome's history. This chapter considers the appearances of the Vestals in what might best be termed the late Republic's and early Empire's own version of Roman history, that is to say the Vestals' appearances in Roman historical accounts of the centuries between the founding of Rome and the end of the Second Punic War. Chapter 7 deals with the various historical appearances of the Vestals from the end of this war to the end of the first century CE for which we have contemporary or almost contemporary sources.

Before we embark on an examination of the Vestals' appearances in the ancient Romans' accounts of their own history, it is important to highlight one point concerning these accounts. The historical appearances of the Vestals discussed in this chapter occurred over a period of some 500 years, and with one single exception all of them took place many years and often centuries before our various ancient sources recorded them. Since these sources are removed in time from the actual events they record and since they are known on other occasions to have reworked or embellished episodes in their accounts of Roman history to fit their own literary or historical agenda, we must accept that their accounts of the Vestals' place in Roman history are not necessarily accurate.[1] What we are dealing with in this chapter, it should be stressed, are the Romans' own beliefs about their earlier history and the Vestals' place in it rather than any absolute and factual account of early Vestal activities.

The Vestals in the Regal Period

The Vestals appear in our ancient sources in connection with three separate episodes during Rome's Regal Period. All three of these episodes emphasize the fact that the Vestals played a central role in the Romans' understanding and construction of the origins of their own culture and identity. Whatever else one says about the Vestals, these priestesses were from the very beginning at the heart of what it was to be Roman. Without them and their cult, ancient Rome as we know it could not have existed.

The earliest Vestal of whom we hear is, of course, Rhea Silvia, the mother of Romulus and Remus.[2] While ancient accounts of the legend of Romulus and Remus differ on some aspects of the story, all are agreed that Rhea Silvia was the Alban king Numitor's daughter, who after her father's deposal was made a Vestal by her uncle in order to prevent her having any sons who might threaten him. Despite her uncle's actions, Rhea Silvia was miraculously impregnated (in most ancient accounts by the god Mars) and gave birth to the twins who grew up to found Rome.

Two particular aspects of this story immediately stand out in relation to the Vestals. First, clearly the Romans of our period believed that this cult and its priestesses (or one particular priestess) were an integral part of the myth of Rome's founding. Without the Vestals and their cult, there would have been no Rome and thus no Romans. Second, the fact that in the Romans' minds the cult clearly pre-existed Rome's founding assumes that it had a prior existence as a non-indigenous cult, one that began elsewhere and only after its arrival in Rome (and Rome's foundation) became Roman.

T. J. Cornell in his book, *The Beginnings of Rome*, writes:

> The Roman foundation legend provides evidence, first and foremost, of how the Romans of later times chose to see themselves, and how they wished to be seen by others. The story carries a strong ideological message. The most revealing sign of this is the way it defines the identity of the Roman people as a mixture of different ethnic groups, and of Roman culture as the product of various foreign influences.[3]

The ancient descriptions of the Vestals' role in the foundation myth of Rome repeat and strengthen the ideological message defined by Cornell. The Vestals who were at the very heart of Rome's beginnings, and without whom Rome's founder would never have existed, were also foreign, and as such a reminder that, as Cornell observes, one part of the Romans' identity was a belief that they were not of indigenous stock but a blending of many peoples and cultures. At the same time, the fact that they partook of the foreignness that was so central to the Romans' own identity emphasizes how intertwined the Vestals and their order were with Rome itself. In the minds of the Romans of our period, the Vestals were inseparable from and in some way the same as Rome itself.

The central role the Vestal order and cult play in ancient accounts of king Numa's establishment of Rome's state religion further emphasizes the Vestals' part in this ideological message.[4] The prominence assigned to the Vestals in ancient accounts of Numa's establishment of this religion suggests that the Romans of our historical period viewed this cult as an integral part of the means by which their ancestors' lawless and warlike society was transformed into their own legal-minded and religiously dutiful state. At the same time, our ancient sources' crediting of Alban Numa with the establishment of the

Roman Vestal order, which many of those same sources also record as originally an Alban priesthood, manifestly reinforces again the message that the Romans and their state were made up of a variety of different peoples and ethnic influences.[5] In this story too, the Vestal cult, which was part of what defined the Romans' own sense of themselves and what it meant to be Roman, began somewhere else and was at the same time both Roman and foreign.

The same message is also to be found in the Vestals' final appearance in ancient accounts of the Regal Period. Dionysius of Halicarnassus records that the first incident of Vestal *incestum* took place under the Roman king, Tarquinius Priscus.[6] The Vestal Pinaria, he writes, was accused and convicted of *incestum* and punished according to a method devised by Priscus himself. The method chosen was, Dionysius observes, the same as that used in later cases:

> [Tarquinius Priscus] seems also to have first invented the punishment which the Pontifices inflict on those Vestals who do not preserve their chastity, motivated either by his own views or, as some believe, following a dream; and this punishment, according to the interpreters of religious rites, was found after his death among the Sibylline oracles. For under his rule the priestess Pinaria, Publius' daughter, was discovered to be performing the rites in a state of unchastity.
>
> (D. H. 3.67.3)

The inventor of the Vestals' punishment, Tarquinius Priscus, was believed to have come to Rome from Etruria and thus serves as yet one more example of the Romans' belief that they and their state were a mixture of many different peoples and cultures. The crediting of Priscus with the invention of the punishment for Vestal *incestum* is thus also one more example of this belief, in that a distinctly Roman tradition is given another ethnic beginning in this story.

Whatever else the Romans wanted to say about their origins and their identity, one aspect of this message was that the Vestals were an integral part of who the Romans were. Wound about and integral in all the Vestals' appearances in the ancient accounts of early Roman history is the theme of their cults' essential foreignness, and its pre-existence of Rome itself. A Vestal was the mother of Rome's founder; the cult itself was brought to Rome from Alba Longa by Numa, and Tarquinius Priscus, the first of Rome's Etruscan kings, was credited with the invention of the best known aspect of this cult, the punishment for Vestal *incestum*. This repeated emphasis on the fact that the priestesses and their cult pre-existed Rome and stemmed from Alba Longa are an inherent reminder that Rome and its culture were made up of foreign rather than indigenous elements. In other words, whatever else one says about the Vestals and their cult, one must recognize that reflected in the Romans' own stories of the early order is the belief that this most essentially Roman institution was of foreign origin, just as the Romans themselves were.

Vestals in the early Republic

Ancient historical accounts of the Vestals' appearances in the early Republic settle into a pattern and in their discussions of the next 350 years or so, with the exception of a single episode, our sources name the Vestals only in connection with accusations of *incestum*. The picture we receive of the Vestals in this period is one of a group of priestesses whose primary function was religious, who did not step out of their cult roles, took no active part in public events and did not even act in their own defence, when it would otherwise seem necessary. With the single exception of their flight from the Gauls in 386 BCE, where the priestesses manifestly acted from necessity and in any case did so within a traditional religious framework (saving Rome's *sacra* surely counts as that), none of the Vestals who appear in the ancient historical accounts of this period emerge as active participants in the episodes recounted by our sources but instead remain passive figures around whom an often tragic drama unfolds. Whether this picture is a historically accurate one is unknown but it is clearly the picture in which the Romans of our period believed, and the picture against which the actions of the Vestals contemporary with our ancient sources were measured.

With the exception of their reports of the Vestals' flight from the Gauls, for which there is nearly contemporary evidence, the historical accuracy of our ancient sources' accounts of the episodes involving the Vestals in this period is unknown. While it is probable that the actual accusations and immolations recorded did take place, given that these events would have been included in the pontifical records, our ancient sources may have known little more than we of the actual events that led up to these incidents. In such a vacuum, it is to be expected that at least some of these sources expanded upon the original pontifical notice of a case of *incestum* with the invention of further details. In other words, while the various accusations and punishments recorded are likely to have occurred, their causes, as well as the events that surrounded them may well have been embellished and many of the details, perhaps even the names of the Vestals involved, invented either by our sources or by our sources' sources.

It must therefore be recognized at the outset of this portion of our discussion that any pattern discovered in these episodes may owe as much to authorial intention as to historical reality.[7] Our ancient sources may well only have included certain episodes of Vestal *incestum* and excluded others that did not fit the structure or intent of their work. Likewise, these same authors may themselves have chosen the Vestal names recorded because these names fit their own agenda rather than because they were historically accurate. In other words, what we have in these accounts is the views of late republican and early imperial sources on the episodes involving these priestesses and not absolute and accurate historical reports.

It is generally assumed nowadays that accusations of, and convictions for, Vestal *incestum* occurred only at moments when Rome was in especially great danger or turmoil.[8] An accused Vestal, most scholars interested in the issue argue, functioned as a scapegoat whose immolation served to reassure Rome's inhabitants that a threatening danger had been avoided.[9] This view, however, is less than accurate. Leaving aside for the moment the whole question of whether this pattern or any other pattern is due more to authorial intention or historical reality, the fact that not all instances of external danger or internal turmoil at Rome in this period resulted in such accusations means that some additional trigger must have been present for each recorded Vestal case of *incestum*. A close examination of these cases in fact reveals that such accusations seem to have been made only when the punishment of a Vestal could serve as an object lesson to some segment of the Roman population with whom the Vestal in question had close connections or whom she could be seen as symbolizing in some way. In other words, Vestals of this period seem to have been accused of *incestum* only when a faction to which they or their family belonged or which they could be seen as representing was involved in the turmoil in question.

Of the nine episodes of possible Vestal *incestum* recorded for the period between the founding of the Republic and the end of the Second Punic War, seven are securely dated. Of these seven, four take place at times when their victims' accusation can be seen as sending a direct and much needed (from the point of view of the authorities in charge) message to a Roman political faction with whom the Vestal in question was closely associated. The remaining three take place at times when Rome's women in particular were under threat from a plague.

The most famous and most discussed charges of Vestal *incestum* in this first period of the Republic are also the last, made in 216 BCE. Livy and others record that shortly after the disaster at Cannae, two Vestals, Opimia and Floronia, were accused and convicted of *incestum*.[10]

> For terrified above all at so great a slaughter together with other *prodigia*, next because two Vestals in the same year, Opimia and Floronia, were convicted of *incestum* and the one was destroyed under the earth at the Colline Gate, as is the custom, while the other contrived her own death; L. Cantilius, one of the Pontifical scribes, whom they now call the lesser Pontifices, who had committed the crime with Floronia, was beaten by the Pontifex Maximus with withies in the *comitium* until he died under the blows.
>
> (Liv. 22.57.2–3)

It is this incident that is most commonly cited as evidence that accusations of Vestal *incestum* were made only at times of great fear and turmoil within Rome, and in this case it is an accurate assessment of Rome's likely state. Hannibal was rampaging through Italy and indeed almost at the gates of Rome. Rome's armies were seemingly able to do little to stop him, and many Roman lives had already been lost. In Livy's own words:

> Among evils the scope of which, great as it was, was still uncertain, they were unable even to form any satisfactory plan, and the clamour of weeping

women disturbed them, for, since the facts were not yet known, the living and the dead were being lamented in almost every house indiscriminately. Therefore Q. Fabius Maximus stated that ... since there were hardly any magistrates remaining in the city, the senators should themselves take steps to calm the tumult and fear that abounded everywhere. They must forbid the matrons the public streets and force them to remain indoors; they must quell the loud lamentation for the dead and bring silence to the city.

(Liv. 22.55)

The *pax romana*, which the Vestals were expected to preserve with their virginity, was without a doubt in danger in Roman eyes. Thus, one reason for these charges is likely to have been, as modern scholars often observe, the Romans' very real fear for their city's future.

At the same time, however, a close examination of Livy's text reveals that above and beyond the general fear engendered by Hannibal's presence, the turmoil at Rome was in large part the result of the behaviour of Rome's women. Instead of remaining at home and silent on public matters, as was proper for respectable Roman mothers, wives and daughters, women had taken to wailing publicly in the streets openly mourning their losses. So great was their lamentation that the Roman senate limited the length of mourning to one month, and the annual rites of Ceres had to be suspended because there were not enough women out of mourning to perform them.[11] Later in the same year, when the senate debated whether or not to ransom the captives from the Battle of Cannae, women mingled publicly with the men listening to the debate. After the senate made the decision not to ransom the captives, the women followed the messengers to the gates of the city openly lamenting and protesting against this decision. All of this combines to suggest an atmosphere where traditional gender barriers were breaking down and women were acting in an increasingly uncontrolled fashion. More than that, though, it suggests an atmosphere where the behaviour of women was of increasing political concern. This raises the possibility that in some measure the condemnation of the two Vestals may again have been an attempt to redress the balance and restore some measure of control over one specific element of Roman society, its women, with the accusation and immolation/suicide of the two Vestals serving as a symbolic correction to the inappropriately uncontrolled behaviour of these same women.

This postulate gains further strength from a consideration of Livy's account of the events of 207 BCE:

more terrifying to the minds of men than all the other portents announced from abroad or seen at home the fire in the *aedes Vestae* went out, and the Vestal who was the guardian that night was beaten with by order of the Pontifex P. Licinius. Although it happened not as a portent from the gods but because of human error, it was nevertheless decided to placate Vesta with a sacrifice of full-grown victims and a supplication.

(Liv. 28.11.6)[12]

In that year, prodigies repeatedly disturbed Rome, still in danger from Hannibal and his army. Among these was the extinguishing of the fire on the hearth of Vesta. Such an occurrence was believed to portend the downfall of Rome, and, as R. Bauman observes, in the frightened atmosphere that still existed at that time in Rome, might well have provoked further accusations of Vestal inchastity.[13] As far as we know it did not, and the lesser punishment of a whipping by the Pontifex Maximus was instead applied. That no graver action seems to have been contemplated, however, gives rise to the question, why?

Bauman wishes to see the growth of the Scipionic party's power as at least partially the reason for this relatively mild reaction and further suggests that it might have been due to Aemilia's influence.[14] Combined with this, though, are also the changed circumstances at Rome. While they were still less than ideal – Hannibal was still in Italy and Rome's safety and indeed its very survival remained uncertain – they had changed in one very important aspect. Women had returned, at least nominally, to their expected places. They were no longer mourning openly in the streets, demonstrating and protesting about the loss of their men, but had retired to their homes and traditional activities.[15] Their behaviour was no longer a political issue, and thus no longer a trigger for Vestal punishment.

The possibility of a political trigger for accusations of Vestal *incestum* is further confirmed by the first immolation of the early Republic recorded for the year 483 BCE. Four separate sources note that in this year a Vestal, whose name these same sources variously give as Oppia, Opimia, Pompilia or Popillia, was accused of *incestum*, found guilty and put to death.[16] Livy, the most detailed of our sources, records that the first suspicion of Vestal *incestum* arose because of various ominous portents occurring in the same year, but the further particulars of the precise circumstances surrounding this accusation, trial and punishment are lacking.

Scholars have generally accepted that the name Oppia, given to the Vestal in question by Livy, is the most likely name of the four provided by our ancient sources.[17] If this is indeed the case, then already at this early date we have a plebeian Vestal.[18] Such a background raises the possibility that a very real political motivation lay behind Oppia's accusation (or, equally possibly, that our sources wished to imply this possibility). Rome was at this time in a state of political unrest over the question of agricultural reform with the patricians taking one side and the plebeians the other.[19] The Pontifices were by definition patrician and as such would most probably have been in the camp of those who supported the status quo and viewed the plebeians' unrest as a worrying development that threatened the very fabric of the state and its continued existence. In light of this, Oppia's immolation takes on an added significance and can be seen in part as the patrician Pontifices' conscious or unconscious reaction to plebeian unrest, one that presumably was meant to send a warning to the plebs of the dangers inherent in overstepping their traditional boundaries.

By itself, the possible relationship between Oppia's immolation and political unrest at Rome is perhaps not enough to suggest that such a relationship is anything other than coincidence or authorial intention. The same pattern, however, is repeated in two other accusations of Vestal *incestum* recorded by our ancient sources for the years of the early Republic. The first accusation is recorded for 420 BCE, when the Vestal Postumia was accused of *incestum* but acquitted:

> In the same year, the Vestal virgin Postumia, although innocent of the crime, was accused of inchastity, coming under suspicion because of her too elegant dress and a manner freer than was suitable for a virgin. After she had been remanded and then acquitted, the Pontifex Maximus, on behalf of the whole college, ordered her to abstain from joking and to practise holiness rather than elegance in her appearance.
>
> (Liv. 4.44.2)[20]

The second is that made against Minucia in 337 BCE:

> In the same year, the Vestal Minucia, suspected first because of her appearance, which was more worldly than appropriate, next accused to the Pontifices by the report of a slave, after she had been commanded by their decree to abstain from the sacred rites and not to sell her slaves, and after judgement had been passed, was buried alive under the earth at the Colline Gate to the right of the *via Strata* in the Campus Sceleratus; I believe that the name of this place comes from the crime of incest.
>
> (Liv. 8.15.7–8)[21]

According to Livy, again the most detailed of our sources, Minucia and her predecessor, Postumia, were both accused of *incestum* because of appearances more elegant than appropriate for Vestals. This explanation, however, is somewhat of a convention in Livy's accounts of Vestal immolation; not only Minucia and Postumia, but also the later Vestals Claudia and Licinia were said by Livy to have suffered because of their too elegant appearance and/or clever tongues.[22] Nor do any of our other sources repeat this explanation in connection with these two immolations, thus raising the likelihood that some other cause lay behind the two accusations.

The names of the two Vestals in question again provide one possible explanation for their respective accusations, one that repeats the pattern established in the first recorded case of Vestal *incestum* for this period. The first of the two Vestals in question, Postumia, was presumably the sister of the military tribune M. Postumius, who was accused and convicted of failure at Veii in 421 BCE.[23] The timing of the charges against Postumia, less than a year after her brother's conviction, seems unlikely to have been pure coincidence. Postumius' failure at Veii put Rome in serious danger and caused enormous resentment of Postumius and his faction among ordinary Romans. This resentment was no doubt extended to the tribune's sister and lay behind the charges raised against her.[24] Equally, the fact that she was found innocent can be attributed to the composition of the Pontifical College, which at this time was still entirely patrician, and thus likely to be supportive of her and her faction.

Contemporary political struggles seem also to lie behind Minucia's accusation and immolation. The years surrounding 337 BCE were again dominated by the ongoing struggle for power between the patricians and the plebeians. Over the preceding thirty years, the plebeians had made increasing inroads in the patricians' traditional power base. In the years between 366 and 351, the first plebeian consul, dictator and censor had held office. In the same year that Minucia was accused, the first plebeian praetor took office. The question of the plebeians' right to various religious offices, which was to result some thirty years later in the *lex Ogulnia*, had already become an issue. Minucia, while not necessarily the first plebeian Vestal, was originally a member of an important and politically active plebeian family.[25] As a member of such a family, Minucia would have been an easy target for the patrician Pontifices. The plebeians would have expected Minucia to demonstrate the plebeians' suitability to hold high religious positions, while those who were against admitting plebeians to positions of religious (or other) authority would have hoped for the opposite, something to prove that plebeians were not suitable candidates. It is thus possible to see in the immolation of Minucia again a purpose having little to do with the supposed facts of the case, and everything to do with contemporary events. Minucia's *incestum*, real or invented, provided the patricians with a golden opportunity to make their point and warn the plebeians of the dangers attendant on overstepping their traditional place, and it is most probably for this reason as much as any actual misdeed that she was found guilty and buried alive.[26]

There remain three accusations of Vestal *incestum* during this period, which can be securely dated. Perhaps because of our limited knowledge of historical events for the times when these three accusations were made, they do not immediately show signs of supporting the pattern of political chastisement delineated above, although it should be stressed that they in no way contradict it. Instead, these three episodes give evidence of a secondary pattern in that they all seem to have been made at a time when some form of plague particularly threatening to women was rampant at Rome. Thus, these accusations too, while not showing signs of being motivated by contemporary political struggles, demonstrate that accusations of Vestal *incestum* occurred only at times when a group with whom the Vestals might be connected in Roman minds – in this case women – was at the root of some serious danger for Rome.

Our sources record that in 472 BCE, the Vestal Orbinia was accused and convicted of *incestum* because of a plague to which women had been particularly vulnerable.[27] As A. Fraschetti recognized, two other accusations of Vestal *incestum* in the same era seem also to have been the result of an outbreak of a similar pestilence at Rome. In 274 or 273 BCE, the Vestal Sextilia was condemned for *incestum* and buried alive.[28] Although the reasons for this accusation are nowhere recorded in our ancient authors, Fraschetti, observing that Orosius records a plague similar to that of 472 in 276 BCE, argued that this plague was still active in 274 BCE, thus raising the possibility that the two events were con-nected.[29] Finally, in 266 BCE, the Vestal Caparronia was accused and convicted of *incestum* but escaped burial alive by hanging herself before her sentence could be carried out.[30] Orosius records that in the same year a plague again raged at Rome. Whether women were mainly the victims of this last plague too is not known, but both Fraschetti and K. Mustakallio argue convincingly for this possibility.[31]

Fraschetti believes that these three immolations of Vestals in response to a plague are evidence that the *incestum* of a Vestal was largely a threat to pregnant women.[32] Mustakallio takes issue with this interpretation, pointing out that the plague in question attacked not only women but also cattle. She wishes to see the *incestum* of a Vestal not as a threat to pregnant women but as a more general threat to Rome's fertility, concluding that these three particular cases of *incestum* took place in the spring and thus polluted the 'fertility and purification rites of this period'.[33]

Neither of these arguments is entirely convincing, if only because other incidents of Vestal *incestum* have no visible connection with either pregnant women in particular or fertility in general. The common thread of a plague whose victims were mainly women, which runs through these three incidents, however, is significant. If it was mainly women whom this plague attacked, then perhaps the Vestals were accused because in the Romans' eyes they were connected with, and indeed represented, women in general. Livy and others record a number of outbreaks of plague at Rome, but only these three specifically are recorded as attacking primarily women. When one combines that fact with the fact that it is also these three alone that result in accusations of Vestal *incestum*, it seems clear that there must be some connection between the two. As we have seen, previous Vestal accusations of this period seem to have occurred because the Vestal in question was connected to and thus could be seen as representing a potentially disruptive faction at Rome. In these three instances, the faction is Rome's women as a whole, whose widespread illness was potentially threatening to Rome's continued existence and status quo.

The final two stories of Vestal *incestum* in this period are perhaps the best known of all such stories. Both involve the miraculous rescue of a Vestal from charges of *incestum* through the intervention of her goddess.[34] Although they are of a less certain date than those discussed previously, on the balance the ancient evidence suggests that both occurred before the Second Punic War; therefore they are both included here.[35]

The more certain of the two episodes in terms of dating is that of the Vestal Tuccia, which most of our sources set to *c.* 230 BCE.[36] In all but one ancient account, Tuccia was accused of *incestum*, but proved her innocence by carrying water in a sieve from the river Tiber to the Forum.[37] The second episode involved the Vestal Aemilia who, also accused of *incestum*, proved her innocence by laying her garment on the hearth of the *aedes Vestae* and miraculously relighting the fire from the dead ashes of this hearth.[38]

Because these two stories are of uncertain date, it is impossible to say whether they follow the same pattern as the instances already discussed. Their miraculous nature, however, sets them off from these other incidents and combined with the uncertainty of their dating suggests that they, even more than the other incidents of *incestum* in this era, should perhaps be viewed rather as legendary tales than as actual historical events. What is particularly significant about these stories is not their historical accuracy but the meaning they would have had to our ancient sources' contemporaries. The actual circumstances surrounding these two accusations are lost to us. What remains is the message contained in the two accounts: when combined, these declared to an ordinary Roman audience that the goddess Vesta was concerned with the conduct of her priestesses and would protect them if such protection became necessary. Conversely, if such protection was not offered, then the priestesses in question were without a doubt guilty and the goddess angry enough to require real and immediate propitiation. Such stories gave added lustre to these priestesses and their cult and emphasized the reality of Vesta's concern for both her cult and Rome as a whole.

Only one Vestal appearance in the period between the founding of the Republic and the beginning of the First Punic War is unconnected with a charge of *incestum*. Our ancient sources record that in 386 BCE, the Gauls besieged Rome itself and sent much of the population in flight from the city.[39] Among those fleeing, these sources note, were the Vestals and the *flamen quirinalis* carrying as many of their *sacra* as they could. A Roman named Lucius Albanius, they add, put his own wife and children out of his wagon and instead took up the priestesses and their *sacra* and carried them to safety in Caere.

This episode may sound like yet another legendary story meant to demonstrate the Romans' devotion to their gods, but it is in fact one for which we have almost contemporary evidence.[40] As such, it provides at least some evidence of contemporary Romans' attitudes toward the Vestals and the Vestals' own attitudes to their *sacra*. It presents us with a group of priestesses who took their duties seriously to the point of being willing to risk their lives to save the *sacra* entrusted to them. Equally importantly, it also offers us the image of an ordinary Roman citizen willing to risk his and his family's lives to save these same priestesses and their *sacra*. Whatever later Vestals thought of their cult and its duties, the Vestals of this period took them seriously. Whatever later Romans thought of the Vestals and their cult, at this period of their history, they regarded the Vestals and their *sacra* with reverence great enough to ensure that at least one Roman was willing to risk his family and his family's future for the priestesses and their cult.

Conclusion

The account we receive of the Vestals' appearances in the first 500 or so years of Rome's existence is less an accurate description of these priestesses' actual historical existence than it is a construction of stories and images that reflects what the Romans of the late Republic and early Empire wished to believe was the truth about these priestesses, their order and their order's role in Rome's past. The picture of the Vestals that emerges for the Regal Period is one that links these priestesses inextricably to and makes them inseparable from the Romans' own definition of their identity. The Vestals were part of Rome from the very beginning, yet at the same time they and their order pre-existed the city and its founding and as such served as a central reminder that Rome was a mixture of ethnic cultures and peoples. The picture that emerges for the early Republic is one of an order focused entirely on cult and religious duties. The Vestals appear in our sources in this period only when they are suspected of polluting their chastity, the preservation of which was an integral part of their religious duties, or in one instance where they attempt to save their *sacra* from invaders. The priestesses who appear in the ancient accounts of this period neither act to defend themselves nor involve themselves in public events or political affairs. Instead they remain within their *aedes*, emerging only when their proper performance of their religious duties is in doubt or when extraordinary danger to their rites makes it necessary. How much of this picture is grounded in reality and how much of it is based on the inventions of our ancient Roman sources is and must remain unknown. What matters, though, is that it is without a doubt this picture of the Vestals in which the Romans of the late Republic and early Empire believed and against which they measured the doings and activities of contemporary Vestals.

Notes

1 See, for example, T. D. McClain 2004, who rightly observes that Livy's description of the accusation of the Vestal Postumia closely parallels and complements two other episodes in Livy's fourth book. See also J. P. Davies 2004; J. Chaplin 2000; G. B. Miles 1995; D. S. Levene 1993; E. Gruen 1992; E. Gabba 1991; R. M. Ogilvie 1970: 577. For a standard modern account of the actual historical events of the period under consideration in this chapter, see H. H. Scullard 1981.
2 See, for example, Liv. 1.3; Ov. *Fast.* 2.382–386; Ov. *Fast.* 3.10–23. For modern discussions of this legend, see H. J. Hillen 2003; M. Fox 1996; T. J. Cornell 1995: 60–63; F. A. López 1991; H. Nesselrath 1990; G. Radke 1986; T. Hemker 1985.
3 T. J. Cornell 1995: 60.
4 See Cic. *Rep.* 2.26; D. H. 2.65; Liv. 1.20. Plu. *Num.* 9–14. For a discussion of Numa's religious reforms, see E. M. Hooker 1963; R. M. Ogilvie 1970: 97–98.
5 See, for example, Liv. 1.20 and Ov. *Fast.* 3.46.
6 Although Dionysius is our only ancient source to include this story of the origins of this punishment, his account should not be dismissed as his own invention. As he himself observes, 'these punishments, according to the interpreters of religious rites, were found after his death among the Sibylline oracles' (D. H. 3.67.3). This suggests, if nothing else, that some such story of the origins of this punishment was

recorded in the Romans' religious annals and was known to contemporary Romans. See H. Hill 1961 on Dionysius and Rome's early history.

7 For a discussion of ancient authors' practices in this respect, again see J. P. Davies 2004; J. Chaplin 2000; G. B. Miles 1995; D. S. Levene 1993; E. Gruen 1992.

8 See, for example, A. Staples 1998: 136.

9 Again, A. Staples 1998: 135.

10 *MRR* 1.253 gives a list of these sources. On Floronia, see also J. Rüpke and A. Glock 2005: 2. 999; J. Saquete 2000: 27. On Opimia, see J. Rüpke and A. Glock 2005: 2. 1184; J. Saquete 2000: 44.

11 Liv. 34.7. See also Rawson 1974 for a discussion of the religious unrest and uncertainty of these years.

12 See also V. Max. 1.1.6–7.

13 R. Bauman 1992: 27.

14 R. Bauman 1992: 27.

15 This is not to say that their roles were unchanged for, as R. Bauman 1994: 34–37 points out, the Punic Wars with their concomitant loss of menfolk gave many women the opportunity to take control of large fortunes and estates. However, to a large extent, surface appearances were retained and women, when they gave up demonstrating and protesting openly, would have seemed to all appearances to have resumed their old places and accepted roles.

16 D. H. 8.89.3–5; Liv. 2.42.11; Liv. *per.* 2. Oros. 2.8.13. On the name Oppia, see R. M. Ogilvie 1970: 349; *MRR* 1.23.

17 R. M. Ogilvie 1970: 349; *MRR* 1.23; F. Münzer 1937–1938: 211–216.

18 The name Oppia, which was given to the Vestal in question by Livy and of which all the other names are likely to be variants, is that of a plebeian gens. For a discussion of this fact, see F. Münzer 1937–1938: 211–216; R. M. Ogilvie 1970: 349.

   The plebeian status of this Vestal has also been used as evidence that the Vestal order was already open to plebeians at this early date. See, for example, T. J. Cornell 1995: 447 n.39. If it is correct, it raises the possibility that the Vestal order alone of all major Roman priesthoods was from the beginning open to members of both the plebeian and patrician classes. If so, there are several possible reasons for this exception. First, the rules that applied to the male priesthoods at Rome may not have applied to the female priesthood of the Vestals, which was so anomalous in other ways. Second, perhaps when a Vestal ceased to be a member of an individual family, she also ceased to be a member of that family's class. Most likely though, the reason is to be found in the Vestals' role as religious representatives of all Rome.

   F. Münzer's 1937–1938: 211–212 argument that this name was a later invention added to the account by opponents of the patricians in the time of the Gracchi, since the true name of the Vestal was lost due to *condemnatio memoriae*, should probably be dismissed. There is no ancient evidence to suggest that *condemnatio memoriae* was ordered in the case of a Vestal convicted of *incestum*. Quite on the contrary in fact, the only names of Vestals that we have for the early Republic are those of condemned Vestals. See Appendix B.

19 Liv. 2.42 describes in some detail the confusion of this year.

20 See also Plu. *Mor.* 89: e–f. For modern discussions of this Vestal and her punishment, see also *MRR* 1951: 71; F. Münzer 1937–1938: 57–59. R. M. Ogilvie 1970: 600–601 supports my argument.

21 Oros. 3.9.5. following Livy writes: 'In the year following this, the Vestal Virgin, Minucia, who had admitted to *incestum* was condemned and buried alive on the field which is now called *sceleratus*'. See also Hier. *Adv. Iovin.* 1.41; Ov. *Fast.* 2.382; *POxy.* 1. 12. col. iii. 33–37. See *MRR* 1.139 for a list of other ancient sources that touch on this immolation and F. Münzer 1937–1938: 61–62. S. P. Oakley 1998: 579–581 also discusses the significance of the Minucii family in this context.

22 See J. Briscoe 1973: 578.

23 R. M. Ogilvie 1970: 602.

24 R. M. Ogilvie 1970: 602.

25 R. Bauman 1992: 17. F. Münzer 1937–1938: 211 does raise the possibility that the Vestal Oppia, who was also accused of *incestum* and immolated in 483 BCE, was also from a plebeian family, but both the uncertainty surrounding her name (see note 18 above) and her early date make this possibility an unlikely one.

26 It should be stressed, though, that it was not necessarily a deliberate decision on the part of the patricians to charge Minucia with inchastity, whether she was guilty or not. They could well have believed in the slave's charges, with their eagerness for ammunition to use against the plebeians only making them more anxious to do so.

27 D. H. 9.40: information was given to the Pontifices by a slave that one of the Vestal Virgins who looked after the eternal fire, Orbinia by name, had lost her virginity and, although unchaste, was performing the sacred rites. The Pontifices removed her from her sacred offices, brought her to trial, and after she had been found guilty, they ordered her to be beaten with withies, carried through the city in a solemn procession and then buried alive. One of the two men who had defiled her killed himself; the other was seized by the Pontifices, who ordered him to be beaten in the Forum as a slave and then put to death. After this action the plague, which had attacked women and caused so many deaths among them, promptly ceased.

Livy makes no mention of this incident. R. M. Ogilvie 1970: 577–578 suggests that this omission 'may be explained as a characteristic instance of his selectivity in the reproduction of real or invented "official material"' and there is some truth in this. At the same time, it begs the question of why Livy omits this (and perhaps a later incident in 266 BCE) from his narrative while including other episodes. This question is important in that it serves to remind us how much our ancient evidence for the Vestals is coloured by authorial intention. The answer to it is no doubt to be found in Livy's focus for the years surrounding 472 BCE and on his not wishing to distract from the main theme of his narrative at this point, which begins in 473 BCE and concludes in 471 BCE.

28 Liv. *per.* 14: Sextilia, the Vestal Virgin, was condemned for *incestum* and buried alive. See also Oros. 4.2.2 and 4.5.6–9. See *MRR* 1.197 for a list of further ancient sources together with F. Münzer 1937–1938: 214 for a second discussion of this incident. See also J. Rüpke and A. Glock 2005: 2. 1287; J. Saquete 2000: 52.

29 A. Fraschetti 1984: 104–106.

30 Oros. 4.5.9. Since the books of Livy's work which cover this date are lost, as are those of Dionysius, we have no earlier sources for this immolation. Nonetheless, there seems to be little risk in including it here, as these three later authors in all the other instances of Vestal *incestum*, which they record, seem to have followed Livy closely in their accounts of this *crimen*. See also J. Rüpke and A. Glock 2005: 2. 858; J. Saquete 2000: 14; *MRR* 1.201; F. Münzer 1937–1938: 215–216.

31 A. Fraschetti 1984: 104–106; K. Mustakallio 1992: 58.

32 A. Fraschetti 1984: 109.

33 K. Mustakallio 1992: 62.

34 Liv. *Per.* 20 claims that Tuccia was convicted but the more usual version of the story has her proving her innocence by carrying a sieve full of water (see, for example, D. H. 2.69–1–3; Plin. *Nat.* 28.12; V. Max. 8.1, abs. 5).

35 F. Münzer 1937–1938: 199–204.

36 The one major exception to this dating is Pliny the Elder, who dates the incident to 145 BCE, a year for which no other sources record such an event. This dating is obviously of some significance to the question of how our ancient sources viewed this incident. On the incident in general, see J. Rüpke and A. Glock 2005: 2. 1327; J. Saquete 2000: 56; *MRR* 1.227; F. Münzer 1937–1938: 203–209.

37 August. *C. D.* 10.16; D. H. 2.69.1–3; Plin. *Nat.* 28.12; Tert. *Apol.* 22; V. Max. 8.1.abs.5; Tertull. *Apol.* 22. Only Liv. *Per.* 20 names Tuccia as guilty. If the account contained in the *Periochae* is not an erroneous recording of Livy's original version of the story, something that seems unlikely, then its existence seems to serve as a solid example of Livy's reworking of Vestal history to suit his own purposes, although perhaps in this case Livy's noted disbelief in the miraculous lay behind his reworking of this story. We unfortunately do not have a Livian version of Aemilia's miraculous rescue with which to compare his account of Tuccia. Whether this is because the book in which it would have been contained is lost or because he deliberately chose not to include it in his work is unclear. If the latter, his ignoring of it is likely to be deliberate and again due to his scepticism of such miraculous incidents. As such, it should serve as a reminder to us of the dangers inherent in taking Livy's accounts of Vestal events as pure, historical fact. On Livy's scepticism (or non-scepticism) towards the many miraculous stories in early Roman history, see D. S. Levene 1993: 10–13.

38 D. H. 2.68.3–5; Prop. 4.11.53–54; V. Max. 1.1.6–7. See J. Rüpke and A. Glock 2005: 2. 734; J. Saquete 2000: 4; *MRR* 2. 486.

39 Liv. 5.40; V. Max.1.1.10. See R. M. Ogilvie 1970: 724 for a discussion of both this rite and its relation to the other sources that also recount it.

40 Plu. *Cam.* 22.3 quotes Aristotle on this point.

7   The Vestals in Roman history

In the century following the end of the Second Punic War, we reach a historical period nearly contemporary with most of our sources. Ancient accounts of the Vestals and their activities in this period and later ones are therefore more likely to be securely rooted in actual historical events than those of the earlier periods of Rome's existence. As such, they can be examined not only for what they reveal that the Romans themselves believed about this priesthood and its history, but also for what they reveal about the actual history of the Vestals and their cult, as well as these priestesses' role in Rome's own history.

The picture that emerges is somewhat of a contrast to that described in Chapter 6. While the Vestals of the late Republic and early Empire continued to take the religious roles that tradition assigned to them, they also began late in the second century BCE to appear as active participants on the Roman historical stage, involving themselves in Rome's politics, working to improve the status and influence of their order, and perhaps even trying to alter the requirement of chastity imposed upon their priesthood. This pattern of public political activity continued into the next century with certain modifications, and indeed remained in effect until the beginning of the First Triumvirate. Thereafter, the Vestals, like many other Romans, largely ceased to figure as active participants in ancient accounts of contemporary political events. They do not, however, disappear entirely from view and we are able from time to time to catch glimpses of them in our ancient sources. These glimpses provide us with a picture of a Vestal order that had a central role in imperial propaganda and at the same time seems to have acquired the added prestige and power that earlier members of the order had sought in the last century of the Republic, as well as perhaps even an unofficial relaxation of the priestesses' commitment to thirty years' chastity.

The Vestals' first interference in Roman public affairs took place in 143 BCE, when the consul Appius Claudius Pulcher asked the senate for permission to celebrate a triumph for his victory over the Salassi and the senate refused his request because he had sustained serious losses during his campaign.[1] Ignoring the senatorial ban, Pulcher decided to celebrate his triumph without official approval. When a tribune tried to halt the procession and physically remove Pulcher from his chariot, the Vestal Claudia, whom our ancient sources variously describe as Pulcher's sister or daughter, threw herself onto the chariot and effectively used her Vestal *sanctitas* to prevent the tribune from halting the procession. In this way, Pulcher was able to proceed with his triumph.

R. Bauman argues that Claudia, possessed of a certain 'legal expertise' and 'in the mainstream of contemporary thinking', was deliberately challenging the expansion of tribunician power by her actions.[2] In his view, Claudia was acting not only from family feeling as some ancient scholars stress, but also from a genuine political interest in limiting a tribune's power.[3] Bauman makes an important point in that he implicitly recognizes that the Vestals, just as other Roman women, might well have had an interest in public affairs above and beyond one based solely on family feeling. He fails to recognize, however, that while Claudia may have acted from a desire to enforce some limitation of tribunician power, it is also possible that she acted out of a wish to expand the power and prestige of her own order. Certainly, the fact that her actions had that effect more than they made any real impact on the use of tribunician power supports such a view.

As Bauman himself observes, one result of Claudia's efforts was the extension of the Vestals' *sanctitas* to something more closely resembling a tribune's *sacrosanctitas*.[4] Traditionally, the Romans had always considered a Vestal *sancta* but this *sanctitas* seems to have been an inactive sort of quality, something that became important only when it was in doubt (when a Vestal was accused of *incestum* for example). There is no real evidence that before Claudia's action, Vestal *sanctitas* had ever had an active application (although arguably the custom of freeing any prisoner who met with a Vestal may have owed something to a belief in the Vestals' *sanctitas*).[5] Afterwards, however, a more active interpretation of the Vestals' *sanctitas* seems to have become generally accepted, with the Vestals more and more frequently taking the role of neutral supplicants on behalf of one threatened Roman or another.[6] That it was this effect rather than a desire to limit tribunician power that Claudia had in mind when she sprang upon her relative's chariot cannot be proven. It is certainly as likely, however, if for no other reason than that her actions resulted in the transformation of Vestal *sanctitas* into a more formidable and effective power, while they seem to have had little or no effect on the limits of tribunician power.

Whatever Claudia's reasons, a second effect of her action was the paving of the way for later Vestals' more active participation in public affairs. Whether Claudia's actions had been motivated by an active desire to improve the Vestals' power or not, the success of these actions undoubtedly suggested to later Vestals the possibility that they might more actively participate in public affairs and affect changes of their own. After Claudia, at any rate, we increasingly see Vestal Virgins acting, at first individually and later collectively, on behalf of themselves, their order or others in the public arena.

The second Vestal public appearance in this century occurred some twenty years later in 123 BCE, when the Vestal Licinia dedicated an altar, *aedicula* and *pulvinar* at the Aventine temple of the *Bona Dea*. Cicero writes of the episode:

When Licinia, a Vestal Virgin born to the noblest family, and offered to the most sacred priesthood, at the time when T. Flaminius and Q. Metellus were consuls, dedicated an altar, an *aediculam* and a *pulvinar* under the Aventine, did not the praetor Sextus Iulius refer the matter to this college by the authority of the senate? Then the Pontifex Maximus P. Scaevola responded on behalf of the college: 'What in a public place, Licinia, the daughter of Gaius, dedicated without the permission of the people I do not consider sacred'. Indeed, with what severity and diligence the senate treated this matter, you know easily from the *senatus consultus* itself.[7]

(Cic. *Dom.* 53.136)

Licinia's dedication took place at a time of renewed political conflict between patricians and plebeians over the question of who should have control of religious power at Rome.[8] Bauman argues that Licinia acted as she did because she wished to support the conservatives in their attempts to preserve the patricians' control over the state religion.[9] He finds it problematic, though, that Licinia's dedication would have been in direct opposition to the plebeian politics of her probable father, Gaius Licinius Crassus, the tribune of 145 BCE, and thus in complete disregard for filial piety. If, however, one begins from the possibility that Licinia believed she had a higher loyalty to her new family, the Vestal order, and that she chose the course she did in order to demonstrate her order's independence from the will of the people, then this difficulty disappears.

This possibility has the advantage that under such an interpretation Licinia would have been following closely in the footsteps of Claudia, whom she almost assuredly had known. Both women's actions can then be seen as attempts to demonstrate and increase the power of the Vestal order – a power that in their eyes did not need to have recourse to and stood above the power of the people. In supporting her father's triumph and preventing a tribunician veto, Claudia had demonstrated that the Vestal's *sanctitas* was above the control of the people's major representatives, the tribunes of the plebs. In dedicating the altar, *aedicula* and *pulvinar* to *Bona Dea*, Licinia was attempting to demonstrate that her actions as a Vestal, and thus implicitly her order's power, were not subjected to the dictates of the people. That her attempt, unlike Claudia's, met with criticism on the part of the general populace and ultimately failed because of this critique should not lessen its significance – a Vestal's actions twice in a relatively short time span seem deliberately intended to increase her order's prestige.

The final incident in this century is recorded for 114 BCE, when a lightning bolt struck the daughter of a knight, while she was riding on her horse, and stripped her naked.[10] This event, which was obviously a prodigy, led to suspicion of the Vestals' inchastity, a suspicion that was confirmed by a slave who revealed that three Vestals, Marcia, Aemilia and Licinia, had all taken lovers. Marcia was accused of having had only one lover, but Aemilia and Licinia were suspected of having taken many, including each other's brothers, and indeed of having participated in group sex. The Pontifical College tried all three women in the traditional manner but only Marcia was found guilty. The case did not end here, however, as this verdict angered the Roman populace, who believed that it threatened Rome's safety. In 113 BCE, a special court (*quaestio*) headed by L. Cassius Longinus was established to reconsider the matter. This court found both Aemilia and Licinia, whom the Pontifices had found innocent, along with a number of their supposed lovers, guilty. All involved were sentenced to death and the sentences carried out.

Bauman argues that the sexual acts of which the three Vestals were accused were in fact the deliberate acts of 'a coterie of rebellious spirits meeting together for some adultery and some sharpening of their wits on the foibles of the world' in much the same way that other similar groups chose to act under the early Principate.[11] Bauman goes on to note that the Vestals' reasons for their actions are likely to have been rooted in a desire to free themselves from a requirement they found both old-fashioned and restrictive, and not, as F. Münzer argues, based on a desire to support their families' populist attitudes towards religion.[12]

The atmosphere of contemporary Rome supports Bauman's argument. As Roman society in general began to question and discard outmoded beliefs and traditions, so too women in particular also began to rebel against the rules and customs that had always bound them. In such an atmosphere, the Vestals are hardly likely to have remained unaffected. Among the most binding restrictions under which they laboured was the requirement of chastity. Girls who became Vestals were chosen at a very young age (between six and ten years) before they could be fully aware of what they were expected to give up. Nor did they have any say in the decision that they become Vestals. Some of them would no doubt have preferred marriage and the more usual women's roles to a religious one, and may perhaps have regretted their loss. Religious belief would not necessarily have been a barrier to such actions either. Many old beliefs were losing or had lost their potency in this period, and the Vestals may well have felt that their enforced chastity was another one of these outmoded superstitions. If the Vestals were guilty as charged, they most probably acted as they did out of a desire to discard the traditional, archaic restraints of their order established in another, more credulous age.

Unfortunately for the Vestals, if their actions were deliberately intended to alter the conditions they lived under, they misjudged their moment. The general Roman populace could not accept such changes and acted swiftly to repel them. Public outcry at the Pontifices' decision was so great that the charges against the two Vestals who had been found innocent were renewed in a different venue.[13] This was a departure from traditional practice and sounds very much like a challenge to pontifical authority, particularly as it took place at a time when the plebeians were demanding and, increasingly, receiving more power in the religious arena, the last bastion of the patricians.[14] The Pontifices' acquittal of two Vestals and their condemnation of only one may well have been seen by the plebeians as yet one more piece of evidence that the religious authorities were biased and that power ought to be removed from the hands of the limited few to the more neutral many, particularly if the Vestals' actions raised a real religious fear among ordinary Romans.

The picture we receive then, of the Vestals in the second half of the second century BCE, is of a group of women increasingly interested in taking a role in public affairs and in improving their own situation. The Vestals appear on three separate occasions in the ancient historical narrative of this period. In the first two instances, individual priestesses stepped forward in ways that were demonstrably meant to improve the public status of their order, while in the last instance fully half of the order seemingly joined together in rebelling against the most central constraint of their priesthood. Their activities met with disapproval on the part of ordinary Romans, but to some extent each of these actions succeeded in making a point, and in the end this disapproval was not so great as to discourage later priestesses from trying and finding more acceptable methods to influence Roman public affairs in the next century.

Vestals in the first century BCE

The Vestals' active participation in public affairs continues and indeed becomes more frequent in the first century BCE. This participation differs from that of the last century, however, in that the Vestals by and large cease to act as individuals bent solely on improving the status and power of their order but instead work together as a group wielding the religious power and prestige of this same order to influence their state's politics. In doing so, they clearly demonstrate that they had found a recipe for success, for so long as they acted as a group within the traditional religious framework of their order, they were generally successful in their attempts to influence public events.

The Vestals first appear in the public arena in this era during the reign of Sulla in connection with that dictator's attacks on Julius Caesar. Suetonius writes of the occasion:

> [He married] Cornelia, daughter of the Cinna who was four times consul, with whom he soon had a daughter, Julia; nor was the dictator Sulla able to force him to repudiate his wife ... He was therefore compelled to go into hiding, and though sick with a severe attack of the quatrain fever, to change hiding places every night, and save himself from informers by bribery, until, with the help of the Vestal virgins and Mamercus Aemilius and Aurelius Cotta, his friends and associates, he sought pardon. Everyone agrees that when Sulla, after he had refused the most friendly and powerful men of his party for a long time and they had obstinately fought for Caesar, was at last worn out, he declared, either divinely inspired or from some chance: that they had won and might have him.
>
> (Suet. *Jul.* 1.2.6)

Suetonius writes as if the Vestal order as a whole was involved in this matter rather than one or two individual priestesses, as had been the case earlier when Vestals involved themselves in public affairs.[15] As such, this is the first time the entire Vestal order is documented as acting as a single unit in a political matter but it is far from the last. Instead of acting as individuals in support of a private cause, the priestesses now chose to act jointly and this joint action established their order as a powerful independent body capable of acting to further its own interests and beliefs and of influencing contemporary Roman politics.

That this new method was something that other Romans could accept seems likely in that, by Suetonius' account, it was clearly the Vestals who had the main responsibility for rescuing Caesar.[16] Suetonius writes that Sulla had refused the earlier requests of others seeking his clemency for Caesar, and that it was only this final appeal by the Vestals and their cohorts that swayed him. The wording of Suetonius' account, which places the Vestals in the most emphatic position in the sentence, sets the Vestals' influence in this matter ahead of that of Aemilius and Cotta. This presents us with an image of a Vestal order who had by acting as a group for the first time found a satisfactory means of influencing Roman public affairs.

That the Vestals were under all circumstances becoming more politically perceptive and sophisticated is shown by the events of 73 BCE, when two Vestals were separately accused of *incestum*. The first, Fabia, was accused of having an affair with Catiline, the second, Licinia, with her cousin M. Licinius Crassus, the consul of 70 BCE.[17] Both women were acquitted – Fabia because of a spirited defence on the part of M. Piso, Cato or Q. Lutatius Catulus (our sources differ on this point); Licinia, because Crassus was able to prove he was interested only in buying a piece of her property.

The general circumstances that surround the levelling of these charges are very similar to those surrounding earlier accusations of *incestum*. Rome was again in the midst of a period of turmoil and fears for the city's safety were great. The long ongoing struggle between patricians and plebeians had been further enflamed by the granting of citizen rights to all Italian communities. Pirate attacks on Roman shipping were frequent, thus decreasing the food supply at Rome. Most worrying of all, the former slave and gladiator, Spartacus, had gathered an army of some 70,000 former slaves and runaways, and was menacing Rome's Italian allies and perhaps even the city itself.

As well though, these accusations seem also at least partially the result of contemporary Roman factional politics. The one Vestal, Fabia, was the half-sister of Cicero's wife, Terentia, and her accused lover was Catiline. In 73 BCE, Catiline had not yet begun on the rebellious actions that were to make him so famous but he was already a member of the political coterie of the Populares and a well-known figure at Rome, famed for his licentious lifestyle. Likewise, Licinia was a member of a family who were important members of the Populares, and her suspected lover was her cousin Crassus, the proconsular general against Spartacus and later member of the First Triumvirate. Since both Fabia's accuser, Clodius and Licinia's accuser, Plotinus, were established members of the Optimates, it is not difficult to see party politics at work here in both instances.

Whatever, the reasons for these accusations though, the results of both were the same. The two Vestals in question were able to prove their innocence and the charges against them were dropped. Bauman argues that this vindication was due to the change in trial venue – no longer did the Pontifices decide an accused Vestal's fate in some closed and arcane court; instead the Vestals defended their innocence with the help of advocates before a secular *quaestio*.[18] The problem with this proposal, however, is that the last Vestals to be found guilty were tried by just such a public court after the Pontifices had found them innocent. Thus, it seems we must look further for the explanation of the Vestals' acquittal.

Most probably, the Vestals' acquittal was due to the priestesses' increased sophistication, and to a change in attitude on the part of the general Roman public. The Vestals of the first century BCE were clearly more independent and willing to act outside the confines of their order and its religious strictures than those of the preceding centuries. They were also apparently in at least some cases wealthy and sophisticated businesswomen who were able to call upon the services of the most distinguished lawyers in Rome for their defence. Certainly, Licinia's possession of enough land to make a real estate transaction with her cousin an acceptable excuse for a private meeting and Fabia's choice of lawyer point in this direction. Their acquittal clearly suggests that these Vestals were no longer the passive Vestals of earlier centuries but knowledgeable, effective women who knew where to look and how to manipulate the system to secure their own acquittal.

At the same time, the Roman public's attitude toward these priestesses and the danger to the city brought on by a possible case of *incestum* must also have altered. Where some fifty years earlier the public had been unwilling to accept a verdict of innocence because of their fears for the future, contemporary Romans were clearly willing to accept such a verdict in this case, despite Rome's evident danger. Whether this was due to a greater trust in the new open court under which the Vestals were tried or simply to a greater sophistication on the part of ordinary Romans and a distaste for the somewhat barbarian practices of their ancestors is unknown. The fact remains, however, that both the Vestals and the public they served had changed and in these two cases, the accused Vestals were found innocent.

The Vestal Virgins and Ciceronian politics

Three times at the height of Cicero's 'struggle of the orders' (63–62 BCE), the Vestal Virgins acted to influence events in favour of Cicero and his supporters. A single action of this sort might be put down to chance, but three separate episodes occurring one after the other in the course of only two years suggest instead that the priestesses had again deliberately chosen to involve themselves as a group in public affairs, and that the priesthood as a whole was solidly in the camp of Cicero and his *boni viri*.

The first of the three episodes occurred in 63 BCE, when the Vestal Virgin Licinia yielded her privileged seat at the games to her cousin, Licinius Murena.[19] At the time, Murena was standing for the consulship of the follow-ing year, backed by Cicero and his faction. Licinia's action in effect bestowed divine sanction on her cousin and suggested to the large audience at the games that his election would find favour with the gods.

The second episode occurred in 63 BCE, when the Roman matrons gathered at the house of the consul, Cicero, for the celebration of the yearly rites of *Bona Dea*.[20] As part of this ritual, a fire that had been lit upon the altar was allowed to die down and extinguish itself. Suddenly, however, it blazed up again. The Vestals, who were present at the celebration of the rites, immediately commanded Cicero's wife, Terentia, to go to her husband and tell him to carry out the decision he had made on behalf of Rome, for the goddess had sent a great light for his protection and glory.

One of the Vestals present at these rites was undoubtedly Fabia, the half-sister of Cicero's wife Terentia. This close family connection makes it likely that the omen was perhaps not the simple chance occurrence that Plutarch assumes but instead was deliberately planned by the Vestals with or without Terentia's knowledge.[21] The timing and setting of the omen both strengthen this possibility, being well calculated to ensure that knowledge of the omen's occurrence spread to all of Rome as every Roman *matrona* was present. These women, the wives of all the respectable voting men at Rome, assuredly could have been expected to repeat the story of such a miraculous event and its interpretation as soon as they arrived home from the rites.

Already, in the following year, 62 BCE, the Vestals again took an active part in public affairs, once more acting collectively in the interests of Cicero and his party. As a number of ancient authors recount, Clodius was accused of disguis-ing himself as a woman and entering the house of the *praetor urbanus*, Julius Caesar, during the rites of the *Bona Dea*, although the presence of anything male at that time was absolutely forbidden.[22] Caesar's mother, Aurelia, was said to have discovered Clodius and reported the affair to the senate, which in turn delegated responsibility for rendering judgement on the nature of Clodius' crime to the Pontifical College and Vestal order. Together the two priesthoods decided that Clodius' act was *nefas* and that a special court (*quaestio*) should be convened to investigate the matter. Although this court subsequently acquitted Clodius, it is clear from the ancient accounts that this was almost certainly due to wide-scale bribing of the jury and that the Vestals and Pontifices had expected Clodius to be found guilty, as his opponents, Cicero among them, clearly would have wished.

Unlike their involvement in the earlier two episodes of this period, the Vestals' original involvement here was due not to a deliberate choice on their part but rather to a decision made by the senate.[23] This decision was no doubt based on religious tradition: the possible sacrilege occurred at a rite celebrated under the aegis of the Vestals and they were therefore automatically responsible for any decisions regarding its expiation.[24] Once the Vestals became involved in this matter, however, they seem to have used this new opportunity to make their political preferences known. There may well have been real religious feeling attached to the Vestals' decision to punish the offender of their rites but at the same time there can be little doubt that their political beliefs and concerns played some role in their decision-making. Not surprisingly, the Vestals once again came down on the side of order and Republican tradition and against the Populares, finding Clodius guilty of sacrilege. Such a finding was clearly what Cicero would have preferred and indeed what he expected.[25] Thus, for a third time in two years, we have the Vestals actively involved in influencing public affairs in favour of Cicero and his *boni viri.*

These three episodes, then, give us an opportunity both to see how the Vestals could and did use their religious position to influence public opinion in this period and also to understand the beliefs and attitudes that motivated them to this action. While the Vestals may have become involved in each instance in part because of family obligations and ties, they also seem to have acted because of a genuine belief in Cicero's *concordia ordium* and because of an active interest in furthering it. These episodes also suggest that as long as the Vestals acted collectively and within the parameters of their religious position they could use the authority this position gave them to influence public opinion without meeting criticism from the Roman public. The one time in this period that a Vestal's use of her religious position in an attempt to influence politics meets with some disapproval is when a single Vestal, Licinia, acting alone, employed one of her traditional privileges in a new way. Similar manipulation, when carried out by the whole order within a traditional religious framework, seems to have been generally accepted by the Romans of the late Republic.

The Vestals under the First and Second Triumvirates

In 60 BCE, Caesar, Crassus and Pompey reached an agreement that resulted in the formation of what modern scholars call the First Triumvirate, effectively limiting the Roman senate's power to make political decisions without reference to the wishes of the three Triumviri and ultimately leading to the civil war of 49 BCE. Not only was the senate's power curtailed, but also many other Romans faded from the active political scene and ceased to play an influential role in public affairs. Among these were the Vestals, who generally disappear from view as active manipulators of public affairs during the Triumviral period.

The last century's Vestal interest in improving the conditions and status of their order together with their desire to influence Roman politics disappears entirely. Instead, they take a more passive role and appear in our historical sources only when some important document is either placed in or released from their keeping. This role, however, is a not unimportant one and the readiness with which both sides of a conflict seem willing to commit their documents to the Vestals and to accept those released by them demonstrates that the high regard in which these priestesses were held in earlier periods clearly remained in force during this period.

Ancient sources record three separate incidents of this sort in the course of the Triumviral period. The first document of which we hear is Julius Caesar's will, released by the Vestals after his death at the request of Lucius Piso, Antonius' father-in-law.[26] The second document entrusted to the Vestals was a public one, the treaty agreed upon by the Second Triumvirate and Sextus Pompeius at Misenum in 39 BCE.[27] Antonius' will was also, according to some ancient sources, taken from the Vestals by Octavian and read aloud in the senate after Antonius' final departure to the east.[28]

In all three of these incidents, our ancient sources imply that the Vestals' possession of the documents was ample evidence of these documents' legitimacy. This means that whatever the realities of the situation, and at least in the case of Antonius' will, we can suspect the Vestals of manipulating Roman public opinion by its timely release,[29] the Vestals' possession of a document was enough to guarantee that document's authenticity to the ordinary Roman. Such a view underscores the Romans' widespread acceptance of the Vestals' neutrality in internecine struggles and simultaneously emphasizes the continuing importance of this Vestal role.

The Vestals' historical role as guardians of so many important documents and the seeming widespread recognition of their impartiality is likely to have its foundation in two aspects of the priestesses' religious roles and status. As we have seen in connection with our study of the Vestals' religious roles, the Vestals were carefully removed from every formal tie to a particular Roman family, and it is this traditional removal that probably lies behind the general acceptance of these priestesses' neutrality. Likewise, one feature of their standard religious cult practices was the protection and care of Rome's figurative *penus*. This religious duty is no doubt at the root of the priestesses' care and protection of important documents. Whether this role was a traditional one for the priestesses or one that was given to their order at this late date is unknown, though it seems likely that such a procedure was of longer standing but first became important on the political stage under the struggles leading up to the establishment of a single man's rule of Rome.

The Vestals and the Julio-Claudians

Already upon Augustus' return to Rome after the Battle of Actium, the Vestals made their first appearance in connection with the new emperor, leading the procession sent out of the city to meet him. Such a role in itself was not a major innovation; in earlier generations, the Vestals had taken part in many processions, including various triumphs.[30] Yet at the same time, this procession was of a new sort, designed to demonstrate a united Rome's welcome of its new leader and to bring home the point that Rome's civil wars were over and peace restored. The Vestals' presence at the head of this procession was without doubt meant as a symbol of the reunited and restored Rome to which Augustus was returning and emphasizes the importance that the Romans attached to these priestesses and their cult as a symbol of Rome itself.

Clearly, Augustus and his successors saw the advantages of using this symbolism as a tool to bind themselves and their family more closely together with Rome itself in the minds of their ordinary subjects. While the Vestals largely disappeared from view as active participants on the public stage in this period, they and their cult played a major role in the propaganda of Augustus and his immediate predecessors. Under the Julio-Claudian emperors, the Vestals received a number of new religious responsibilities directly associated with the imperial family and its cult while more traditional aspects of their cult were joined directly to the imperial family and its residence. All of these changes seem designed to emphasize how inseparable the fate of the imperial family was from Rome's.

According to Augustus' *res gestae*, in 13 BCE the senate ordered the building of an *ara pacis* and commanded that the 'magistrates, priests and Vestal virgins make a yearly sacrifice' there (*R.G.* 11).[31] This command gave the Vestals a new duty and was the first signal that a new task had been added to their traditional concern with Rome's safety, the care and protection of the emperor and his family on a religious level. Augustus' safety was henceforth to be synonymous with and inseparable from Rome's, and the inclusion of the Vestals in the task of preserving this safety was a sure means of demonstrating this fact.

Augustus' actions in 12 BCE reinforced this association. Shortly after the death of Lepidus at the end of the previous year, Augustus had been elected Pontifex Maximus. Traditionally, the Pontifex Maximus had always lived in the *regia*, a public, official building located next to the Vestals' house and *aedes*, and closely connected with it. Augustus, however, was unwilling to move from his own house on the Palatine. At the same time, presumably recognizing the necessity of seeming to conform to long established tradition, he made over part of his house to the state and 'dedicated an image and [shrine] of Vesta' there.[32] This dedication effectively joined the official hearth of the Roman state, with all its associations with Rome's continued success, to that of Augustus. 'The emperor (and the emperor's house) could now be claimed to stand for the state', as Beard, North and Price write.[33]

At the same time as he drew the Vestal order and its cult more closely into the sphere of the imperial family, Augustus also clearly went out of his way to increase the order's prestige and importance. When one Vestal died and another had to be chosen in her place, Augustus, rebuking the senators for not offering their own daughters, declared that if he had had a granddaughter of a suitable age, he would have put her forward immediately. He also gave the Vestals special seats at the gladiatorial games and ensured that they too received the same rights that other women gained under the *ius trium liberorum* passed in 18 BCE.[34] As well, according to Dio, the Vestals were awarded the privilege of accompaniment by a single lictor, ostensibly after one was insulted on the way home from a party (D.C. 47.19.4).[35] Augustus also continued the practice of earlier important men and entrusted his own will to the Vestals.[36]

Finally, the repeated emphasis that contemporary writers place on the close relationship between Augustus and Vesta strengthen the impression that the enhancement of this close relationship was a deliberate policy on the part of Augustus and his supporters. Ovid for example goes so far as to describe Augustus as a relative of Vesta,[37] while Virgil and others highlight the importance of Vesta to Augustus and his ancestors.[38]

Tiberius, Caligula and Claudius continued the process begun by Augustus and bound the Vestals and the imperial family ever more closely together. In particular, the first two emperors intensified and strengthened the associations between the Vestals and the women of the imperial family, while Claudius, in keeping with his general practices, returned to a more traditional method of reinforcing the relationship between the imperial house and the Vestals.

Both Tiberius and Caligula granted Vestal privileges to close female relatives, Tiberius providing Augusta with a seat among the priestesses at the games,[39] while in 37 CE Caligula granted his grandmother, Antonia, as well as his three sisters Vestal privileges.[40] In choosing to make use of the Vestals' privileges in this way, the two emperors were no doubt partially motivated by the fact that the Vestals were the one group of Roman women who already had a public status, familiar and thus presumably acceptable to ordinary Romans. At the same time, however, Tiberius' placement of Augusta in the Vestal box implies that, like Augustus, he too was interested in binding the Vestal cult and the imperial family more closely together, an interest which is also demonstrated by his gift of a million sesterces as a consolation to a rejected Vestal candidate.[41] Caligula's gift of Vestal privileges to his grandmother and three sisters goes even further in that he provided all the women of his immediate family with the same status as the Vestals, not just the wife of the emperor himself. Finally, while Claudius did not draw any immediate connections between the living women of the imperial family and the Vestals, his choice of the Vestals as the appropriate religious officials to take responsibility for the cult of Augusta nevertheless demonstrates his intentions of continuing his predecessors' ever closer association of the Vestals and the imperial family.[42] In choosing these priestesses for this role rather than appointing a new priesthood as had been done in connection with the cult of Divus Augustus, Claudius was following the pattern established by Augustus, and continued by Tiberius and Caligula, of repeatedly reinforcing the close connections between the Vestal cult and the imperial family.

The last of the Julio-Claudians, Nero, also showed an interest in the Vestals and their cult, increasing the privileges of the Vestal order by inviting them to the athletic contests because, so Suetonius says, 'it was permitted for the priestesses of Ceres to watch at Olympia' (Suet. *Ner.* 12.4). In his case, however, it seems likely that he granted this privilege to the Vestals not because he wished to increase their status or the close connections between his family and their order, but because he was intent on heightening the importance of the Greek goddess Ceres (Demeter) and her priestesses.

It is clear from our ancient sources that Ceres and her cult were of some importance to Nero, particularly after a coup attempt made in connection with the goddesses' games failed.[43] After this abortive overthrow, Nero established additional horse races in the goddess' honour and changed the name of the month in which her games were held to his own name.[44] Whether he invited the Vestals to the contests at the same point is unknown, but it is unlikely that the invitation was issued before this date as Nero showed little interest in the cult of Ceres before the attempt on his life. His extension of this invitation to the Vestals in any case seems likely to be based on thinking similar to that which lay behind his predecessors' attribution of Vestal honours to their family members; a closer connection between the Vestals and any other body or individual was enough to add substantially to the prestige of that body or individual, in this case Ceres.

In each of these instances, the emperor in question made use of the Vestals and their privileges in order to strengthen the prestige of a person or group close to him. Tiberius used the Vestals to increase the status of his mother, Caligula his grandmother and sisters, Claudius his deified grandmother and Nero the goddess Ceres, his rescuer. Their use of the Vestal order in every instance reinforces a fact implicitly recognized already by Augustus. The Vestals and their cult were at the very centre of what it was to be Roman. As long as they were included in and accepted any new innovations, then these innovations could be expected to prove palatable to ordinary Romans, for the Vestals' presence and acceptance of these innovations meant that Rome itself was present and accepted them. Even during the early Empire, the Vestals continued to symbolize Rome itself in a very real way.

While the Vestal order and the enhancement or use of its traditional privileges figure most frequently in ancient accounts of the early Empire, we do occasionally hear of individual Vestals in this period. Under Tiberius, two senators offered their daughters when a new Vestal was needed, and the girl who was not chosen was consoled with a gift of a million sesterces.[45] At roughly the same time, the Vestal Urgulania, no doubt demonstrating her power and that of her order – as Tacitus himself observes '[her] power was too great for the state' (Tac. *Ann.* 2.34) – refused to appear as a witness in open court and demanded that a Praetor come to her home to hear her evidence. He did so. Under Claudius, the Vestals once again emerge as actors on the political scene pleading (though unsuccessfully) for Messilina.[46] Finally, Tacitus tells us that during the reign of Nero, the Vestal Laelia died and was replaced by Cornelia Cossa,[47] while Suetonius notes that the emperor Nero included among his other crimes the rape of the Vestal Rubria.[48]

While not all of these Vestals take an active role in events, their various appearances further reinforce the image of the great respect with which the Vestals were viewed under the early Empire. As well, both Urgulania's exhibition of her power and the Vestals' pleading on behalf of Messilina demonstrate that at least some imperial Vestals continued to believe that their order could and should play a role in public affairs.

The Vestals in the year of the four emperors and after

The Vestals appear only twice in ancient historical accounts of the period between the death of Nero and the death of Vespasian. In the first instance, they briefly resume their role as suppliants interceding unsuccessfully for the life of Vitellius with Vespasian's general, Antonius.[49] In the second instance, they appear helping to dedicate the Capitol after its rebuilding.[50] Both appearances are very much in keeping with earlier, pre-imperial Vestal roles. This suggests that whatever expanded role they had had in the imperial propaganda of the Julio-Claudian period, this role disappeared under Vespasian and Titus, with the Vestals once again returning to their traditional duties and roles and once again being largely active only within their traditional religious framework.

Domitian

The accounts of the Vestals under Domitian, however, shatter this picture, suggesting as they do that while the Vestals may have seemed to return to their traditional religious duties and place under Vespasian and Titus, they had in fact broken with the most binding rule of their order and generally ignored the requirement of chastity.

Suetonius writes that under Domitian, three Vestals, Varronilla and the sisters Oculatae, were tried and found guilty of *incestum* but were allowed by the emperor to choose their own means of death.[51] He further observes that 'the *incestum* of the Vestal Virgins, overlooked also by his father and brother, [Domitian] punished variously and severely' (Suet. *Dom.* 8.3), and adds that a fourth Vestal, the *virgo maxima* Cornelia, who had originally been acquitted, presumably at the same time as the other three Vestals were punished, was found guilty and buried alive at a later date.[52] The same Cornelia's punishment is recorded in detail by Pliny the Younger in a letter to Cornelius Minucianus:

> For when he desired to bury alive Cornelia the Senior Vestal, as he judged that by examples of this sort he might adorn his age, by his right as Pontifex Maximus, or more likely by the immense licence of a tyrant, he called the other Pontifices not to the Regia but to his Alban villa. . . . He condemned her for incest absent and, unheard. . . . The Pontifices were immediately dispatched to see to her death and burial. She raising her hands now to Vesta, now to the other gods, cried out many things, but this especially: 'Caesar thinks that I am impure, I who have performed so many rites, by which he conquered and triumphed!'. . . She repeated this until she was led away to punishment, whether she was innocent or not, I do not know, but she certainly acted innocent. For even when she was sent down

into the underground chamber, and her *stola* caught as she descended, she turned and collected herself, and when the executioner would have given her a hand, she refused.

(Plin, *Ep.* 4.11)[53]

From the ancient accounts of these two episodes, it sounds as if at least the first three Vestals were in fact guilty as charged and that in fact the Vestal order as a whole had long since given up worrying about the preservation of their chastity. Suetonius states explicitly that Vespasian and Titus had looked the other way in this matter. Even Pliny, somewhat coyly, remarks that he himself cannot comment on Cornelia's real or supposed innocence. Reading between the lines, it sounds as if the letter writer would like to be able to claim that her burial alive was yet another unjustified act on the part of Domitian, but recognizes that there may well have been some truth to the accusations.

If our sources are correct in their observations, then this gives a new tint to the Vestals' activities under the Flavians. On the surface, these priestesses may well have returned to their traditional religious roles and concerns, appearing only infrequently in the ancient historical accounts of this period. Behind the scenes, however, the Vestals had perhaps discarded the most limiting strictures of their order and were living a life similar to other upper-class women of their time. That they did so and were allowed to do so by the Roman authorities suggests that both they and these authorities, if not the Roman public as a whole, viewed this most central restriction and duty of the Vestal order as an anachronism that had little to do with the realities of contemporary Rome and its affairs.

Conclusion

An examination of the Vestals' historical appearances reveals that the Vestals' attitudes to their cult and to their own role in Roman society were no more static than the attitudes and roles of other Romans. Just as ordinary Romans' thinking altered as they and their society were exposed to new and different cultures over time, the Vestals' did also. Early Vestals appear only infrequently and then in their traditional religious roles. By the end of the second century BCE, however, the priestesses had begun acting publicly, trying to improve the status and power of their order. By the middle of the first century BCE, the Vestals had expanded their interests to public affairs, increasingly frequently acting on behalf of one Roman or another and using their position to try to influence the outcome of contemporary events. During the early Empire, the priestesses again largely disappeared from view as active participants on the Roman public stage, but their cult plays a major role in the propaganda of the earlier Julio-Claudians functioning as a symbol of the Roman state in its joining with the imperial family. Once this role is firmly established, the cult also largely disappears from view and we hear of the Vestals only when their long established roles require them to appear as part of historical events.

As well, while the question of a Vestal's actual innocence or guilt in cases of *incestum* can rarely be determined from the information found in our ancient sources, it is evident that the Vestals' attitudes towards the chastity enforced upon them by their priesthood varied greatly, and that this variety depended as much on the tenor of their times as it did on any other factor. At least once during the late Republic (Aemilia, Marcia and Licinia), we have evidence that some concerted effort was made on the part of the Vestals to break with this most constricting rule of their order. Likewise, under the later Julio-Claudians and early Flavians, the Vestals seem to have flouted this rule openly without any retribution on the part of the authorities.

Notes

1 Cic. *Cael.* 34; Suet. *Tib.* 2.4; V. Max. 5.4.6. See also D. C. fr. 74; Oros. 5.4.7. On Claudia, see J. Rüpke and A. Glock 2005: 2. 874; *MRR* 1.471 and 473. On Appius' reputation in general, see J. McDougall 1992b.
2 R. Bauman 1992: 47.
3 R. Bauman 1992: 230 n.21.
4 R. Bauman 1992: 47.
5 Plu. *Num.* 10.
6 See, for example, Cic. *Font.* 17; D.C. 65.18; Suet. *Jul.* 1; Suet. *Vit.* 16; Tac. *Ann.* 3.69; Tac. *Ann.* 9.32; Tac. *Hist.* 3.81.
7 A Vestal Licinia is also named in Cic. *Brut.* 160, where he praises the eloquence of the lawyer who defended her. Whether this is the same Licinia is uncertain. On Licinia, see J. Rüpke and A. Glock 2005: 2.1103; J. Saquete 2000: 34; *MRR* 1.515 and 534.
8 For a discussion of the religious struggles of this period, see Rawson 1974.
9 R. Bauman 1992: 52–53.
10 For ancient accounts of various aspects of this affair, see Asc. 39–40; Cic. *Brut.*122; D. C. fr.87.1–5; Liv. *per.* 63a; Macr. 1.10.5–6; Obseq. 37; Oros. 5.15.20–22; Plu. *Mor.* 284. For a discussion of the dating of this event, see E. S. Gruen 1968. On Marcia, see J. Rüpke and A. Glock 2005: 2.1134; J. Saquete 2000: 37; *MRR* 1.534; F. Münzer 1920: 243–245. On Aemilia, see J. Rüpke and A. Glock 2005: 2.734; J. Saquete 2000: 3; *DnP* 1.175; MRR 1.534; F. Münzer 1920: 243–245. On Licinia, see above, note 7.
11 R. Bauman 1994: 56.
12 R. Bauman 1994: 57. See also F. Münzer 1920: 244.
13 So R. Bauman 1994: 55–57, F. Münzer 1920: 219–221 and others assume. But for the view that this court was a one-time affair, see R. G. Lewis 2001:142.
14 B. A. Marshall 1985: 196–197. T. J. Cornell 1981: 28 n.6 maintains that the whole affair should be seen as a drawn-out expiation for Cato's losses to the Scordisci, while J. P. Hallett 1984: 87 claims that it was due to the desire of various families to secure priesthoods for their unmarried daughters. Neither of these arguments is especially convincing.
15 See F. Münzer 1937–1938: 221; R. Bauman 1992: 62.
16 Again see R. Bauman 1992: 62.
17 For Fabia, see Asc. *tog. cand.* 70, 28–31; Oros. 6.3.1; Plu. *Cat. Mi.* 19.3; Sal. *Cat.* 15.1; J. Rüpke and A. Glock 2005: 966; J. Saquete 2000: 24; *MMR* 2.114 and 136. For Licinia, see Cic. *Cat.* 3.9; Macr. 3.13.10; Plu. *Crass.* 1.2; J. Rüpke and A. Glock 2005: 1103; J. Saquete 2000: 34; *MMR* 2.114 and 135. For a discussion of Catalina's part in the affair, see also R. G. Lewis 2001.

18 R. Bauman 1994: 61–62.
19 Cic.*Mur.* 73. For a bibliography on Licinia, see above, note 17.
20 Plu. *Cic.* 20.
21 Such human interference with the gods' wishes was not uncommon among the Romans. For example, Augustus arranged a duplication of Romulus' portent of twelve vultures to inaugurate his first consulship after Caesar's death (Suet. *Aug.* 95). There was in fact no sacrilege involved in such tampering. The gods were, after all, more powerful than mere humans and could certainly halt any humanly devised omen they did not wish to occur.
22 Cic. *Att.* 1.13.3; D. C. 37.45.2; Plu. *Caes.* 110.9; *Cic.* 29.9; Suet. *Jul.* 74.2. For modern discussions, see J. Tatum 1990; H. Brouwer 1989: 361–370; D. Mulroy 1988; P. Moreau 1982; J. P. V. D. Balsdon 1966.
23 Although it is perhaps just possible that either the Vestals worked behind the scenes to ensure their inclusion, or Cicero and his supporters in the senate actively pressed for the Vestals' inclusion in the process of judgement, there is no evidence to support or refute either possibility. If it were the latter instance, the effort perhaps was made in an attempt to ensure that an order that had already shown its support of the *concordia ordium* would be included in the judgement process rather than a more neutral group. The pontifical order, after all, included Julius Caesar, who while certainly an offended party, was a member of the *Populares*, and one who might overlook the personal insult in the broader interests of his party.
24 After all, the rites were women's rites celebrated under the aegis of the Vestal order and, as such, it was surely suitable that the priestesses too be consulted.
25 See Cic. *Att.* 1.16. D. R. Shackleton Bailey 1965–1970 discusses this issue.
26 Suet. *Iul.* 83.
27 App. *B. Civ.* 5.73; D. C. 48.37.
28 For Antonius, see Suet. *Tib.* 76.
29 F. A. Sirianni 1984 and J. R. Johnson 1976, 1978 argue strongly for the view that Antonius's will was at least a partial forgery, but see J. Crook 1989 for an opposing opinion.
30 J. Scheid 1986: 219.
31 *R. G.*11. See F. Bömer 1987.
32 M. Beard *et al.* 1998: 189; A. De Grassi 1955: 452. For further discussions, see A. Fraschetti 1999; D. Fishwick 1992; M. Guarducci 1964, 1971; H. G. Kolbe 1966–1967.
33 M. Beard *et al.* 1998: 191.
34 It has been asked why Augustus felt it necessary to grant something to the Vestals that in effect they already had. The answer to this question is no doubt to be found in the Romans' cautious legalistic and religious mindset. In granting other women rights similar to those held by the Vestals, Augustus risked unintentionally infringing the Vestals' rights. The Vestals, as women who did not have three children, could have been seen to fall under the limitations of this new law. The granting of this right to the Vestals is likely to have been a rider to the *ius trium liberorum*, intended to make clear that despite the change in other women's legal status, this change in no way affected the Vestals. What they had had before they were to continue to have, even though similar rights had now been granted to other Roman women. This right was a cautionary clause designed to ensure that the Vestals' former legal position was in no way unintentionally limited or affected by the new law.
35 For another account of this Vestal privilege, see Plu. *Num.* 10.
36 Tac. *Ann.* 1.8.
37 Ov. *Fast.* 3.423–426. For a somewhat special discussion of Ovid's treatment of the Vestals in relation to Augustus, see C. Korten 1992.

38 See also D. H. 2.65.2; Ov.*Fast.* 1.527–528; 3.29, 6.227; Ov. *Met.* 15.730–731; Prop. 4.4.69 and Verg. *A.*2.296, 567.

39 Tac. *Ann.* 4.16

40 *PIR* 319.

41 Tac. *Ann.* 4.16.

42 C. D. 60.5.2.

43 Tac. *Ann.* 15.52–53. See B. Spaeth 1996: 28.

44 Tac. *Ann.* 15. 74.

45 Tac. *Ann.* 2.86.

46 Tac. *Ann.* 11.32: 'and Vibidia, the oldest of the Vestal virgins, begged to approach the ears of the Pontifex Maximus and seek his clemency'.

47 Tac. *Ann.* 15.22. On Laelia, see J. Rüpke and A. Glock 2005: 1090; J. Saquete 2000: 33 and *PIR* [2]L58. On Cornelia Cossa, see *CIL* 6.17179; Suet. *Dom.* 8.4; J. Rüpke and A. Glock 2005: 905; J. Saquete 2000: 21; *PIR* [2]C1480/1481; *DnP* 3.167.

48 Suet. *Nero* 28.1. J. Rüpke and A. Glock 2005: 1254; J. Saquete 2000: 50.

49 Tac. *Hist.* 3.81.

50 Tac. *Hist.* 4.53.

51 Suet. *Dom.* 8.3.

52 For a discussion of the identity of this Cornelia, see J. Pigon 1999. See also above, note 46.

53 A. N. Sherwin-White 1966: 282–283 discusses this passage in detail and arrives at similar conclusions about Cornelia's possible guilt.

Conclusion

The central concern of this work has been the Vestal Virgins of the late Republic and early Empire (from roughly 100 BCE to 200 CE), their cult and history as described to us by our ancient literary sources. As such, this work spans a broad variety of topics, which can be difficult to bind into a single whole. Nevertheless, certain thematic points do emerge.

First, I have argued that the Vestals were at the same time members of the Roman *virgines* and non-members of Rome's family structure and that this was done to ensure that the Vestals could represent Rome as a whole on the religious level, without any risk of pollution from a family cult. The only person in Rome who had the potential to be removed from a family's *potestas*, and thus from that family's cult without immediately coming under another's or receiving *potestas*, was a virgin at the moment of transition from one family to another. Men either were under the *potestas* of their fathers or had themselves *potestas*. Daughters were under the *potestas* of their fathers or a senior male relative, wives under that of their husband or a senior male relative. Only at the time of their marriage were women momentarily in a liminal state, transferred out of their birth family's cult but not yet transferred into their marital family's cult. By preserving the Vestals at this moment of transition, the restrictions with which they were surrounded ensured that these priestesses could represent all Rome.

This theory satisfactorily explains many aspects of the Vestal order that have puzzled modern scholars. The choice of women rather than men to represent Rome as a whole, these women's extended virginity, the care that was paid to a girl's family background before she was selected as a priestess, all of these features of the Vestal cult devolved from the necessity of ensuring the Vestals' special status. Likewise, the many anomalous aspects of the Vestals' legal and financial position arose from the same need, while their dress and hairstyle served as visible markers of these priestesses' special liminal status.

Second, the rituals that the Vestals performed on behalf of the Roman state were neither fertility rites nor reflections of traditional female activities as has so often been postulated. Instead they were rites concerned with purification, storage and the preparation of harvested grain for food use, or sometimes a combination of all three areas at once. Most frequently, we see the Vestals using water and fire in one rite to prepare a purificatory substance for use in another later rite, but we also see them performing rituals to purify their own religious precincts and Rome's citizens, storing religious substances and other items (the various wills mentioned in our historical accounts for example) and drying and baking grain and salt for religious uses.

Third, while many of the ritual aspects of the Vestals' cult seem to have been static, changing little, if at all, over time, the Vestals' own attitude to their cult and the world around them was anything but static. Instead, just as ordinary Romans' attitudes changed as they and their society were exposed to new and different cultures through the expansion of their empire, the Vestals' ideas and attitudes also changed. The Romans of our historical period seem to have believed that the Vestals of the earlier periods stayed very much within the confines of their religious role, performing the rituals required of them and appearing only infrequently on the public stage. By the time of the late Republic, however, this pattern has begun to change, until by the middle of the first century BCE, we see the Vestals appearing more and more frequently on behalf of one Roman or another and using their position to try to influence Roman public affairs. Under the early Empire, this pattern continues, with the Vestals often functioning as emissaries for one imperial suppliant or another.

At the same time that the Vestals increasingly become more active on the public stage, they also become more independent in their own affairs, both personal and cultic, until by the end of the Republic we find Vestals effectively defending themselves against charges of *incestum* and making their own decisions on other matters. By the middle of the first century CE, we even have evidence that the Vestals were ignoring one of the major restrictions of their cult – the requirement that they remain virgins.

Appendix A
Original texts of translated passages

Asconius *In Miloniam* 43

virgines pro populo Romano sacra fecerant

Asconius *In Miloniam* 46

totumque collegium pontificum male iudicasse de incesto virginum Vestalium, quod unam modo Aemiliam damnaverat, absolverat autem duas Marciam et Liciniam, populus hunc Cassium creavit qui de eisdem virginibus quaereret. Isque et ultrasque eas et praeterea complures alias nimia etiam, ut existimatio est, asperitate usus damnavit.

Asconius 70t.

L. Cassius fuit, sicut iam saepe diximus, summae vir severitatis. Is quotiens quaesitor iudicii alicuius esset in quo quaerebatur de homine occiso suadebat atque etiam praeibat iudicibus hoc quod Cicero nunc admonet, ut quaereretur cui bono fuisset perire eum de cuius morte quaeritur. Ob quam severitatem, quo tempore Sex. Peducaeus tribunus plebis criminatus est L. Metellum pontificem max. totumque collegium pontificum male iudicasse de incesto virginum Vestalium, quod unam modo Aemiliam damnaverat, absolverat autem duas Marciam et Liciniam, populus hunc Cassium creavit qui de eisdem virginibus quaereret. Isque et ultrasque eas et praeterea complures alias nimia etiam, ut existimatio est, asperitate usus damnavit.

Augustine *Civitas Dei* 10.16

quod virgo Vestalis, de cuius corruptione quaestio vertebatur, aqua impleto cribro de Tiberi neque perfluente abstulit controversiam, haec ergo atque huius modi nequaquam illis, quae in populo Dei facta legimus, virtute ac magnitudine conferenda sunt . . .

Cicero *Ad Atticum* 1.13.3

idque sacrificium cum virgines instaurassent.

Cicero *Brutus* [160]

defendit postea Liciniam virginem, cum annos xxvii natus esset. in ea ipsa causa fuit eloquentissimus orationisque eius scriptas quasdam partes reliquit. voluit adulescens in colonia Narbonensi causae popularis aliquid adtingere eamque coloniam, ut fecit, ipse deducere; exstat in eam legem senior, ut ita dicam, quam aetas illa ferebat oratio. multae deinde causae; sed ita tacitus tribunatus ut, nisi in eo magistratu cenavisset apud praeconem Granium idque nobis bis narravisset Lucilius, tribunum plebis nesciremus fuisse.

Cicero *Brutus* 236

deinde ex virginum iudicio magnam laudem est adeptus et ex eo tempore quasi revocatus in cursum tenuit locum tam diu, quam ferre potuit laborem; postea quantum detraxit ex studio tantum amisit ex gloria ...

Cicero *De Domo* 53.136

Cum Licinia, virgo Vestalis summo loco nata, sanctissimo sacerdotio praedita, T. Flaminio Q. Metello consulibus aram et aediculam et pulvinar sub Saxo dedicasset, nonne eam rem ex auctoritate senatus ad hoc conlegium Sex. Iulius praetor rettulit? cum P. Scaevola pontifex maximus pro conlegio respondit, QUOD IN LOCO PUBLICO LICINIA, GAI FILIA, INIUSSU POPULI DEDICASSET SACRUM NON VIDERIER. Quam quidem rem quanta *tractaverit* severitate quantaque diligentia senatus, ex ipso senatus consulto facile cognoscetis.

Cumque Vesta quasi focum urbis, ut Graeco nomine est appellata, quod nos prope idem Graecum, non interpretatum nomen tenemus, conplexa sit, ei colendae uirgines praesint, ut advigiletur facilius ad custodiam ignis et sentiant mulieres in illis naturam feminarum omnem castitatem pati.

Cicero *de haruspicum responso* 13.3

Nego umquam post sacra constituta, quorum eadem est antiquitas quae ipsius urbis, ulla de re, ne de capite quidem virginum Vestalium, tam frequens conlegium iudicasse.

Cicero *de haruspicum responso* 17.37

quod quidem sacrificium nemo ante P. Clodium omni memoria violavit, nemo umquam adiit, nemo neglexit, nemo vir aspicere non horruit, quod fit per virgines Vestalis, fit pro populo Romano, fit in ea domo quae est in imperio, fit incredibili caerimonia, fit ei deae cuius ne nomen quidem viros scire fas est, quam iste idcirco Bonam dicit quod in tanto sibi scelere ignoverit.

Cicero *De Legibus* 2.20

Virginesque Vestales in urbe custodiunto ignem foci publici sempitemum . . .

Cicero *De Legibus* 2.29

Quomque Vesta quasi focum urbis, ut Graeco nomine est appellata – quod nos prope idem <ac> Graecum, <non> interpretatum nomen tenemus –, conplexa sit, ei colendae <VI> virgines praesint, ut advigiletur facilius ad custodiam ignis, et sentiant mulieres <in> naturam feminarum omnem castitatem pati.

Cicero *De Re Publica* 2.26

Pompilius et auspiciis maioribus inventis ad pristinum numerum duo augures addidit, et sacris e principum numero pontifices quinque praefecit, et animos propositis legibus his quas in monumentis habemus ardentis consuetudine et cupiditate bellandi religionum caerimoniis mitigavit, adiunxitque praeterea flamines Salios virginesque Vestales, omnisque partis religionis statuit sanctissime.

Cicero *De Re Publica* 3.10.17

[voconia lex] quidem ipsa lex utilitatis virorum gratia rogata in mulieres plena est iniuriae. Cur enim pecuniam non habeat mulier? Cur virgini Vestali sit heres, non sit matri suae?

Cicero *Philippics* 11.24

. . . ut illud signum, quod de caelo delapsum Vestae custodiis continetur; quo salvo salvi sumus futuri.

Cicero *Pro Caelio* 34

virgo illa Vestalis Claudia quae patrem complexa triumphantem ab inimico tribuno plebei de curru detrahi passa non est?

Cicero *Pro Murena* 73

si virgo Vestalis, huius propinqua et necessaria, locum suum gladiatorium concessit huic, non et illa pie fecit et hic a culpa est remotus. Omnia haec sunt officia necessarium, commoda tenuiorum . . .

Cicero *Pro Scauro* 48.4

Metelli, pontificis maximi, qui, cum templum illud arderet, in medios se iniecit ignis et eripuit flamma Palladium illud quod quasi pignus nostrae salutis atque imperi custodiis Vestae continetur. qui utinam posset parumper exsistere! eriperet ex hac flamma stirpem profecto suam, qui eripuisset ex illo incendio di . . .

Dio Cassius 37.45

κἀν τούτῳ ὁ Καῖσαρ, τοῦ Κλωδίου τοῦ Πουπλίου τὴν γυναῖκα αὐτοῦ ἔν τε τῇ οἰκίᾳ καὶ παρὰ τὴν ποίησιν τῶν ἱερῶν, ἅπερ αἱ ἀειπαρθένοι παρά τε τοῖς ὑπάτοις καὶ παρὰ τοῖς στρατηγοῖς ἄγνωστα ἐκ τῶν πατρίων ἐς πᾶν τὸ ἄρρεν ἐπετέλουν, αἰσχύναντος, ἐκείνῳ μὲν οὐδὲν ἐνεκάλεσεν (καὶ γὰρ εὖ ἠπίστατο ὅτι οὐχ ἁλώσεται διὰ τὴν ἑταιρείαν), τὴν δὲ δὴ γυναῖκα ἀπεπέμψατο, εἰπὼν ἄλλως μὲν μὴ πιστεύειν τῷ λεγομένῳ, μὴ μέντοι καὶ συνοικῆσαι ἔτ' αὐτῇ δύνασθαι, διότι καὶ ὑπωπτεύθη ἀρχὴν μεμοιχεῦσθαι· τὴν γὰρ σώφρονα χρῆναι μὴ μόνον μηδὲν ἁμαρτάνειν, ἀλλὰ μηδ' ἐς ὑποψίαν αἰσχρὰν ἀφικνεῖσθαι.

Dio Cassius 47.19

ταῖς δὲ ἀειπαρθένοις ῥαβδούχῳ ἑνὶ ἑκάστῃ χρῆσθαι, ὅτι τις αὐτῶν ἀπὸ δείπνου πρὸς ἑσπέραν οἴκαδε ἐπανιοῦσα ἠγνοήθη τε καὶ ὑβρίσθη.

Dio Cassius 48.12

καὶ ταῦτά τε ἐς δέλτους γράψαντες καὶ κατασημηνάμενοι ταῖς ἀειπαρθένοις φυλάττειν ἔδοσαν.

Dio Cassius 60.5

τήν τε τήθην τὴν Λιουίαν οὐ μόνον ἵππων ἀγῶσιν ἐτίμησεν ἀλλὰ καὶ ἀπηθανάτισεν, ἄγαλμά τέ τι αὐτῆς ἐν τῷ Αὐγουστείῳ ἱδρύσας καὶ τὰς θυσίας ταῖς ἀειπαρθένοις ἱεροποιεῖν προστάξας.

Dionysius Halicarnassus 1.38.3

τοῦτο δὲ καὶ μέχρις ἐμοῦ ἔτι διετέλουν Ῥωμαῖοι δρῶντες ὀσέτῃ μικρὸν ὕστερον τῆς ἐαρινῆς ἰσημερίας ἐν μηνὶ Μαΐῳ ταῖς καλουμέναις εἰδοῖς, διχομήνιδα βουλόμενοι ταύτην εἶναι τὴν ἡμέραν, ἐν ᾗ προθύσαντες ἱερὰ τὰ κατὰ τοὺς νόμους οἱ καλούμενοι ποντίφικες, ἱερέων οἱ διαφανέστατοι, καὶ σὺν αὐτοῖς αἱ τὸ ἀθάνατον πῦρ διαφυλάττουσαι παρθένοι στρατηγοί τε καὶ τῶν ἄλλων πολιτῶν οὓς παρεῖναι ταῖς ἱερουργίαις θέμις εἴδωλα μορφαῖς ἀνθρώπων εἰκασμένα, τριάκοντα τόν ἀριθμόν, ἀπὸ τῆς ἱερᾶς γεφύρας βάλλουσιν εἰς τὸ ῥεῦμα τοῦ Τεβέριος, Ἀργείους αὐτὰ καλοῦντες.

Dionysius Halicarnassus 2.66–69

Νόμας δὲ τὴν ἀρχὴν παραλαβὼν τὰς μὲν ἰδίας οὐκ ἐκίνησε τῶν φρατριῶν ἑστίας, κοινὴν δὲ κατεστήσατο πάντων μίαν ἐν τῷ μεταξὺ τοῦ τε Καπιτωλίου καὶ τοῦ Παλατίου χωρίῳ, συμπεπολισμένων ἤδη τῶν λόφων ἑνὶ περιβόλῳ καὶ μέσης ἀμφοῖν οὔσης τῆς ἀγορᾶς, ἐν ᾗ κατεσκεύασται τὸ ἱερόν, τήν τε φυλακὴν τῶν ἱερῶν κατὰ τὸν πάτριον τῶν Λατίνων νόμον διὰ παρθένων ἐνομοθέτησε γίνεσθαι· ἔχει δέ τινας ἀπορίας καὶ τὸ φυλαττόμενον ἐν τῷ ἱερῷ τί δήποτέ ἐστι καὶ διὰ τί πρόσκειται παρθένοις. τινὲς μὲν οὖν οὐδὲν ἔξω τοῦ φανεροῦ πυρὸς εἶναί φασι τὸ τηρούμενον, τὴν δὲ φυλακὴν αὐτοῦ παρθένοις ἀνακεῖσθαι μᾶλλον ἢ ἀνδράσι ποιοῦνται κατὰ τὸ εἰκός, ὅτι πῦρ μὲν ἀμίαντον, παρθένος δ' ἄφθαρτον, τῷ δ' ἁγνοτάτῳ τῶν θείων τὸν καθαρώτατον εἰκός, ὅτι πῦρ μὲν ἀμίαντον, παρθένος δ' ἄφθαρτον, τῷ δ' ἁγνοτάτῳ τῶν θείων τὸν καθαρώτατον τῶν θνητῶν φίλον. Ἑστίᾳ δ' ἀνακεῖσθαι τὸ πῦρ νομίζουσιν, ὅτι γῆ τε οὖσα ἡ θεὸς καὶ τὸν μέσον κατέχουσα τοῦ κόσμου τόπον τὰς ἀνάψεις τοῦ μεταρσίου ποιεῖται πυρὸς ἀφ' ἑαυτῆς. εἰσὶ δέ τινες οἵ φασιν ἔξω τοῦ πυρὸς ἀπόρρητα τοῖς πολλοῖς ἱερὰ κεῖσθαί τινα ἐν τῷ τεμένει τῆς θεᾶς, ὧν οἵ τε ἱεροφάνται τὴν γνῶσιν ἔχουσι καὶ αἱ παρθένοι, τεκμήριον οὐ μικρὸν παρεχόμενοι τοῦ λόγου τὸ συμβὰν περὶ τὴν ἔμπρησιν τοῦ ἱεροῦ κατὰ τὸν Φοινικικὸν πόλεμον τὸν πρῶτον συστάντα Ῥωμαίοις πρὸς Καρχηδονίους περὶ Σικελίας. ἐμπρησθέντος γὰρ τοῦ τεμένους καὶ τῶν παρθένων φευγουσῶν ἐκ τοῦ πυρὸς τῶν ἱεροφαντῶν τις Λεύκιος Καικίλιος ὁ καλούμενος Μέτελλος ἀνὴρ ὑπατικός, ὁ τὸν ἀοίδιμον ἐκ Σικελίας ἀπὸ Καρχηδονίων καταγαγὼν ὀκτὼ καὶ τριάκοντα καὶ ἑκατὸν ἐλεφάντων θρίαμβον, ὑπεριδὼν τῆς ἰδίας ἀσφαλείας τοῦ κοινῇ συμφέροντος ἕνεκα παρεκινδύνευσεν εἰς τὰ καιόμενα βιάσασθαι καὶ τὰ καταλειφθέντα ὑπὸ τῶν παρθένων ἁρπάσας ἱερὰ διέσωσεν ἐκ τοῦ πυρός· ἐφ' ᾧ τιμὰς παρὰ τῆς πόλεως ἐξηνέγκατο μεγάλας, ὡς ἡ τῆς εἰκόνος αὐτοῦ τῆς ἐν Καπιτωλίῳ κειμένης ἐπιγραφὴ μαρτυρεῖ. τοῦτο δὴ λαβόντες ὁμολογούμενον ἐπισυνάπτουσιν αὐτοὶ στοχασμούς τινας ἰδίους, οἱ μὲν ἐκ τῶν ἐν Σαμοθράκῃ λέγοντες ἱερῶν μοῖραν εἶναί τινα φυλαττομένην τὴν ἐνθάδε, Δαρδάνου μὲν εἰς τὴν ὑφ' ἑαυτοῦ κτισθεῖσαν πόλιν ἐκ τῆς νήσου τὰ ἱερὰ μετενεγκαμένου, Αἰνείου δέ, ὅτ' ἔφυγεν ἐκ τῆς Τρῳάδος ἅμα τοῖς ἄλλοις καὶ ταῦτα κομίσαντος εἰς Ἰταλίαν, οἱ δὲ τοῖς ἄλλοις καὶ ταῦτα κομίσαντος εἰς Ἰταλίαν, οἱ δὲ τὸ διοπετὲς Παλλάδιον ἀποφαίνοντες εἶναι τὸ παρ' Ἰλιεῦσι γενόμενον, ὡς Αἰνείου κομίσαντος αὐτὸ δι' ἐμπειρίαν, Ἀχαιῶν δὲ τὸ μίμημα αὐτοῦ λαβόντων κλοπῇ· περὶ οὗ πολλοὶ σφόδρα εἴρηνται ποιηταῖς τε καὶ συγγραφεῦσι λόγοι. ἐγὼ δὲ τὸ μὲν εἶναί τινα τοῖς πολλοῖς ἄδηλα ἱερὰ φυλαττόμενα ὑπὸ τῶν παρθένων καὶ οὐ τὸ πῦρ μόνον ἐκ πολλῶν πάνυ καταλαμβάνομαι, τίνα δὲ ταῦτ' ἐστὶν οὐκ ἀξιῶ πολυπραγμονεῖν οὔτ' ἐμαυτὸν οὔτε ἄλλον οὐδένα τῶν βουλομένων τὰ πρὸς θεοὺς ὅσια τηρεῖν.

Αἱ δὲ θεραπεύουσαι τὴν θεὸν παρθένοι τέτταρες μὲν ἦσαν κατ' ἀρχὰς τῶν βασιλέων αὐτὰς αἱρουμένων ἐφ' οἷς κατεστήσατο δικαίοις ὁ Νόμας, ὕστερον δὲ διὰ πλῆθος τῶν ἱερουργιῶν ἃς ἐπιτελοῦσιν ἓξ γενόμεναι μέχρι τοῦ καθ' ἡμᾶς διαμένουσι χρόνου δίαιταν ἔχουσαι παρὰ τῇ θεῷ, ἔνθα δι' ἡμέρας μὲν οὐδεὶς ἀπείργεται τῶν βουλομένων εἰσιέναι, νύκτωρ δὲ οὐδενὶ τῶν ἀρρένων ἐναυλίσασθαι θέμις. χρόνον δὲ τριακονταετῆ μένειν αὐτὰς ἀναγκαῖον ἁγνὰς γάμων θυηπολούσας τε καὶ τἆλλα θρησκευούσας κατὰ νόμον, ἐν ᾧ δέκα μὲν ἔτη μανθάνειν αὐτὰς ἔδει, δέκα δ' ἐπιτελεῖν τὰ ἱερά, τὰ δὲ λοιπὰ δέκα διδάσκειν ἑτέρας. ἐκπληρωθείσης δὲ τῆς τριακονταετίας οὐδὲν ἦν τὸ κωλῦσον τὰς βουλομένας ἀποθείσας τὰ στέμματα καὶ τὰ λοιπὰ παράσημα τῆς ἱερωσύνης γαμεῖσθαι. καὶ ἐποίησάν τινες τοῦτο πάνυ ὀλίγαι, αἷς ἄζηλοι συνέβησαν αἱ τελευταὶ τῶν βίων καὶ οὐ πάνυ εὐτυχεῖς, ὥστε δι' οἰωνοῦ λαμβάνουσαι τὰς ἐκείνων συμφορὰς αἱ λοιπαὶ παρθένοι μένουσι.

παρὰ τῇ θεῷ μέχρι θανάτου, τότε δὲ εἰς τὸν τῆς ἐκλιπούσης ἀριθμὸν ἑτέρα πάλιν ὑπὸ τῶν ἱεροφαν⁻ τῶν ἀποδείκνυται. τιμαὶ δὲ αὐταῖς ἀποδέδονται παρὰ τῆς πόλεως πολλαὶ καὶ καλαί, δι' ἃς οὔτε παίδων αὐταῖς ἐστι πόθος οὔτε γάμων, τιμωρίαι τε ἐπὶ τοῖς ἁμαρτανομένοις κεῖνται μεγάλαι, ὧν ἐξετασταί τε καὶ κολασταὶ κατὰ νόμον εἰσὶν οἱ ἱεροφάνται, τὰς μὲν ἄλλο τι τῶν ἐλαττόνων ἁμαρτανούσας ῥάβδοις μαστιγοῦντες, τὰς δὲ φθαρείσας αἰσχίστῳ τε καὶ ἐλεεινοτάτῳ παραδιδόντες θανάτῳ. ζῶσαι γὰρ ἔτι πομπεύουσιν ἐπὶ κλίνης φερόμεναι τὴν ἀποδεδειγμένην τοῖς νεκροῖς ἐκφοράν, ἀνακλαιομένων αὐτὰς καὶ προπεμπόντων φίλων τε καὶ συγγενῶν, κομισθεῖσαι δὲ μέχρι τῆς Κολλίνης πύλης, ἐντὸς τείχους εἰς σηκὸν ὑπὸ γῆς κατεσκευασμένον ἅμα τοῖς ἐνταφίοις κόσμοις τίθενται καὶ οὔτ' ἐπιστήματος οὔτ' ἐναγισμῶν οὔτ'ἄλλου τῶν νομίμων οὐδενὸς τυγχάνουσι. πολλὰ μὲν οὖν καὶ ἄλλα δοκεῖ μηνύματα εἶναι τῆς οὐχ ὁσίως ὑπηρετούσης τοῖς ἱεροῖς, μάλιστα δὲ ἡ σβέσις τοῦ πυρός, ἣν ὑπὲρ ἅπαντα τὰ δεινὰ Ῥωμαῖοι δεδοίκασιν ἀφανισμοῦ τῆς πόλεως σημεῖον ὑπολαμβάνοντες, ἀφ' ἧς ποτ' ἂν αἰτίας γένηται, καὶ πολλαῖς αὐτὸ θεραπείαις ἐξιλασκόμενοι κατάγουσι πάλιν εἰς τὸ ἱερόν· ὑπὲρ ὧν κατὰ τὸν οἰκεῖον καιρὸν ἐρῶ.

Πάνυ δ' ἄξιον καὶ τὴν ἐπιφάνειαν ἱστορῆσαι τῆς θεᾶς, ἣν ἐπεδείξατο ταῖς ἀδίκως ἐγκληθείσαις παρθένοις, πεπίστευται γὰρ ὑπὸ Ῥωμαίων, εἰ καὶ παράδοξά ἐστι, καὶ πολὺν πεποίηνται λόγον ὑπὲρ αὐτῶν οἱ συγγραφεῖς. ὅσοι μὲν οὖν τὰς ἀθέους ἀσκοῦσι φιλοσοφίας, εἰ δὴ καὶ φιλοσοφίας αὐτὰς δεῖ καλεῖν, ἁπάσας διασύροντες τὰς ἐπιφανείας τῶν καλεῖν, ἁπάσας διασύροντες τὰς ἐπιφανείας τῶν θεῶν τὰς παρ' Ἕλλησιν ἢ βαρβάροις γενομένας καὶ ταύτας εἰς γέλωτα πολὺν ἄξουσι τὰς ἱστορίας ἀλαζονείαις ἀνθρωπίναις αὐτὰς ἀνατιθέντες, ὡς οὐδενὶ θεῶν μέλον ἀνθρώπων οὐδενός. ὅσοι δ' οὐκ ἀπολύουσι τῆς ἀνθρωπίνης ἐπιμελείας τοὺς θεούς, ἀλλὰ καὶ τοῖς ἀγαθοῖς εὐμενεῖς εἶναι νομίζουσι καὶ τοῖς κακοῖς δυσμενεῖς διὰ πολλῆς ἐληλυθότες ἱστορίας,οὐδὲ ταύτας ὑπολήψονται τὰς ἐπιφανείας εἶναι ἀπίστους. λέγεται δή ποτε τοῦ πυρὸς ἐκλιπόντος δι' ὀλιγωρίαν τινὰ τῆς τότε αὐτὸ φυλαττούσης Αἰμιλίας ἑτέρᾳ παρθένῳ τῶν νεωστὶ κατειλεγμένων καὶ ἄρτι μανθανουσῶν παραδούσης τὴν ἐπιμέλειαν ταραχὴ πολλὴ γενέσθαι κατὰ τὴν πόλιν ὅλην καὶ ζήτησις ὑπὸ τῶν ἱεροφαντῶν, μή τι μίασμα περὶ τὸ πῦρ τῆς ἱερείας ἐτύγχανε γεγονός· ἔνθα δή φασι τὴν

Αἰμιλίαν ἀναίτιον μὲν οὖσαν, ἀπορουμένην δ' ἐπὶ τῷ συμβεβηκότι παρόντων τῶν ἱερέων καὶ τῶν ἄλλων παρθένων τὰς χεῖρας ἐπὶ τὸν βωμὸν ἐκτείνασαν εἰπεῖν· Ἑστία τῆς Ῥωμαίων πόλεως φύλαξ, εἰ μὲν ὁσίως καὶ δικαίως ἐπιτετέλεκά σοι τὰ ἱερὰ χρόνον ὀλίγου δέοντα τριακονταετοῦς καὶ ψυχὴν ἔχουσα καθαρὰν καὶ σῶμα ἁγνόν, ἐπιφάνηθί μοι καὶ βοήθησον καὶ μὴ περιίδῃς τὴν σεαυτῆς ἱέρειαν τὸν οἴκτιστον μόρον ἀποθανοῦσαν· εἰ δὲ ἀνόσιόν τι πέπρακταί μοι ταῖς ἐμαῖς τιμωρίαις τὸ τῆς πόλεως ἄγος ἀφάγνισον. ταῦτ' εἰποῦσαν καὶ περιρρήξασαν ἀπὸ τῆς καρπασίνης ἐσθῆτος, ἣν ἔτυχεν ἐνδεδυκυῖα, βαλεῖν τὸν τελαμῶνα ἐπὶ τὸν βωμὸν μετὰ τὴν εὐχὴν λέγουσι καὶ ἐκ τῆς κατεψυγμένης πρὸ πολλοῦ καὶ οὐδένα φυλαττούσης σπινθῆρα τέφρας ἀναλάμψαι φλόγα πολλὴν τούσης σπινθῆρα τέφρας ἀναλάμψαι φλόγα πολλὴν διὰ τῆς καρπάσου, ὥστε μηδὲν ἔτι δεῆσαι τῇ πόλει μήτε ἁγνισμῶν μήτε νέου πυρός.

Ἔτι δὲ τούτου θαυμασιώτερόν ἐστι καὶ μύθῳ μᾶλλον ἐοικὸς ὃ μέλλω λέγειν. κατηγορῆσαί τινά φασιν ἀδίκως μιᾶς τῶν παρθένων τῶν ἱερῶν Τυκκίας ὄνομα, ἀφανισμὸν μὲν πυρὸς οὐκ ἔχοντα προφέρειν, ἄλλας δέ τινας ἐξ εἰκότων τεκμηρίων καὶ μαρτυριῶν ἀποδείξεις φέροντα οὐκ ἀληθεῖς· κελευσθεῖσαν δ' ἀπολογεῖσθαι τὴν παρθένον τοῦτο μόνον εἰπεῖν, ὅτι τοῖς ἔργοις ἀπολύσεται τὰς διαβολάς· ταῦτα δ' εἰποῦσαν καὶ τὴν θεὸν ἐπικαλεσαμένην ἡγεμόνα τῆς ὁδοῦ γενέσθαι προάγειν ἐπὶ τὸν Τέβεριν ἐπιτρεψάντων μὲν αὐτῇ τῶν ἱεροφαντῶν, τοῦ δὲ κατὰ τὴν πόλιν ὄχλου συμπροπέμποντος γενομένην δὲ τοῦ ποταμοῦ πλησίον τὸ παροιμιαζόμενον ἐν τοῖς πρώτοις τῶν ἀδυνάτων τόλμημα ὑπομεῖναι, ἀρυσαμένην ἐκ τοῦ ποταμοῦ καινῷ κοσκίνῳ καὶ μέχρι τῆς ἀγορᾶς ἐνέγκασαν παρὰ τοὺς πόδας τῶν ἱεροφαντῶν ἐξερᾶσαι τὸ ὕδωρ. καὶ μετὰ ταῦτά φασι τὸν κατήγορον αὐτῆς πολλῆς ζητήσεως γενομένης μήτε ζῶντα εὑρεθῆναι μήτε νεκρόν. ἀλλ' ὑπὲρ μὲν τῶν ἐπιφανειῶν τῆς θεᾶς ἔχων ἔτι πολλὰ λέγειν καὶ ταῦτα ἱκανὰ εἰρῆσθαι νομίζω.

Dionysius Halicarnassus 3.67

ἔπειτα ταῖς ἱεραῖς παρθένοις, ὑφ' ὧν τὸ ἄσβεστον φυλάττεται πῦρ, τέτταρσιν οὔσαις δύο προσκατέλεξεν ἑτέρας· πλειόνων γὰρ ἤδη συντελουμένων ὑπὸ τῆς ἑτέρας· πλειόνων γὰρ ἤδη συντελουμένων ὑπὸ τῆς πόλεως ἱερουργιῶν, αἷς ἔδει τὰς τῆς Ἑστίας παρεῖναι θυηπόλους, οὐκ ἐδόκουν αἱ τέτταρες ἀρκεῖν. Ταρκυνίου δὲ ἄρξαντος ἠκολούθουν οἱ λοιποὶ βασιλεῖς,καὶ μέχρι τῶν καθ' ἡμᾶς χρόνων ἓξ ἀποδείκνυνται τῆς Ἑστίας ἀμφίπολοι. δοκεῖ δὲ καὶ τὰς τιμωρίας, αἷς κολάζονται πρὸς τῶν ἱεροφαντῶν αἱ μὴ φυλάττουσαι τὴν παρθενίαν, ἐκεῖνος ἐξευρεῖν πρῶτος εἴτε κατὰ λογισμὸν εἴτε ὡς οἴονταί τινες ὀνείρῳ πειθόμενος, ἃς μετὰ τὴν ἐκείνου τελευτὴν ἐν τοῖς Σιβυλλείοις εὑρεθῆναι χρησμοῖς οἱ τῶν ἱερῶν ἐξηγηταὶ λέγουσιν· ἐφωράθη γάρ τις ἐπὶ τῆς ἐκείνου βασιλείας ἱέρεια Πιναρία Ποπλίου θυγάτηρ οὐχ ἁγνὴ προσιοῦσα τοῖς ἱεροῖς.

Dionysius Halicarnassus 8.89.3–5

ἔδοξε μέντοι καὶ λόγος ἦν ἐν τῇ ῾Ρώμῃ πολύς, ὡς δυναμένη τότε νικᾶν ἡ ῾Ρωμαίων δύναμις ἑκουσία μηδὲν ῾ἦν᾽ ἐργάσασθαι λαμπρὸν διὰ μῖσός τε τοῦ ὑπάτου καὶ ὀργήν, ἣν εἶχε πρὸς τοὺς πατρικίους ἐπὶ τῷ φενακισμῷ τῆς κληρουχίας. αὐτοὶ δ᾽ οἱ στρατιῶται τὸν ὕπατον ὡς οὐχ ἱκανὸν στρατηγεῖν ἠτιῶντο, γράμματα πέμποντες ὡς τοὺς ἐπιτηδείους ἑαυτῶν ἕκαστοι. καὶ τὰ μὲν ἐπὶ στρατοπέδου γινόμενα τοιαῦτ᾽ ἦν· ἐν αὐτῇ δὲ τῇ ῾Ρώμῃ πολλὰ δαιμόνια σημεῖα ἐφαίνετο δηλωτικὰ θείου χόλου κατά τε φωνὰς καὶ ὄψεις ἀήθεις. πάντα δ᾽ εἰς τοῦτο συνέτεινεν, ὡς οἵ τε μάντεις καὶ οἱ τῶν ἱερῶν ἐξηγηταὶ συνενέγκαντες τὰς ἐμπειρίας ἀπεφαίνοντο, ῾ὅτι᾽ θεῶν [χολοῦσθαί] τινες οὐ κομίζονται τὰς νομίμους τιμὰς οὐ καθαρῶς οὐδὲ ὁσίως ἐπιτελουμένων αὐτοῖς τῶν ἱερῶν. ζήτησις οὐδὲ ὁσίως ἐπιτελουμένων αὐτοῖς τῶν ἱερῶν. ζήτησις δὴ μετὰ τοῦτο πολλὴ ἐκ πάντων ἐγίνετο, καὶ σὺν χρόνῳ μήνυσις ἀποδίδοται τοῖς ἱεροφάνταις, ὅτι τῶν παρθένων μία τῶν φυλαττουσῶν τὸ ἱερὸν πῦρ, Ὀπιμία ὄνομα αὐτῇ, τὴν παρθενίαν ἀφαιρεθεῖσα μιαίνει τὰ ἱερά. οἱ δ᾽ ἔκ τε βασάνων καὶ τῶν ἄλλων ἀποδείξεων μαθόντες, ὅτι τὸ μηνυόμενον ἦν ἀδίκημα ἀληθές, αὐτὴν μὲν τῆς κορυφῆς ἀφελόμενοι τὰ στέμματα καὶ πομπεύσαντες δι᾽ ἀγορᾶς ἐντὸς τείχους ζῶσαν κατώρυξαν· δύο δὲ τοὺς ἐξελεγχθέντας διαπράξασθαι τὴν φθορὰν μαστιγώσαντες ἐν φανερῷ παραχρῆμα ἀπέκτειναν καὶ μετὰ τοῦτο καλὰ τὰ ἱερὰ καὶ τὰ μαντεύματα ὡς ἀφεικότων αὐτοῖς τῶν θεῶν τὸν χόλον, ἐγίνετο.

Dionysius Halicarnassus 9.40

ὅτι μία τῶν ἱεροποιῶν παρθένων τῶν φυλαττουσῶν τὸ ἀθάνατον πῦρ Ὀρβινία τὴν παρθενίαν ἀπολώλεκε καὶ τὰ ἱερὰ θύει τὰ τῆς πόλεως οὐκ οὖσα καθαρά. κἀκεῖνοι μεταστήσαντες αὐτὴν ἀπὸ τῶν ἱερῶν καὶ προθέντες δίκην, ἐπειδὴ καταφανὴς ἐγένετο ἐλεγχθεῖσα, ῥάβδοις τ᾽ ἐμαστίγωσαν καὶ πομπεύσαντες διὰ τῆς πόλεως ζῶσαν κατώρυξαν. τῶν δὲ διαπραξαμένων τὴν ἀνοσίαν φθορὰν ὁ μὲν ἕτερος ἑαυτὸν διεχρήσατο, τὸν δ᾽ ἕτερον οἱ τῶν ἱερῶν ἐπίσκοποι συλλαβόντες ἐν ἀγορᾷ μάστιξιν αἰκισάμενοι καθάπερ ἀνδράποδον ἀπέκτειναν. ἡ μὲν οὖν νόσος ἡ κατασκήψασα εἰς τὰς γυναῖκας καὶ ὁ πολὺς αὐτῶν φθόρος μετὰ τοῦτο τὸ ἔργον εὐθὺς ἐπαύσατο.

Festus p. 14 L

Argeos vocabant scirpeas effigies, quae per virgines Vestales annis singulis iaciebantur in Tiberim.

Festus p. 57 L

Casta mola genus sacrificii, quod Vestales virgines faciebant.

Festus p. 94 L

Ignis Vestae si quando interstinctus esset, virgines verberibus adficiebantur a pontifice, quibus mos erat tabulam felicis materiae tam diu terebrare, quosque exceptum ignem cribro aeneo virgo in aedem ferret.

Festus p. 152 L

Muries est, quemadmodum Veranius docet, ea quae fit ex sali sordido, in pila pisato, et in ollam fictilem coniecto, ibique operto gypsatoque et in furno percocto; cui virgines Vestales serra ferrea secto, et in seriam coniecto, quae est intus in aede Vestae in penu exteriore, aquam iugem, vel quamlibet, praeterquam quae per fistulas venit, addunt, atque ea demum in sacrificiis utuntur.

Festus p. 190 L

October equus appellatur, qui in campo Martio mense Octobri immolatur quotannis Marti, bigarum victricum dexterior. De cuius capite non levis contentio solebat esse inter Subaraneses, et Sacravienses, ut hi in regiae pariete, illi ad turrim mamiliam id figerent; euisdemque coda tanta celeritate perfertur in regiam, ut ex ea sanguis destillet in focum, participandae rei divinae gratia.

Festus p. 277 L

Probrum virginis Vestalis ut capite puniretur, vir, qui eam incestavisset, verberibus necaretur: lex fixa in atrio Libertatis cum multi<s> alis legibus incendio consumpta est, ut ait M. Cato in ea oratione, quae de augribus inscribitur. Adicit quoque virgines Vestales sacerdotio ex augurali …

Festus p. 296 L

<*Penus* v>ocatur locus intimus in aede Vestae tegetibus saeptus qui certis diebus circa Vestalia aperitur. i dies religiosi habentur.

Festus p. 310 L

<Q.S.D.F. Quandoc ster>cus delatum fas, eo<dem modo in fastis notatur di>es, qui talis est, ut <*aedes Vestae purgetur,* s>tercusque in alvum ca … cum id factum sit … ta.

Festus p. 448/449 L

Sceleratus campus app<ellatur prope portam Col>linam in quo virgin<es Vestales, quae incestum> fecerunt, defossae sunt v>ivae …

Festus p. 454 L

Senis crinibus nubentes ornantur, quod [h]is ornatus vetussimus fuit. Quidam quod eo Vestales virgines ornentur, quarum castitatem viris suis †sponoe * * * a ceteris ...

Festus p. 468 L

Sex Vestae sacerdotes constitutae sunt, ut populus pro sua quaque parte haberet ministram sacrorum; quia civitas Romana in sex est distributa partis: in primos secundosque Titienses, Ramnes, Luceres.

Festus p. 474 L

Suffibulum est vestimentum al<bum praetextum, qua>drangulum, oblongum, quod in ca<pite virgines Ve>stales, cum sacrificant, semper <*habere solent, i*>dque fibula conprehenditur.

Florus *Epitome* 1.1.105

Succedit Romulo Numa Pompilius, quem Curibus Sabinis agentem ultro petiverunt ob inclitam viri regionem. Ille sacra et caerimonias omnemque cultum deorum inmortalium docuit, ille pontifices, augures, Salios ceteraque sacerdotia creavit annumque in duodecim menses, fastos dies nefastoque discriptis, ille ancilia atque Palladium, secreta quaedam imperii pignora, Ianumque geminum fidem pacis ac belli, in primis focum Vestae virginibus colendum dedit, ut ad simulacrum caelestium siderum custos imperii flamma vigilaret: haec omnia quasi monitu deae Egeriae, quo magis barbari acciperet.

Gaius *Institutes* 1.145

Itaque si quis filio filiaeque testamento tutorem dederit, et ambo ad pubertatem pervenerint, filius quidem desinit habere tutorem, filia vero nihilo minus in tutela permanet: Tantum enim ex lege Iulia et Papia Poppaea iure liberorum a tutela liberantur feminae. Loquimur autem exceptis virginibus Vestalibus, quas etiam veteres in honorem sacerdotii liberas esse voluerunt: Itaque etiam lege XII tabularum cautum est.

Aulus Gellius *Noctes Atticae* 1.12

Virgo Vestae quid aetatis et ex quali familia et quo ritu quibusque caerimoniis ac religionibus ac quo nomine a pontifice maximo capiatur et quo statim iure esse incipiat, simul atque capta est; quodque, ut Labeo dicit, nec intestato cuiquam nec eius intestatae quisquam iure heres est.
I. Qui de virgine capienda scripserunt, quorum diligentissime scripsit Labeo

Antistius, minorem quam annos sex, maiorem quam annos decem natam negaverunt capi fas esse;

II. item quae non sit patrima et matrima;

III. item quae lingua debili sensuve aurium deminuta aliave qua corporis labe insignita sit;

IV. item quae ipsa aut cuius pater emancipatus sit, etiamsi vivo patre in avi potestate sit;

V. item cuius parentes alter ambove servitutem servierunt aut in negotiis sordidis versantur.

VI. Sed et eam, cuius soror ad id sacerdotium lecta est, excusationem mereri aiunt; item cuius pater flamen aut augur aut quindecimvirum sacris faciundis aut septemvirum epulonum aut Salius est.

VII. Sponsae quoque pontificis et tubicinis sacrorum filiae vacatio a sacerdotio isto tribui solet.

VIII. Praeterea Capito Ateius scriptum reliquit neque eius legendam filiam, qui domicilium in Italia non haberet, et excusandam eius, qui liberos tres haberet.

IX. Virgo autem Vestalis, simul est capta atque in atrium Vestae deducta et pontificibus tradita est, eo statim tempore sine emancipatione ac sine capitis minutione e patris potestate exit et ius testamenti faciundi adipiscitur.

X. De more autem rituque capiundae virginis litterae quidem antiquiores non exstant, nisi, quae capta prima est, a Numa rege esse captam.

XI. Sed Papiam legem invenimus, qua cavetur, ut pontificis maximi arbitratu virgines e populo viginti legantur sortitioque in contione ex eo numero fiat et, cuius virginis ducta erit, ut eam pontifex maximus capiat eaque Vestae fiat.

XII. Sed ea sortitio ex lege Papia non necessaria nunc videri solet. Nam si quis honesto loco natus adeat pontificem maximum atque offerat ad sacerdotium filiam suam, cuius dumtaxat salvis religionum observationibus ratio haberi possit, gratia Papiae legis per senatum fit.

XIII. "Capi" autem virgo propterea dici videtur, quia pontificis maximi manu prensa ab eo parente, in cuius potestate est, veluti bello capta abducitur.

XIV. In libro primo Fabii Pictoris, quae verba pontificem maximum dicere oporteat, cum virginem capiat, scriptum est. Ea verba haec sunt: "Sacerdotem Vestalem, quae sacra faciat, quae ius siet sacerdotem Vestalem facere pro populo Romano Quiritibus, uti quae optima lege fuit, ita te, Amata, capio."

XV. Plerique autem "capi" virginem solam debere dici putant. Sed flamines quoque Diales, item pontifices et augures "capi" dicebantur.

XVI. L. Sulla rerum gestarum libro secundo ita scripsit: "P. Cornelius, cui primum cognomen Sullae impositum est, flamen Dialis captus."

XVII. M. Cato de Lusitanis, cum Servium Galbam accusavit: "Tamen dicunt deficere voluisse. Ego me nunc volo ius pontificium optime scire; iamne ea causa pontifex capiar? si volo augurium optime tenere, ecquis me ob eam rem augurem capiat?"

XVIII. Praeterea in commentariis Labeonis, quae ad duodecim tabulas composuit, ita scriptum est: "Virgo Vestalis neque heres est cuiquam intestato,

neque intestatae quisquam, sed bona eius in publicum redigi aiunt. Id quo iure fiat, quaeritur."
XIX. "Amata" inter capiendum a pontifice maximo appellatur, quoniam, quae prima capta est, hoc fuisse nomen traditum est.

Aulus Gellius *Noctes Atticae* 7.7.2

Et Taraciam quidem virginem Vestae fuisse lex Horatia testis est, quae super ea ad populum lata. Qua lege ei plurimi honores fiunt, inter quos ius quoque testimonii dicendi tribuitur testabilisque uns omnium feminarum ut sit datur. Id verbum est legis ipsius Horatiae; contrarium est in *duodecim tabulis* scriptum: "Inprobus intestabilis esto." Praeterea si quadriaginta annos nata sacerdotio abire ac nubere voluisset, ius ei potestasque exaugurandi atque nubendi facta est munificentiae et beneficii gratia, quod campum Tiberinum sive Martium populo condonasset.

Aulus Gellius *Noctes Atticae* 10.15.31

Verba praetoris ex **edicto perpetuo** de flamine Diali et de sacerdote adscripsi: "Sacerdotem Vestalem et flaminem Dialem in omni mea iurisdictione iurare non cogam."

Horace *Odes* 3.30.8–9

usque ego postera
crescam laude recens, dum Capitolium
scandet cum tacita uirgine pontifex.

Hyginus, *De condicionibus agrorum*, C. 82

ex anti*qui*tate[m] recipiunt hoc [est], ut et nominibus vetustis utantur, ut vectigalis ager virginum Vestae, <et> aris templis sepulchris et his similibus.

Juvenal 4.9–10

incestus, cum quo nuper vittata iacebat
sanguine adhuc vivo terram subitura sacerdos?

Livy 1.3

Addit sceleri scelus: stirpem fratris virilem interemit, fratris filiae Reae Silviae per speciem honoris cum Vestalem eam legisset perpetua virginitate spem partus adimit.
    Sed debebatur, ut opinor, fatis tantae origo urbis maximique secundum

deorum opes imperii principium. Vi compressa Vestalis cum geminum partum edidisset, seu ita rata seu quia deus auctor culpae honestior erat, Martem incertae stirpis patrem nuncupat. Sed nec di nec homines aut ipsam aut stirpem a crudelitate regia vindicant: sacerdos vincta in custodiam datur, pueros in profluentem aquam mitti iubet.

Livy 1.20

virginesque Vestae legit, Alba oriundum sacerdotium et genti conditoris haud alienum. His ut adsiduae templi antistites essent stipendium de publico statuit; virginitate aliisque caerimoniis venerabiles ac sanctas fecit.

Livy 2.42.11

qui terrores tamen eo evasere ut Oppia virgo Vestalis damnata incesti poenas dederit.

Livy 4.44.2

Eodem anno Postumia virgo vestalis de incestu causam dixit, crimine innoxia, ab suspicione propter cultum amoeniorem ingeniumque liberius quam virginem decet parum abhorrens. Eam ampliatam, deinde absolutam pro collegii sententia pontifex maximus abstinere iocis colique sancte potius quam scite iussit.

Livy 5.40

Flamen interim Quirinalis uirginesque Vestales omissa rerum suarum cura, quae sacrorum secum ferenda, quae quia uires ad omnia ferenda deerant relinquenda essent consultantes, quisue ea locus fideli adseruaturus custodia esset, optimum ducunt condita in doliolis sacello proximo aedibus flaminis Quirinalis, ubi nunc despui religio est, defodere; cetera inter se onere partito ferunt uia quae sublicio ponte ducit ad Ianiculum. In eo cliuo eas cum L. Albinius de plebe Romana homo conspexisset plaustro coniugem ad liberos uehens inter ceteram turbam quae inutilis bello urbe excedebat, saluo etiam tum discrimine diuinarum humanarumque rerum religiosum ratus sacerdotes publicas sacraque populi Romani pedibus ire ferrique, se ac suos in uehiculo conspici, descendere uxorem ac pueros iussit, uirgines sacraque in plaustrum imposuit et Caere quo iter sacerdotibus erat peruexit.

Livy 8.15.7–8

Eo anno Minucia Vestalis, suspecta primo propter mundiorem iusto cultum, insimulata deinde apud pontifices ab indice servo, cum decreto eorum iussa esset sacris abstinere familiamque in potestate habere, facto iudicio viva sub terram ad portam Collinam dextra viam stratam defossa Scelerato campo; credo ab incesto id ei loco nomen factum.

Livy 22.57.2–3

Territi etiam super tantas clades cum ceteris prodigiis, tum quod duae Vestales eo anno, Opimia atque Floronia, stupri compertae et altera sub terra, uti mos est, ad portam Collinam necata fuerat, altera sibimet ipsa mortem consciverat; L. Cantilius scriba pontificius, quos nunc minores pontifices appellant, qui cum Floronia stuprum fecerat, a pontifice maximo eo usque virgis in comitio caesus erat ut inter verbera exspiraret.

Livy 28.11.6

plus omnibus aut nuntiatis peregre aut uisis domi prodigiis terruit animos hominum ignis in aede Uestae exstinctus, caesaque flagro est Uestalis cuius custodia eius noctis fuerat iussu P. Licini pontificis. id quamquam nihil portendentibus dis ceterum neglegentia humana acciderat, tamen et hostiis maioribus procurari et supplicationem ad Uestae haberi placuit.

Livy *Periochae* 14

Sextilia, virgo Vestalis, damnata incesti viva defossa est.

Livy *Periochae* 20

Tuccia, uirgo Vestalis, incesti damnata est.

Livy *Periochae* 63a

Aemilia, Licinia, Marcia, uirgines Vestales, incesti damnatae sunt, idque incestum quem ad modum et commissum et deprehensum et uindicatum sit re fertur.

Macrobius *Saturnalia* 1.10.5–6

Masurius et alii uno die, id est quarto decimo Kalendas Ianuarias fuisse Saturnalia crediderunt: quorum sententiam Fenestella confirmat, dicens Aemiliam virginem XV. Kal. Ianuar.

Macrobius *Saturnalia* 1.12.6

Huius etiam prima die ignem novum Vestae aris accendebant, ut incipiente anno cura denuo servandi novati ignis inciperet.

Orosius 3.9.5

Anno autem post hunc subsequente Minucia virgo Vestalis ob admissum incestum damnata est vivaque obruta in campo, qui nunc sceleratus vocatur.

Orosius 4.5.9

Eodem tempore Caparronia virgo Vestalis incesti rea suspendio periit corruptor eius consciique servi supplicio adfecti.

Orosius 5.15.22

Parvo post hoc intercessu temporis L. Veterius eques Romanus Aemiliam virginem Vestalem furtivo stupro polluit. duas praeteraea virgines Vestales eadem Aemilia ad participationem incesti sollicitatas contubernalibus sui corruptoris exposuit ac tradidit. indicio per servum factosuppliciumde omnibus sumptumest.

Ovid *Fasti* 1.527–528

iam pius Aeneas sacra et, sacra altera, patrem
adferet: Iliacos accipe, Vesta, deos.

Ovid *Fasti* 2.382–386

Silvia Vestalis caelestia semina partu
ediderat, patruo regna tenente suo;
is iubet auferri parvos et in amne necari:
quid facis? ex istis Romulus alter erit.

Ovid *Fasti* 3.11–30

Silvia Vestalis (quid enim vetat inde moveri?)
sacra lavaturas mane petebat aquas.
ventum erat ad molli declivem tramite ripam;
ponitur e summa fictilis urna coma:
fessa resedit humo, ventosque accepit aperto
pectore, turbatas restituitque comas.
dum sedet, umbrosae salices volucresque canorae
fecerunt somnos et leve murmur aquae;
blanda quies furtim victis obrepsit ocellis,
et cadit a mento languida facta manus.
Mars videt hanc visamque cupit potiturque cupita,
et sua divina furta fefellit ope.
somnus abit, iacet ipsa gravis; iam scilicet intra

viscera Romanae conditor urbis erat.
languida consurgit, nec scit cur languida surgat,
et peragit tales arbore nixa sonos:
'utile sit faustumque, precor, quod imagine somni
vidimus: an somno clarius illud erat?
ignibus Iliacis aderam, cum lapsa capillis
decidit ante sacros lanea vitta focos'.

Ovid *Fasti* 3.141–144

Vesta quoque ut folio niteat velata recenti,
cedit ab Iliacis laurea cana focis.
adde quod arcana fieri novus ignis in aede
dicitur, et vires flamma refecta capit.

Ovid *Fasti* 3.423–426

di veteris Troiae, dignissima praeda ferenti,
qua gravis Aeneas tutus ab hoste fuit,
ortus ab Aenea tangit cognata
numina: cognatum, Vesta, tuere caput.

Ovid *Fasti* 4.629–640

Tertia post Veneris cum lux surrexerit Idus,
pontifices, forda sacra litate bove.
forda ferens bos est fecundaque dicta ferendo:
hinc etiam fetus nomen habere putant.
nunc gravidum pecus est, gravidae quoque semine terrae:
Telluri plenae victima plena datur.
pars cadit arce Iovis, ter denas curia vaccas
accipit et largo sparsa cruore madet.
ast ubi visceribus vitulos rapuere ministri,
sectaque fumosis exta dedere focis,
igne cremat vitulos quae natu maxima Virgo est,
luce Palis populos purget ut ille cinis.

Ovid *Fasti* 4.721–734

Nox abiit, oriturque aurora: Parilia poscor;
non poscor frustra, si favet alma Pales.
alma Pales, faveas pastoria sacra canenti,
prosequor officio si tua festa meo.
certe ego de vitulo cinerem stipulasque fabales
saepe tuli plena, februa tosta, manu;

certe ego transilui positas ter in ordine flammas,
udaque roratas laurea misit aquas.
mota dea est, operique favet. navalibus exit
puppis; habent ventos iam mea vela suos.
 i, pete virginea, populus, suffimen ab ara;
Vesta dabit, Vestae munere purus eris.
sanguis equi suffimen erit vitulique favilla,
tertia res durae culmen inane fabae.

Ovid *Fasti* 5.621–622

Tum quoque priscorum Virgo simulacra virorum
mittere roboreo scirpea ponte solet.

Ovid *Fasti* 6.226–234

nam mihi sic coniunx sancta Dialis ait:
'donec ab Iliaca placidus purgamina Vesta
detulerit flavis in mare Thybris aquis,
non mihi detonso crinem depectere buxo,
non ungues ferro subsecuisse licet,
non tetigisse virum, quamvis Iovis ille sacerdos,
quamvis perpetua sit mihi lege datus.
tu quoque ne propera: melius tua filia nubet
ignea cum pura Vesta nitebit humo.'

Ovid *Fasti* 6.267–268

Vesta eadem est et terra: subest vigil ignis utrique:
significant sedem terra focusque suam.

Ovid *Fasti* 6.282–318

cur sit virginibus, quaeris, dea culta ministris?
inveniam causas hac quoque parte suas.
ex Ope Iunonem memorant Cereremque creatas
semine Saturni; tertia Vesta fuit.
utraque nupserunt, ambae peperisse feruntur;
de tribus impatiens restitit una viri.
quid mirum, virgo si virgine laeta ministra
admittit castas ad sua sacra manus?
nec tu aliud Vestam quam vivam intellege flammam;
nataque de flamma corpora nulla vides.
iure igitur virgo est, quae semina nulla remittit
nec capit, et comites virginitatis amat.

esse diu stultus Vestae simulacra putavi,
mox didici curvo nulla subesse tholo.
ignis inexstinctus templo celatur in illo:
effigiem nullam Vesta nec ignis habet.
stat vi terra sua: vi stando Vesta vocatur;
causaque par Grai nominis esse potest.
at focus a flammis et quod fovet omnia dictus;
qui tamen in primis aedibus ante fuit.
hinc quoque vestibulum dici reor; inde precando
praefamur Vestam, quae loca prima tenet.
Ante focos olim scamnis considere longis
mos erat, et mensae credere adesse deos;
nunc quoque, cum fiunt antiquae sacra Vacunae,
ante Vacunales stantque sedentque focos.
venit in hos annos aliquid de more vetusto:
fert missos Vestae pura patella cibos.
Ecce coronatis panis dependet asellis,
et velant scabras florida serta molas.
sola prius furnis torrebant farra coloni
(et Fornacali sunt sua sacra deae):
subpositum cineri panem focus ipse parabat,
strataque erat tepido tegula quassa solo.
inde focum servat pistor dominamque focorum
et quae pumiceas versat asella molas.

Ovid *Fasti* 6.457–460

nullaque dicetur vittas temerasse sacerdos
hoc duce, nec viva defodietur humo:
sic incesta perit, quia, quam violavit, in illam
conditur: est Tellus Vestaque numen idem.

Ovid *Fasti* 6.713–714

haec est illa dies qua tu purgamina Vestae,
Thybri, per Etruscas in mare mittis aquas.

Ovid *Metamorphoses* 15.729–731

huc omnis populi passim matrumque patrumque
obvia turba ruit, quaeque ignes, Troica, servant,
Vesta, tuos, laetoque deum clamore salutant.

Pliny *Epistulae* 4.11

Nam cum Corneliam Vestalium maximam defodere vivam concupisset, ut qui illustrari saeculum suum eiusmodi exemplis arbitraretur, pontificis maximi iure, seu potius immanitate tyranni licentia domini, reliquos pontifices non in Regiam sed in Albanam villam convocavit. Nec minore scelere quam quod ulcisci videbatur, absentem inauditamque damnavit incesti, cum ipse fratris filiam incesto non polluisset solum verum etiam occidisset; nam vidua abortu periit. Missi statim pontifices qui defodiendam necandamque curarent. Illa nunc ad Vestam, nunc ad ceteros deos manus tendens, multa sed hoc frequentissime clamitabat: 'Me Caesar incestam putat, qua sacra faciente vicit triumphavit!' Blandiens haec an irridens, ex fiducia sui an ex contemptu principis dixerit, dubium est. Dixit donec ad supplicium, nescio an innocens, certe tamquam innocens ducta est. Quin etiam cum in illud subterraneum demitteretur, haesissetque descendenti stola, vertit se ac recollegit, cumque ei manum carnifex daret, aversata est et resiluit foedumque contactum quasi plane a casto puroque corpore novissima sanctitate reiecit omnibusque numeris pudoris 'pollên pronoian eschen euschêmôn pesein?'. Praeterea Celer eques Romanus, cui Cornelia obiciebatur, cum in comitio virgis caederetur, in hac voce perstiterat: 'Quid feci? nihil feci.'

Pliny *Historia Naturalis* 16.235

Romae vero lotos in Lucinae area, anno, qui fuit sine magistratibus, CCCLXXIX urbis aede condita. incertum, ipsa quanto vetustior; esse quidem vetustiorem non est dubium, cum ab eo luco Lucina nominetur. haec nunc D circiter annum habet. antiquior, sed incerta eius aetas, quae capillata dicitur, quoniam Vestalium virginum capillus ad eam defertur.

Pliny *Historia Naturalis* 18.7

Numa instituit deos fruge colere et mola salsa supplicare atque, ut auctor est Hemina, far torrere, quoniam tostum cibo salubrius esset, id uno modo consecutus, statuendo non esse purum ad rem divinam nisi tostum.

is et Fornacalia instituit farris torrendi ferias et aeque religiosas Terminis agrorum.

Pliny, *Historia Naturalis* 28.7.39

... et fascinus, imperatorum quoque, non solum infantium, custos, qui deus inter sacra Romana a Vestalibus colitur, et currus triumphantium, sub his pendens, defendit medicus invidiae ...

Pliny *Historia Naturalis* 28.12

extat Tucciae Vestalis incesti deprecatio, qua usa aquam in cribro tulit anno
urbis DXVIIII. boario vero in foro Graecum Graecamque defossos aut aliarum
gentium, cum quibus tum res esset, etiam nostra aetas vidit. cuius sacri
precationem, qua solet praeire XVvirum collegii magister, si quis legat,
profecto vim carminum fateatur, omnia ea adprobantibus DCCCXXX
annorum eventibus.

Pliny *Historia Naturalis* 34.25

invenitur statua decreta et Taraciae Gaiae sive Fufetiae virgini Vestali, ut
poneretur ubi vellet, quod adiectum non minus honoris habet quam feminae
esse decretam. meritum eius ipsis ponam annalium verbis: quod campum
Tiberinum gratificata esset ea populo.

Plutarch *Camillus* 20

Καὶ πλεῖστος μὲν λόγος κατεῖχε τὸ Τρωϊκὸν ἐκεῖνο Παλλάδιον ἀποκεῖσθαι
δι' Αἰνείου κομισθὲν εἰς Ἰταλίαν· εἰσὶ δ† οἱ τὰ Σαμοθράκια μυθολογοῦντες
Δάρδανον μὲν εἰς Τροίαν ἐξενεγκάμενον ὀργιάσαι καὶ καθιερῶσαι κτίσαντα
τὴν πόλιν, Αἰνείαν δὲ περὶ τὴν ἅλωσιν ἐκκλέψαντα διασῶσαι μέχρι τῆς ἐν
Ἰταλίᾳ κατοικήσεως. Οἱ δὲ προσποιούμενοι πλέον ἐπίστασθαί τι περὶ
τούτων δύο φασὶν οὐ μεγάλους ἀποκεῖσθαι πίθους, ὧν τὸν μὲν ἀνεῳγότα
καὶ κενὸν, τὸν δὲ πλήρη καὶ κατασεσημασμένον, ἀμφοτέρους δὲ ταῖς
παναγέσι μόναις παρθένοις ὁρατοὺς εἶναι.

Plutarch *Cato Maior* 20.5–7

αὐτὴ γὰρ ἔτρεφεν ἰδίῳ γάλακτι· πολλάκις δὲ καὶ τὰ τῶν δούλων παιδάρια
τῷ μαστῷ προσιεμένη, κατεσκεύαζεν εὔνοιαν ἐκ τῆς συντροφίας πρὸς τὸν
υἱόν. ἐπεὶ δ' ἤρξατο συνιέναι, παραλαβὼν αὐτὸς ἐδίδασκε γράμματα.
καίτοι χα- ρίεντα δοῦλον εἶχε γραμματιστὴν ὄνομα Χίλωνα, πολ λοὺς
διδάσκοντα παῖδας· οὐκ ἠξίου δὲ τὸν υἱόν, ὥς φησιν αὐτός, ὑπὸ δούλου
κακῶς ἀκούειν ἢ τοῦ ὠτὸς ἀνατείνεσθαι μανθάνοντα βράδιον, οὐδέ γε
μαθήματος τηλικούτου ⟦τω⟧ δούλῳ χάριν ὀφείλειν, ἀλλ' αὐτὸς μὲν ἦν
γραμματιστής, αὐτὸς δὲ νομοδιδάκτης, αὐτὸς δὲ γυμναστής, οὐ μόνον
ἀκοντίζειν οὐδ' ὁπλομαχεῖν οὐδ' ἱππεύειν διδάσκων τὸν υἱόν, ἀλλὰ καὶ
τῇ χειρὶ πὺξ παίειν καὶ καῦμα καὶ ψῦχος ἀνέχεσθαι καὶ τὰ δινώδη καὶ
τραχύνοντα τοῦ ποταμοῦ διανηχόμενον ἀποβιάζεσθαι. καὶ τὰς ἱστορίας
ποταμοῦ διανηχόμενον ἀποβιάζεσθαι. καὶ τὰς ἱστορίας δὲ συγγράψαι
φησὶν αὐτὸς ἰδίᾳ χειρὶ καὶ μεγάλοις γράμμασιν, ὅπως οἴκοθεν ὑπάρχοι
τῷ παιδὶ πρὸς ἐμπειρίαν.
τῶν παλαιῶν καὶ πατρίων ὠφελεῖσθαι· τὰ δ' αἰσχρὰ τῶν ῥημάτων οὐχ
ἧττον ἐξευλαβεῖσθαι τοῦ παιδὸς παρόντος ἢ τῶν ἱερῶν παρθένων ἃς
Ἑστιάδας καλοῦσι· συλλούσασθαι δὲ μηδέποτε.

Plutarch *Cato Minor* 19.3–9

οὔτε γὰρ δόξης χάριν οὔτε πλεονεξίας οὔτ' αὐτομάτως καὶ κατὰ τύχην ὥσπερ ἕτεροί τινες ἐμπεσὼν εἰς τὸπράττειν τὰ τῆς πόλεως, ἀλλ' ὡς ἴδιον ἔργον ἀνδρὸς ἀγαθοῦ τὴν πολιτείανἑλόμενος, μᾶλλον ᾤετο δεῖν προσέχειν τοῖς κοινοῖς ἢ τῷ κηρίῳ τὴν μέλιτ ταν· ταν· ὅς γε καὶ τὰ τῶν ἐπαρχιῶν πράγματα καὶ δόγματα καὶ κρίσεις [καὶπράξεις] τὰς μεγίστας ἔργον πεποίητο διὰ τῶν ἑκασταχόθι ξένων καὶ φίλων πέμπεσθαι πρὸς αὐτόν. ἐνστὰς δέ ποτε Κλωδίῳ τῷ δημαγωγῷ, κινοῦντι καὶ πράττοντι μεγάλων ἀρχὰς νεωτερισμῶν, καὶ διαβάλλοντι πρὸς τὸν δῆμον ἱερεῖς καὶ ἱερείας, ἐν οἷς καὶ Φαβία Τερεντίας ἀδελφὴ τῆς Κικέρωνος γυναικὸς ἐκινδύνευσε, τὸν μὲν Κλώδιον αἰσχύνη περιβαλὼν ἠνάγκασεν ὑπεκστῆναι τῆς πόλεως, τοῦ δὲ Κικέρωνος εὐχαριστοῦντος, τῇ πόλει δεῖν ἔχειν ἔφη χάριν αὐτόν, ὡς ἐκείνης ἕνεκα πάντα ποιῶν καὶ πολιτευόμενος. ἐκ τούτου μεγάλη δόξα περὶ αὐτὸν ἦν, ὥστε ῥήτορα μὲν‹ἐν δίκῃ τινὶ μαρτυρίας μιᾶς φερομένης εἰπεῖν πρὸς τοὺς δικαστάς, ὡς ἑνὶ μαρτυροῦντι προσέχειν οὐδὲ Κάτωνι καλῶς ἔχει, πολλοὺς δ' ἤδη περὶ τῶν ἀπίστων καὶ παραδόξων ὥσπερ ἐν παροιμίᾳ τινὶ λέγειν, ὅτι τοῦτο μὲν οὐδὲ Κάτωνος λέγοντος πιθανόν ἐστι. μοχθηροῦ δ' ἀνθρώπου καὶ πολυτελοῦς λόγον ἐν συγκλήτῳ διαθεμένου πρὸς εὐτέλειαν καὶ σωφρονισμόν, ἐπαναστὰς Ἀμναῖος ϛlῶ ἄνθρωπ' εἶπε, ϛltιϛ ἀνέξεταί σου, δειπνοῦντος μὲν ὡς Κράσσου, οἰκοδομοῦντος δ' ὡς Λευκόλλου, δημηγοροῦντος δ'ἡμῖν ὡς Κάτωνος; καὶ τῶν ἄλλων δὲ τοὺς φαύλους καὶ ἀκολάστους,τοῖς λόγοις δὲ σεμνοὺς καὶ αὐστηρούς, χλευάζοντες ἐκάλουν Ψευδοκάτωνας.

Plutarch *Cicero* 19

θύεται δαὐτῇ κατ' ἐνιαυτὸν ἐν τῇ οἰκίᾳ τοῦ ὑπάτου διὰ γυναικὸς ἢ μητρὸς αὐτοῦ, τῶν Ἑστιάδων παρθένων παρουσῶν.

Plutarch *Cicero* 20

Ταῦτα τοῦ Κικέρωνος διαποροῦντος, γίνεταί τι ταῖς γυναιξὶ σημεῖον θυούσαις. Ὁ γὰρ βωμός, ἤδη τοῦ πυρὸς κατακεκοιμῆσθαι δοκοῦντος, ἐκ τῆς τέφρας καὶ τῶν κεκαυμένων φλοιῶν φλόγα πολλὴν ἀνῆκε καὶ λαμπράν. Ὑφ' ἧς αἱ μὲν ἄλλαι διεπτοήθησαν, αἱ δ' ἱεραὶ παρθένοι τὴν τοῦ Κικέρωνος γυναῖκα Τερεντίαν ἐκέλευσαν ᾗ τάχος χωρεῖν πρὸς τὸν ἄνδρα καὶ κελεύειν οἷς ἔγνωκεν ἐγχειρεῖν ὑπὲρ τῆς πατρίδος, ὡς μέγα πρός τε σωτηρίαν καὶ δόξαν αὐτῷ τῆς θεοῦ φῶς διδούσης.

Plutarch *Numa* 3.4

ὅπως λαμβάνουσαι καθ ἡμέραν ἁγνίζωσι καὶ ῥαίνωσι τὸ ἀνάκτορον . . .

Plutarch Numa 9–11

Ὁ δὲ μέγιστος τῶν Ποντιφίκων οἷον ἐξηγητοῦ καὶ προφήτου, μᾶλλον δὲ ἱεροφάντου τάξιν εἴληχεν, οὐ μόνον τῶν δημοσίᾳ δρωμένων ἐπιμελούμενος, ἀλλὰ καὶ τοὺς ἰδίᾳ θύοντας ἐπισκοπῶν καὶ κωλύων παρεκβαίνειν τὰ νενομισμένα, καὶ διδάσκων ὅτου τις δέοιτο πρὸς θεῶν τιμὴν ἢ παραίτησιν. ἦν δὲ καὶ τῶν ἱερῶν παρθένων ἐπίσκοπος, ἃς Ἑστιάδας προσαγορεύουσι. Νομᾷ γὰρ δὴ καὶ τὴν τῶν Ἑστιάδων παρθένων καθιέρωσιν καὶ ὅλως τὴν περὶ τὸ πῦρ τὸ ἀθάνατον, ὃ φυλάττουσιν αὗται, θεραπείαν τε καὶ τιμὴν ἀποδιδόασιν, εἴτε ὡς καθαρὰν καὶ ἄφθαρτον τὴν τοῦ πυρὸς οὐσίαν ἀκηράτοις καὶ ἀμιάντοις παρατιθεμένου σώμασιν, εἴτε τὸ ἄκαρπον καὶ ἄγονον τῇ παρθενίᾳ συνοικειοῦντος. ἐπεί τοι τῆς Ἑλλάδος ὅπου πῦρ ἄσβεστόν ἐστιν, ὡς Πυθοῖ καὶ Ἀθήνησιν, οὐ παρθένοι, γυναῖκες δὲ πεπαυμέναι γάμων ἔχουσι "σβεστόν ἐστιν, ὡς Πυθοῖ καὶ Ἀθήνησιν, οὐ παρθένοι, γυναῖκες δὲ πεπαυμέναι γάμων ἔχουσι τὴν ἐπιμέλειαν· ἐὰν δὲ ὑπὸ τύχης τινὸς ἐκλίπῃ, καθάπερ Ἀθήνησι μὲν ἐπὶ τῆς Ἀριστίωνος λέγεται τυραννίδος ἀποσβεσθῆναι τὸν ἱερὸν λύχνον, ἐν Δελφοῖς δὲ τοῦ ναοῦ καταπρησθέντος ὑπὸ Μήδων, περὶ δὲ τὰ Μιθριδατικὰ καὶ τὸν ἐμφύλιον Ῥωμαίων πόλεμον ἅμα τῷ βωμῷ τὸ πῦρ ἠφανίσθη, οὔ φασι δεῖν ἀπὸ ἑτέρου πυρὸς ἐναύεσθαι, καινὸν δὲ ποιεῖν καὶ νέον, ἀνάπτοντας ἀπὸ τοῦ ἡλίου φλόγα καθαρὰν καὶ ἀμίαντον. ἐξάπτουσι δὲ μάλιστα τοῖς σκαφείοις, ἃ κατασκευάζεται μὲν ἀπὸ πλευρᾶς ἰσοσκελοῦς ὀρθογωνίου τριγώνου κοιλαινόμενα, συννεύει δ᾽ εἰς ἓν ἐκ τῆς περιφερείας κέντρον. ὅταν οὖν θέσιν ἐναντίαν λάβῃ πρὸς τὸν ἥλιον, ὥστε τὰς αὐγὰς πανταχόθεν ἀνακοπτομένας ἀθροίζεσθαι καὶ συμπλέκεσθαι περὶ τὸ κέντρον, αὐτόν τε διακρίνει τὸν ἀέρα λεπτυνόμενον, καὶ τὰ κουφότατα καὶ ξηρότατα τῶν προστιθεμένων ὀξέως ἀνάπτει κατὰ τὴν ἀντέρεισιν, σῶμα καὶ πληγὴν πυρώδη τῆς αὐγῆς λαβούσης. ἔνιοι μὲν οὖν οὐδὲν ὑπὸ τῶν ἱερῶν παρθένων ἀλλ᾽ ἢ τὸ ἄσβεστον ἐκεῖνο φρουρεῖσθαι πῦρ νομίζουσιν· ἔνιοι δὲ εἶναί τινά φασιν ἀθέατα τοῖς ἄλλοις ἱερὰ κρυπτόμενα, περὶ ὧν ὅσα καὶ πυθέσθαι καὶ φράσαι θεμιτὸν ἐν τῷ Καμίλλου βίῳ γέγραπται.

Πρῶτον μὲν οὖν ὑπὸ Νομᾶ καθιερωθῆναι λέγουσι Γεγανίαν καὶ Βερηνίαν, δεύτερον δὲ Κανουληΐαν καὶ Ταρπηΐαν· ὕστερον δὲ Σερβίου δύο προσθέντος ἄλλας τῷ ἀριθμῷ διατηρεῖσθαι μέχρι τῶν χρόνων τούτων τὸ πλῆθος. ὡρίσθη δὲ ταῖς ἱεραῖς παρθένοις ὑπὸ τοῦ βασιλέως ἁγνεία τριακονταέτις, ἐν ᾗ τὴν μὲν πρώτην δεκαετίαν ἃ χρὴ δρᾶν μανθάνουσι, τὴν δὲ μέσην ἃ μεμαθήκασι δρῶσι, τὴν δὲ τρίτην ἑτέρας αὐταὶ διδάσκουσιν.

εἶτα ἀνεῖται τῇ βουλομένῃ μετὰ τὸν χρόνον τοῦτον ἤδη καὶ γάμου μεταλαμβάνειν καὶ πρὸς ἕτερον τραπέσθαι βίον, ἀπαλλαγείσῃ τῆς ἱερουργίας. λέγονται δὲ οὐ πολλαὶ ταύτην ἀσπάσασθαι τὴν ἄδειαν, οὐδὲ ἀσπασαμέναις χρηστὰ πράγματα συντυχεῖν, ἀλλὰ μετανοίᾳ καὶ κατηφείᾳ συνοῦσαι τὸν λοιπὸν βίον ἐμβαλεῖν τὰς ἄλλας εἰς δεισιδαιμονίαν, ὥστε μέχρι γήρως καὶ θανάτου διατελεῖν ἐγκαρτερούσας καὶ παρθενευομένας. Τιμὰς δὲ μεγάλας ἀπέδωκεν αὐταῖς, ὧν ἔστι καὶ τὸ διαθέσθαι ζῶντος ἐξεῖναι πατρὸς καὶ τἆλλα πράττειν ἄνευ προστάτου διαγούσας, ὥσπερ αἱ τρίπαιδες. ῥαβδουχοῦνται δὲ προϊοῦσαι· κἂν ἀγομένῳ τινὶ πρὸς θάνατον αὐτομάτως συντύχωσιν, οὐκ ἀναιρεῖται. δεῖ δὲ ἀπομόσαι τὴν παρθένον ἀκούσιον καὶ τυχαίαν καὶ οὐκ ἐξεπίτηδες γεγονέναι τὴν ἀπάντησιν. ὁ δὲ ὑπελθὼν κομιζομένων ὑπὸ τὸ φορεῖον ἀποθνήσκει. κόλασις δὲ τῶν μὲν ἄλλων ἁμαρτημάτων πληγαὶ ταῖς παρθένοις, τοῦ μεγίστου Ποντίφικος κολάζοντος ἔστιν ὅτε καὶ γυμνὴν τὴν πλημμελήσασαν, ὀθόνης ἐν παλινσκίῳ παρατεινομένης· ἡ δὲ τὴν παρθενίαν καταισχύνασα ζῶσα κατορύττεται παρὰ τὴν Κολλίνην λεγομένην πύλην· ἐν ᾗ τις ἔστιν ἐντὸς τῆς πόλεως ὀφρὺς γεώδης παρατείνουσα πόρρω· Κολλίνην λεγομένην πύλην· ἐν ᾗ τις ἔστιν ἐντὸς τῆς πόλεως ὀφρὺς γεώδης παρατείνουσα πόρρω· καλεῖται δὲ χῶμα διαλέκτῳ τῇ Λατίνων. ἐνταῦθα κατασκευάζεται κατάγειος οἶκος οὐ μέγας, ἔχων ἄνωθεν κατάβασιν. κεῖται δὲ ἐν αὐτῷ κλίνη τε ὑπεστρωμένη καὶ λύχνος καιόμενος, ἀπαρχαί τε τῶν πρὸς τὸ ζῆν ἀναγκαίων βραχεῖαί τινες, οἷον ἄρτος, ὕδωρ ἐν ἀγγείῳ, γάλα, ἔλαιον, ὥσπερ.

ἀφοσιουμένων τὸ μὴ λιμῷ διαφθείρειν σῶμα ταῖς μεγίσταις καθιερωμένον ἁγιστείαις. αὐτὴν δὲ τὴν κολαζομένην εἰς φορεῖον ἐνθέμενοι καὶ καταστεγάσαντες ἔξωθεν καὶ καταλαβόντες ἱμᾶσιν, ὡς μηδὲ φωνὴν ἐξάκουστον γενέσθαι, κομίζουσι δι᾽ ἀγορᾶς. ἐξίστανται δὲ πάντες σιωπῇ καὶ παραπέμπουσιν ἄφθογγοι μετά τινος δεινῆς κατηφείας· οὐδὲ ἐστὶν ἕτερον θέαμα φρικτότερον, οὐδ᾽ ἡμέραν ἡ πόλις ἄλλην ἄγει στυγνοτέραν ἐκείνης. ὅταν δὲ πρὸς τὸν τόπον κομισθῇ τὸ φορεῖον, οἱ μὲν ὑπηρέται τοὺς δεσμοὺς ἐξέλυσαν, ὁ δὲ τῶν ἱερέων ἔξαρχος εὐχάς τινας ἀπορρήτους ποιησάμενος καὶ χεῖρας ἀνατείνας θεοῖς πρὸ τῆς ἀνάγκης, ἐξάγει (συγκεκαλυμμένην καὶ καθίστησιν ἐπὶ κλίμακος εἰς τὸ οἴκημα κάτω φερούσης. εἶτα αὐτὸς μὲν ἀποτρέπεται μετὰ τῶν ἄλλων ἱερέων· τῆς δὲ καταβάσης ἥ τε κλίμαξ ἀναιρεῖται καὶ κατακρύπτεται τὸ οἴκημα γῆς πολλῆς ἄνωθεν ἐπιφορουμένης, ὥστε ἰσόπεδον τῷ λοιπῷ χώματι γενέσθαι τὸν τόπον. οὕτω μὲν αἱ προέμεναι τὴν ἱερὰν παρθενίαν κολάζονται.

Νομᾶς δὲ λέγεται καὶ τὸ τῆς Ἑστίας ἱερὸν ἐγκύκλιον περιβαλέσθαι τῷ ἀσβέστῳ πυρὶ φρου‑ ἐγκύκλιον περιβαλέσθαι τῷ ἀσβέστῳ πυρὶ φρουράν, ἀπομιμούμενος οὐ τὸ σχῆμα τῆς γῆς ὡς Ἑστίας οὔσης, ἀλλὰ τοῦ σύμπαντος κόσμου, οὗ μέσον οἱ Πυθαγορικοὶ τὸ πῦρ ἱδρῦσθαι νομίζουσι, καὶ τοῦτο Ἑστίαν καλοῦσι καὶ μονάδα· τὴν δὲ γῆν οὔτε ἀκίνητον οὔτε ἐν μέσῳ τῆς περιφορᾶς οὖσαν, ἀλλὰ κύκλῳ περὶ τὸ πῦρ αἰωρουμένην οὐ τῶν τιμιωτάτων οὐδὲ τῶν πρώτων τοῦ κόσμου μορίων ὑπάρχειν. ταῦτα δὲ καὶ Πλάτωνά φασι πρεσβύτην γενόμενον διανενοῆσθαι περὶ τῆς γῆς ὡς ἐν ἑτέρᾳ χώρᾳ καθεστώσης, τὴν δὲ μέσην καὶ κυριωτάτην ἑτέρῳ τινὶ κρείττονι προσήκουσαν.

Plutarch *Publius* 8.8

ρίον ὁμοροῦν ἐκείνῳ Ταρκυνίας ἀνείσης. ἡ δὲ Ταρκυνία παρθένος ἦν ἱέρεια, μία τῶν Ἑστιάδων, ἔσχε δὲ τιμὰς ἀντὶ τούτου μεγάλας, ἐν αἷς ἦν καὶ τὸ μαρτυρίαν αὐτῆς δέχεσθαι μόνης γυναικῶν· τὸ δ᾽ ἐξεῖναι γαμεῖσθαι ψηφισαμένων οὐ προσεδέξατο. καὶ ταῦτα μὲν οὕτω γενέσθαι μυθολογοῦσι.

Plutarch *Romulus* 3.3–4

Τοῦ δὲ πίστιν ἔχοντος λόγου μάλιστα καὶ πλείστους μάρτυρας τὰ μὲν κυριώτατα πρῶτος εἰς τοὺς Ἕλληνας ἐξέδωκε Διοκλῆς Πεπαρήθιο, ᾧ καὶ Φάβιος ὁ Πίκτωρ ἐν τοῖς πλείστοις ἐπηκολούθηκε. γεγόνασι δὲ καὶ περὶ τούτων ἕτεραι διαφοραί τύπῳ δ' εἰπεῖν τοιοῦτός ἐστι. τῶν ἀπ' Αἰνείου γεγονότων ἐν Ἄλβῃ βασιλέων εἰς ἀδελφοὺς δύο, Νομήτορα καὶ Ἀμούλιον, ἡ διαδοχὴ καθῆκεν. Ἀμουλίου δὲ νείμαντος τὰ πάντα δίχα, τῇ δὲ βασιλείᾳ τὰ χρήματα καὶ τὸν ἐκ Τροίας κομισθέντα χρυσὸν ἀντιθέντος, εἵλετο τὴν βασι λείαν ὁ Νομήτωρ. ἔχων οὖν ὁ Ἀμούλιος τὰ χρήματα καὶ πλέον ἀπ' αὐτῶν δυνάμενος τοῦ Νομήτορος, τήν τε βασιλείαν ἀφείλετο ῥᾳδίως, καὶ φοβούμενος ἐκ τῆς θυγατρὸς αὐτοῦ γενέσθαι παῖδας, ἱέρειαν τῆς Ἑστίας ἀπέδειξεν, ἄγαμον καὶ παρθένον ἀεὶ βιωσομένην. ταύτην οἱ μὲν Ἰλίαν, οἱ δὲ Ῥέαν, οἱ δὲ Σιλουίαν ὀνομάζουσι. φωρᾶται δὲ μετ' οὐ πολὺν χρόνον κυοῦσα παρὰ τὸν καθεστῶτα ταῖς Ἑστιάσι νόμον, καὶ τὸ μὲν ἀνήκεστα μὴ παθεῖν αὐτὴν ἡ τοῦ βασιλέως θυγάτηρ Ἀνθὼ παρῃτήσατο, δεηθεῖσα τοῦ πατρός, εἵρχθη δὲ καὶ δίαιταν εἶχεν ἀνεπίμεικτον, ὅπως μὴ λάθοι τεκοῦσα τὸν Ἀμούλιον. ἔτεκε δὲ δύο παῖδας ὑπερφυεῖς μεγέθει καὶ κάλλει. δι' ὃ καὶ μᾶλλον ὁ Ἀμούλιος φοβηθείς, ἐκέλευσεν αὐτοὺς ὑπηρέτην λαβόντα ῥῖψαι. τοῦτον ἔνιοι Φαιστύλον ὀνομάζεσθαι λέγουσιν, οἱ δ' οὐ τοῦτον, ἀλλὰ τὸν ἀνελόμενον. ἐνθέμενος σιν, οἱ δ' οὐ τοῦτον, ἀλλὰ τὸν ἀνελόμενον. ἐνθέμενος οὖν εἰς σκάφην τὰ βρέφη, κατέβη μὲν ἐπὶ τὸν ποταμὸν ὡς ῥίψων, ἰδὼν δὲ κατιόντα πολλῷ ῥεύματι καὶ τραχυνόμενον, ἔδεισε προσελθεῖν, ἐγγὺς δὲ τῆς ὄχθης καταθεὶς ἀπηλλάσσετο. τοῦ δὲ ποταμοῦ κατακλύζοντος ἡ πλημμύρα τὴν σκάφην ὑπολαβοῦσα καὶ μετεωρίσασα πράως κατήνεγκεν εἰς χωρίον ἐπιεικῶς μαλθακόν, ὃ νῦν Κερμαλὸν καλοῦσι, πάλαι δὲ Γερμανόν, ὡς ἔοικεν ὅτι καὶ τοὺς ἀδελφοὺς γερμανοὺς ὀνομάζουσιν.

⁵Ἦν δὲ πλησίον ἐρινεός, ὃν Ῥωμινάλιον ἐκάλουν, ἢδιὰ τὸν Ῥωμύλον ὡς οἱ πολλοὶ νομίζουσιν, ἢ διὰ τὸ τὰ μηρυκώμενα τῶν θρεμμάτων ἐκεῖ διὰ τὴν σκιὰν ἐνδιάζειν, ἢ μάλιστα διὰ τὸν τῶν βρεφῶν θηλασμόν, ὅτι τήν τε θηλὴν ῥοῦμαν ὠνόμαζον οἱ παλαιοί, καὶ θεόν τινα τῆς ἐκτροφῆς τῶν νηπίων ἐπιμελεῖσθαι δοκοῦσαν ὀνομάζουσι Ῥουμίναν, καὶ θύουσιν αὐτῇ νηφάλια, καὶ γάλα τοῖς ἱεροῖς ἐπισπένδουσιν. ἐνταῦθα δὴ τοῖς βρέφεσι κειμένοις τήν τε λύκαιναν ἱστοροῦσι θηλαζομένην καὶ δρυοκολάπτην τινὰ παρεῖναι συνεκτρέφοντα καὶ φυλάττοντα. νομίζεται δ' Ἄρεως ἱερὰ τὰ ζῷα, τὸν δὲ δρυοκολάπτην καὶ διαφερόντως Λατῖνοι σέβονται καὶ τιμῶσιν· ὅθεν οὐχ ἥκιστα πίστιν ἔσχεν ἡ τεκοῦσα τὰ βρέφη τεκεῖν ἐξ Ἄρεως φάσκουσα. καίτοι τοῦτο παθεῖν αὐτὴν ἐξαπατηθεῖσαν λέγουσιν, ὑπὸ τοῦ Ἀμουλίου διαπαρθενευθεῖσαν, ἐν ὅπλοις ἐπιφανέντος αὐτῇ καὶ συναρπάσαντος. οἱ δὲ τοὔνομα τῆς τροφοῦ δι' ἀμφιβολίαν ἐπὶ τὸ μυθῶδες ἐκτροπὴν τῇ φήμῃ παρασχεῖν· λούπας γὰρ ἐκάλουν οἱ Λατῖνοι τῶν τε θηρίων τὰς λυκαίνας καὶ τῶν γυναικῶν τὰς ἑταιρούσας· εἶναι δὲ τοιαύτην τὴν Φαιστύλου γυναῖκα τοῦ τὰ βρέφη θρέψαντος, Ἄκκαν Λαρεντίαν ὄνομα. ταύτῃ δὲ καὶ θύουσι θρέψαντος, Ἄκκαν Λαρεντίαν ὄνομα. ταύτῃ δὲ καὶ θύουσι Ῥωμαῖοι,

καὶ χοὰς ἐπιφέρει τοῦ ᾿Απριλίου μηνὸς αὐτῇ ὁ τοῦ ῎Αρεως ἱερεύς, καὶ Λαρεντάλίαν καλοῦσι τὴν ἑορτήν.

Propertius 4.1.21–22

Vesta coronatis pauper gaudebat asellis,
ducebant macrae uilia sacra boues.

Propertius 4.4.69

nam Vesta, Iliacae felix tutela fauillae.

Propertius 4.11.53–54

uel cuius rasos cum Vesta reposceret ignis,
exhibuit uiuos carbasus alba focos.

Sallust *Catilina* 15.1

Iam primum adulescens Catilina multa nefanda stupra fecerat, cum virgine nobili, cum sacerdote Vestae, alia huiusce modi contra ius fasque.

Servius *in Aeneidas* 7.150

HAEC FONTIS STAGNA NUMICI ista iam ab incolis discuntur. Quod autem ait 'stagna' verum est: nam Numicus ingens ante fluvius fuit, in quo repertum est cadaver Aeneae et consecratum. Post paulatim decrescens in fontem redactus est, qui et ipse siccatus est sacris interceptus: Vestae enim libari non nisi de hoc fluvio licebat.

Servius *in Aeneidas* 339

NON FUTILLIS AUCTOR non inanis: nam futtile vas quodam est lato ore, fundo angusto, quo utebantur in sacris Vestae, quia aqua ad sacra *Vestae* hausta in terra non ponitur, quod si fiat, piaculum est: unde excogitatum vas est, quod stare non posset, sed positum statim effunderetur.

Servius *in Aeneidas* 4.57

. . . olim enim hostiae "immolatae" dicebantur **mola salsa** tacta...

Servius *in Aeneidas* 10.228

VIGILASNE DEUM GENS AENEA VIGILA verba sunt sacrorum; nam virgines Vestae certa die ibant ad regem sacrorum et dicebant "vigilasne rex? vigila."

Servius *in Aeneidas* 11.206

finitimos tollunt in agros qui enim e longinquo venerant, referri non poterant. **urbique** remittunt deest 'unicuique'. et meminit antiquae consuetudinis: nam ante etiam in civitatibus sepeliebantur, quod postea Duellio consule senatus prohibuit et lege cavit, ne quis in urbe sepeliretur: unde imperatores et virgines Vestae quia legibus non tenentur, in civitate habent sepulchra. denique etiam nocentes virgines Vestae, *quia* legibus non tenentur, licet vivae, tamen intra urbem in campo scelerato obruebantur.

Servius *in Vergilis Eclogae* 8.82

Virgines Vestales tres maximae ex nonis Maiis ad pridie idus Maias alternis diebus spicas adoreas in corbibus messuariis ponunt easque spicas ipsae virgines torrent, pinsunt, molunt atque ita molitum condunt. Ex eo farre virgines ter in anno molam faciunt, Lupercalibus, Vestalibus, idibus septembribus, adiecto sale cocto et sale duro.

Suetonius *Augustus* 44.3

solis virginibus Vestalibus locum in theatro separatim et contra praetoris tribunal dedit.

Suetonius *Augustus* 101

Post quae rettulit Caesar capiendam virginem in locum Occiae, quae septem et quinquaginta per annos summa sanctimonia Vestalibus sacris praesederat; egitque grates Fonteio Agrippae et Domitio Pollioni quod offerendo filias de officio in rem publicam certarent. praelata est Pollionis filia, non ob aliud quam quod mater eius in eodem coniugio manebat; nam Agrippa discidio domum imminuerat. et Caesar quamvis posthabitam decies sestertii dote solatus est.

Suetonius *Domitian* 8.3

incesta Vestalium virginum, a patre quoque suo et fratre neglecta, varie ac severe coercuit, priora capitali supplicio, posteriora more veteri. Nam cum Oculatis sororibus, item Varronillae liberum mortis permisisset arbitrium corruptoresque earum relegasset, mox Corneliam maximam virginem, absolutam olim, dein longo intervallo repetitam atque convictam defodi imperavit, stupratoresque virgis in comitio ad necem caedi, excepto praetorio viro; cui, dubia etiam tum causa et incertis quaestionibus atque tormentis de semet professo, exilium indulsit.

Suetonius *Iulius* 2.6

Corneliam Cinnae quater consulis filiam duxit uxorem . . . neque ut repudiaret compelli a dictatore Sulla ullo modo potuit. Quare et sacerdotio et uxoris dote et gentilicis hereditatibus multatus diversarum partium habebatur, ut etiam discedere e medio et quamquam morbo quartanae adgravante prope per singulas noctes commutare latebras cogeretur seque ab inquisitoribus pecunia redimeret, donec per virgines Vestales perque Mamercum Aemilium et Aurelium Cottam propinquos et adfines suos veniam impetravit. Satis constat Sullam, cum deprecantibus amicissimis et ornatissimis viris aliquamdiu denegasset atque illi pertinaciter contenderent, expugnatum tandem proclamasse sive divinitus sive aliqua coniectura: "vincerent ac sibi haberent, dum modo scirent eum, quem incolumem tanto opere cuperent, quandoque optimatium partibus, quas secum simul defendissent, exitio futurum; nam Caesari multos Mario inesse.

Suetonius *Iulius* 83

Postulante ergo Lucio Pisone socero testamentum eius aperitur recitaturque in Antoni domo, quod Idibus Septembribus proximis in Lauicano suo fecerat demandaueratque uirgini Vestali maximae.

Suetonius *Nero* 12.4

Ad athletarum spectaculum invitavit et virgines Vestales, quia Olympiae quoque Cereris sacerdotibus spectare conceditur.

Suetonius *Nero* 28.1

Super ingenuorum paedagogia et nuptarum concubinatus Vestali virgini Rubriae vim intulit.

Suetonius *Tiberius* 2

Etiam virgo Vestalis fratrem iniussu populi triumphantem ascenso simul curru usque in Capitolium prosecuta est, ne vetare aut intercedere fas cuiquam tribunorum esset.

Suetonius *Tiberius* 76

Postulante ergo Lucio Pisone socero testamentum eius aperitur recitaturque in Antoni domo, quod Idibus Septembribus proximis in Lauicano suo fecerat demandaueratque uirgini Vestali maximae.

Tacitus *Annales* 1.8

... Augusti, cuius testamentum inlatum per Virgines Vestae Tiberium et Liviam heredes habuit.

Tacitus *Annales* 2.34

ceterum Vrgulaniae potentia adeo nimia civitati erat ut testis in causa quadam, quae apud senatum tractabatur, venire dedignaretur: missus est praetor qui domi interrogaret, cum virgines Vestales in foro et iudicio audiri, quotiens testimonium dicerent, vetus mos fuerit.

Tacitus *Annales* 2.86

Post quae rettulit Caesar capiendam virginem in locum Occiae, quae septem et quinquaginta per annos summa sanctimonia Vestalibus sacris praesederat; egitque grates Fonteio Agrippae et Domitio Pollioni quod offerendo filias de officio in rem publicam certarent. praelata est Pollionis filia, non ob aliud quam quod mater eius in eodem coniugio manebat; nam Agrippa discidio domum imminuerat. et Caesar quamvis posthabitam decies sestertii dote solatus est.

Tacitus *Annales* 4.16

utque glisceret dignatio sacerdotum atque ipsis promptior animus foret ad capessendas caerimonias decretum Corneliae virgini, quae in locum Scantiae capiebatur, sestertium viciens, et quotiens Augusta theatrum introisset ut sedes inter Vestalium consideret.

Tacitus *Annales* 11.32

... et Vibidiam, virginum Vestalium vetustissimam, oravit pontificis maximi auris adire, clementiam expetere.

Tacitus Annales 15.22

defunctaque virgo Vestalis Laelia, in cuius locum Cornelia ex familia Cossorum capta est.

Tacitus *Historiae* 3.81

obviae fuere et virgines Vestales cum epistulis Vitellii ad Antonium scriptis: eximi supremo certamini unum diem postulabat: si moram interiecissent, facilius omnia conventura. virgines cum honore dimissae; Vitellio rescriptum Sabini caede et incendio Capitolii dirempta belli commercia.

Tacitus *Historiae* 4.53

[Vespasian] Curam restituendi Capitolii in Lucium Vestinum confert, equestris ordinis virum, sed auctoritate famaque inter proceres. ab eo contracti haruspices monuere ut reliquiae prioris delubri in paludes aveherentur, templum isdem vestigiis sisteretur: nolle deos mutari veterem formam. XI kalendas Iulias serena luce spatium omne quod templo dicabatur evinctum vittis coronisque; ingressi milites, quis fausta nomina, felicibus ramis; dein virgines Vestales cum pueris puellisque patrimis matrimisque aqua e fontibus amnibusque hausta perluere.

Tertullian *De Spectaculiss* 5.7

Et nunc ara Conso illi in circo defossa est ad primas metas sub terra cum inscriptione huiusmodi: CONSUS CONSILIO MARS DUELLO LARES COILLO POTENTES. Sacrificant apud eam nonis Iuliis sacerdotes publici, XII kalend. Septembres Flamen Quirinalis et virgines.

Valerius Maximus 1.1.6–7

Adiciendum his quod P. Licinio pontifici maximo uirgo Vestalis, quia quadam nocte parum diligens ignis aeterni custos fuisset, digna uisa est quae flagro admoneretur. Maximae uero uirginis Aemiliae discipulam extincto igne tutam ab omni reprehensione Vestae numen praestitit. qua adorante, cum carbasum, quem optimum habebat, foculo inposuisset, subito ignis emicuit.

Valerius Maximus 1.1.10

Quod animi iudicium in priuatorum quoque pectoribus uersatum est: urbe enim a Gallis capta, cum flamen Quirinalis uirginesque Vestales sacra onere partito ferrent, easque pontem sublicium transgressas et cliuum, qui ducit ad Ianiculum, ascendere incipientes L. Albanius plaustro coniugem et liberos uehens aspexisset, propior publicae religioni quam priuatae caritati suis ut plaustro descenderent inperauit atque in id uirgines et sacra inposita omisso coepto itinere Caere oppidum peruexit, ubi cum summa ueneratione recepta. grata memoria ad hoc usque tempus hospitalem humanitatem testatur: inde enim institutum est sacra caerimonias uocari, quia Caeretani ea infracto rei publicae statu perinde ac florente sancte coluerunt. quorum agreste illud et sordidius plaustrum tempestiue capax cuiuslibet fulgentissimi triumphalis currus uel aequauerit gloriam uel antecesserit.

Valerius Maximus 4.4.11

namque per Romuli casam perque ueteris Capitolii humilia tecta et aeternos Vestae focos fictilibus etiam nunc uasis contentos iuro nullas diuitias talium uirorum paupertati posse praeferri.

Valerius Maximus 5.4.6

Magna sunt haec virilis pietatis opera, sed nescio an his omnibus valentius et animosius Claudiae Vestalis virginis factum. quae, cum patrem suum triumphantem e curru violenta tribuni *pl.* manu *detrahi* animadvertisset, mira celeritate utrisque se interponendo amplissimam potestatem inimicitiis accensam depulit. igitur alterum triumphum pater in Capitolium alterum filia in aedem Vestae duxit, nec discerni potuit utri plus laudis tribueretur, cui victoria an cui pietas comes aderat.

Valerius Maximus 6.1. ext. 3

Post quae rettulit Caesar capiendam virginem in locum Occiae, quae septem et quinquaginta per annos summa sanctimonia Vestalibus sacris praesederat; egitque grates Fonteio Agrippae et Domitio Pollioni quod offerendo filias de officio in rem publicam certarent. praelata est Pollionis filia, non ob aliud quam quod mater eius in eodem coniugio manebat; nam Agrippa discidio domum imminuerat. et Caesar quamvis posthabitam decies sestertii dote solatus est.

Valerius Maximus 8.1.abs.5

Eodem auxilii genere Tucciae uirginis Vestalis incesti criminis reae castitas infamiae nube obscurata emersit. quae conscientia certa sinceritatis suae spem salutis ancipiti argumento ausa petere est: arrepto enim cribro "Vesta" inquit, "si sacris tuis castas semper admoui manus, effice ut hoc hauriam e Tiberi aquam et in aedem tuam perferam." audaciter et temere iactis uotis sacerdotis rerum ipsa natura cessit.

Varro *Linguae Latinae* 6.21

Opsconsiva dies ab dea Ops Consiva, cuius in Regia sacrarium quod adeo artum, ut eo praeter virgines Vestales et sacerdotem publicum introeat nemo. "Is cum eat, suffibulum ut habeat," scriptum: id dicitur ut ab suffi<g>endo subfigabulum.

Varro *Linguae Latinae* 6.32

Dies qui vocatur, "Quando stercum delatum fas" ab eo appellatus, quod eo die ex Aede Vestae stercus everritur et per Capitolium Clivum in locum defertur certum.

Vergil *Aeneid* 2.296–297

sic ait et manibus uittas Vestamque potentem
aeternumque adytis effert penetralibus ignem.

Vergil *Aeneid* 2.567–70

Iamque adeo super unus eram, cum limina Vestae
seruantem et tacitam secreta in sede latentem
Tyndarida aspicio; dant claram incendia lucem
erranti passimque oculos per cuncta ferenti.

Appendix B

List of known Vestals in chronological order

Rhea Silvia *c.* 770 BCE (legendary)
Pinaria *c.* 600 BCE (legendary)
Oppia immolated 483 BCE
Postumia acquitted of *incestum* in 420 BCE
Minucia immolated 337 BCE
Tuccia third century BCE
Sextilia immolated 274 BCE
Caparronia immolated 266 BCE
Opimia immolated 216 BCE
Floronia immolated 216 BCE
Aemilia served as Vestal from *c.* 210 – post 178 BCE
Claudia post 143 BCE
Aemilia served as Vestal from *c.* 140–114 BCE
Licinia C. f. served as Vestal from *c.* 140–113 BCE
Marcia immolated 113 BCE
Popillia served as Vestal from *c.* 100–70 BCE
Perpennia served as Vestal from *c.* 100–70 BCE
Licinia served as Vestal from pre 73 to post 63 BCE.
Fabia served as Vestal from 73 to pre 58 BCE
Arruntia served as Vestal post 70 BCE
Fonteia served as Vestal pre 69 BCE
Scantia served as Vestal from *c.* 40 BCE – CE 23
Occia served as Vestal from *c.* 40 BCE – CE 19
Valeria served as Vestal some time in the first century CE
Lepida served as Vestal in the first half of the first century CE
Domitia Pollionis f. served as Vestal from *c.* 10 – post 19 CE
Cornelia served as Vestal some time post 23 CE
Aurelia Q. Aurelii Filia served as Vestal some time post 30 CE
Vibidia served as Vestal some time pre 48 CE
Iunia C. Silani f. Torquata served as Vestal some time post 48 CE
Cornelia served as Vestal from *c.* 50 – 91 CE
Rubria 54 CE
Laelia 62 CE

Varronilla served as Vestal some time from *c.* 10 – 83 CE
Aelia Oculata 83 CE
Licinia Praetextata Crassi f. post 92 CE
Iunia 107 CE
Octavia Honorata served as Vestal in the third century CE
Bellicia Modesta served as Vestal in the third century CE
Calpurnia Praetextata served as Vestal in the third century CE
Teia Euphrosyne Ruffina *c.* 200 CE
Vettenia Sabinilla 200 CE
Numisia L. f. served as Vestal post 204 CE
Clodia Laeta *c.* 213 CE
Pomponia Rufina 213 CE
Aurelia Severa post 213 CE
Cannutia Crescentina post 213 CE
Flavia L. f. Publicia post 213 CE
Terentia Flavola post 215 CE
Aquilia Severa 218 CE
Campia Severina post 240 CE
Flavia Mamilia post 240 CE
Terentia Rufilla served as Vestal 250 – 301 CE
Claudia post 364 CE
Coelia Concordia post 385 CE

Vestals of unknown date

Sossia Maxima
Coelia Claudiana

Bibliography

Adkins, L. and Adkins, R. A. (1996) *Dictionary of Roman Religion*. New York: Facts on File.

Ampolo, C. (1988) 'La nascità della città', in *Storia di Roma I: Roma in Italia*. Turin: Einaudi.

Assis de Rojo, M. E. (1998) 'La matrona romana', *Argos*, 22: 11–25.

Auer, H. (1888) 'Das Haus der Vestalinnen am Forum Romanum', in *Denkschriften der kaiserlichen Akademie der Wissenschaften im Wien*, 36(2): 3.

Bailey, C. P. (1921) *Ovidi Nasonis Fastorum Liber III*. Oxford: Clarendon Press.

Bailey, D. R. Shackleton (1965–1970) *Cicero's Letters to Atticus*, 7 vols. Cambridge: Cambridge University Press.

Baldwin, B. (1978) 'Festus the historian', *Historia*, 27: 197–217.

Balsdon, J. P. V. D. (1962) *Roman Women: Their History and Habits*. London: Bodley Head.

Balsdon, J. P. V. D. (1966) 'Fabula Clodiana', *Historia*, 15: 65–73.

Bartoli, A. (1959) 'I pozzi nell'area sacra di Vesta', *MonAnt*, 45: 2–143.

Baudy, D. (2001) 'Der dumme Teil des Volkes (Ov, Fast. 2, 531)', *MH*, 58: 32–39.

Baudy, G. J. (1995) 'Cereal diet and the origins of man', in J. Wilkins, D. Harvey and M. Dobson (eds) *Food in Antiquity*. Exeter: Exeter University Press.

Bauman, R. A. (1992) *Women and Politics in Ancient Rome*. London: Routledge.

Bauman, R. A. (1994) 'Tanaquil-Livia and the death of Augustus', *Historia*, 43: 177–188.

Bayet, J. (1971) *Croyances et rites dans la Rome antique*. Paris: Payot.

Beard, M. (1980) 'The sexual status of Vestal Virgins', *JRS*, 70: 12–27.

Beard, M. (1987) 'A complex of times: no more sheep on Romulus' birthday', *PCPS*, 213: 1–15.

Beard, M. (1988a) 'Rituel, texte, temps, les Parilia romains', in A. M. Blondeau and K. Schipper (eds) *Essais sur le rituel*. Paris: Bibliothèque de l'Ecole des hautes études.

Beard, M. (1988b) 'Roman priesthoods', in M. Grant and R. Kitzinger (eds) *Civilizations of the Ancient Mediterranean. Greece and Rome*, vol. 2. London: Scribner's.

Beard, M. (1995) 'Re-reading (Vestal) virginity', in R. Hawley and B. Levick (eds) *Women in Antiquity: New Assessments*. London: Routledge.

Beard, M. and North, J. (1990) *Pagan Priests*. Ithaca, NY: Cornell University Press.

Beard, M., North, J. and Price, S. (1998) *Religions of Rome*, 2 vols. Cambridge: Cambridge University Press.

Bernstein, F. (1997) 'Verständnis-und Entwicklungsstufen der archaischen Consualia', *Hermes*, 125(4): 413–446.

Bettini, M. (1992) *Familie und Verwandtschaft im antiken Rom*. Frankfurt am Main: Peter Lang.

Blanck, H. (1997) 'Die instita der Matronenstola', in *Festschrift T. Lorenz*. Vienna: Phoebus.

Bloch, H. (1936) 'I bolli laterizi e la storia edilizia romana', *BullCom*, 64: 141–225.

Bodeüs, R. (1983) 'Par delà les spéculations sur la déesse Vesta', *LEC*, 51: 233–239.

Boldrini, S. (1995) 'Verginità delle vestali: la prova', in *Vicende e figure femminili*. Ancona: Commissione per le pari opportunità tra uomo e donna della Regione Marche.

Bömer, F. (1957) *Ovidius Naso Die Fasten*, 2 vols. Heidelberg: C. Winter.

Bömer, F. (1987) 'Wie ist Augustus mit Vesta verwandt? Zu Ovid fast. III, 425 f. und IV, 949f.', *Gymnasium*, 94: 525–528.

Bomgardner, D. L. (2000) *The Story of the Roman Amphitheatre*. London: Routledge.

Boni, G. (1900) 'Il sacrario di Vesta', *NSc.*, 172–183.

Boren, H. C. (1983) 'Studies relating to the stipendium militum', *Historia*, 32: 427–460.

Bradley, K. R. (1978) *Suetonius' Life of Nero*. Brussels: Latomus.

Brauer, G. C. (1975) 'Vestal types on Roman coins', *San.*, 7: 24–27.

Braun, T. (1995) 'Barley cakes and emmer bread', in J. Wilkins, D. Harvey and M. Dobson (eds) *Food in Antiquity*. Exeter: Exeter University Press.

Brelich, A. (1949) *Vesta*. Zurich: Rhein-Verlag.

Brind'amour, P. (1983) *Le Calendrier romain*. Ottawa, Ont.: Editions de l'Université d'Ottawa.

Briscoe, J. (1973) *A Commentary on Livy Books XXXI–XXXIII*. Oxford: Clarendon Press.

Briscoe, J. (1981) *A Commentary on Livy Books XXXIV–XXXVII*. Oxford: Clarendon Press.

Brothwell, D. R. and Brothwell, P. (1969) *Food in Antiquity: A Survey of the Diet of Early Peoples*. London: Thames & Hudson.

Broughton, T. R. S. (1951–1956) *The Magistrates of the Roman Republic*, 3 vols. New York: American Philological Association.

Brouwer, H. H. J. (1989) *Bona Dea: The Sources and a Description of the Cult*. Leiden, The Netherlands: E. J. Brill.

Brouwers, A. (1933) 'A progos de la formule de la "captio" des Vestales', *Rev. Belge de phil. et hist.* 12: 1080 ff.

Butrica, J. L. (2000) 'Propertius on the Parilia (4.4.73-8)', *CQ*, NS 50(2): 472–478.

Cameron, A. and Kuhrt, E. (eds) (1983) *Images of Women in Antiquity*. Detroit, IL: Wayne State University Press.

Campbell, B. (2000) *The Writings of the Roman Land Surveyors: Introduction, Text, Translation and Commentary*. London: Society for the Promotion of Roman Studies.

Camps, W. A. (1965) *Propertius Elegies, Book IV*. New York: Arno Press.

Cancik, H. and Schneider, H. (eds) (1997–2004) *Der neue Pauly*. Stuttgart, Germany: J. B. Metzler.

Cancik-Lindemaier, H. (1990) 'Kultische Privilegierung und gesellschaftliche Realität: Ein Beitrag zur Sozialgeschichte der uirgines Vestae', *Saeculum*, 41: 1–16.

Cantarella, E. (1987) *Pandora's Daughters*, M. Fant (trans.). Baltimore, MD: Johns Hopkins University Press.

Capdeville, G. (1993a) 'Jeux athlétiques et rituels de fondation', in *Spectacles sportifs et scéniques*. Rome: Ecole française de Rome.

Capdeville, G. (1993b) 'Les institutions religieuses de la Rome primitive d'après Denys d'Halicarnasse', *Pallas*, 39: 153–172.

Cardauns, B. (1976) *M. Terentius Varro: Antiquitates rerum divinarum*. Mainz: Akademie der Wissenschaften und der Literatur.

Carettoni, G. (1978–1980) 'La Domus Virginum Vestalium e la Domus Publica del periodo repubblicano', *RendPontAcc*, 51–52: 325–355.

Cecamore, C. (1994–1995) 'Apollo e Vesta sul Palatino fra Augusto e Vespasiano', *BCAR*, 96: 9–32.

Chaplin, J. D. (2000) *Livy's Exemplary History*. Oxford: Oxford University Press.

Christman, E. (1999) 'Überlegungen zu Entwicklungen im Vesta-kult', in W. Schubert (ed.) *Ovid: Werk und Wirkung*. Frankfurt am Main: Peter Lang.

Clark, G. (1989) *Women in the Ancient World*. Oxford: Oxford University Press.

Cohen, D. (1992) 'The Augustan law on adultery: the social and cultural context', in D. L. Kertzer and R. P. Saller (eds) *The Family in Italy from Antiquity to the Present*. New Haven, CT: Yale University Press.

Colonna, G. (1980) 'Appendice: Le iscrizioni strumentali latine del 6 e 5 secolo a.Cr', in C. Stibbe, G. Colonna, C. De Simone and H. R. Versnel (eds) *Lapis Satricanus: Archaeological, Epigraphical, Linguistic and Historical Aspects of the New Inscription from Satricum*. Gravenhage: Ministerie van Cultur, Recreatie en Maatschappelijk Werk.

Cornell, T. J. (1981) 'Some observations on the crimen incesti', in M. Torelli (ed.) *Le Délit religieux dans la cité antique*. Rome: Ecole française de Rome.

Cornell, T. J. (1995) *The Beginnings of Rome: Italy and Rome from the Bronze Age to the Punic Wars, c. 1000–264 BC*. London: Routledge.

Craik, E. (ed.) (1984) *Marriage and Property*. Aberdeen: Aberdeen University Press.

Crook, J. (1967a) 'Patria potestas', *CQ*, 17: 113–122.

Crook, J. (1967b) *Law and Life of Rome*. Ithaca, NY: Cornell University Press.

Crook, J. (1973) 'Intestacy in Roman society', *PCPS*, 199: 38–44.

Crook, J. (1989) 'A negative point about Mark Antony's will', *AC*, 58: 221–223.

Cubberley, A. (1995) 'Bread-baking in ancient Italy', in J. Wilkins, D. Harvey and M. Dobson (eds) *Food in Antiquity*. Exeter: Exeter University Press.

Curtis, R. (1991) *Garum and Salsamenta*. Leiden: E. J. Brill.

Daremberg, C. and Saglio, E. (eds) (1877 on) *Dictionnaire des Antiquités Grecques et Romains*. Graz, Austria: Akademische Druck- u. Verlagsanstalt.

Davies, J. P. (2004) *Rome's Religious History: Livy, Tacitus and Ammianus and their Gods*. Cambridge: Cambridge University Press.

De Cazanove, O. (1987) 'exesto. L'incapacité sacrificielle des femmes a Rome', *Phoenix*, 41: 159–173.

De Grassi, A. (1955) 'Esistette sul palatino un tempio di Vesta?' *RM*, 62: 144–54.

De Grassi, A. (1963) *Epigraphica I*. Rome.

De Grassi, A. (1965) *Inscriptiones Latinae Liberae Rei Publicae*, 2nd edn. Berlin: Gruyter.

Dessau, H. (1892–1916) *Inscriptiones Latinae Selectae*, 3 vols. Berlin.

De Witt, N. W. (1960) 'Vesta unveiled', in *Studies in Honor of Ullman*. St Louis, MO: St Louis University, Classical Bulletin.

Dixon, S. (1988) *The Roman Mother*. Norman, OK: University of Oklahoma Press.

Dixon, S. (1991) 'The sentimental ideal of the Roman family', in B. Rawson (ed.) *Marriage, Divorce, and Children in Ancient Rome*. Oxford: Clarendon Press.

Dixon, S. (1992) *The Roman Family*. Baltimore, MD: Johns Hopkins University Press.

Douglas, M. (1966) *Purity and Danger*. London: Routledge & Kegan Paul.

Dragendorff, H. (1896) 'Die Amtstracht der Vestalinnen', *RM*, 51: 281–302.

Düll, R. (1953) 'Privatrechtsprobleme im Bereich der virgo Vestalis', *Zeitschrift der Savigny-Stiftung for Rechtsgeschichte Romanistische Abteilung*, 70: 380–390.

Dumézil, G. (1954) *Aedes Rotundae Vestae*, in *Rituels indo-européens a Rome*. Paris: Librairie C. Klincksieck.

Dumézil, G. (1959) 'QII 7, Trois regles de l'aedes Vestae', *Revue des etudes*, 37: 94–102.

Dumézil, G. (1963) 'QII 18, Te, amata, capio', *REL*, 41: 89–91.

Dumézil, G. (1970) *Archaic Roman Religion*. Chicago, IL: University of Chicago Press.

Eitrem, S. (1915) *Opferritus und Voropfer der Griechen und Römer*. Kristiania: In kommission bei J. Dybwad.

Eliade, M. (1984) *The History of Religions*. London: Macmillan.

Euing, L. (1933) *Die sage von Tanaquil*. Frankfurt am Main: V. Klostermann.

Evans, J. D. (1992) *The Art of Persuasion: Political Propaganda from Aeneas to Brutus*. Ann Arbor, MI: University of Michigan Press.

Evans, J. K. (1991) *War, Women and Children in Ancient Rome*. London: Routledge.

Fantham, E. (1983) 'Sexual comedy in Ovid's *Fasti*: sources and motivations', *HSCPh*, 87: 185–216.

Fantham, E. (1998) *Fasti: Book IV*. Cambridge: Cambridge University Press.

Fauth, W. (1978) 'Römische Religion im Spiegel der "Fasti" des Ovid', *ANRW*, 2.16.1: 104–186.

Fehrle, E. (1910) *Die kultische Keuschkeit im Altertum*. Naumburg a.S.: Druck von Lippert.

Feichtinger, B. (1993) 'Casta matrona-puella fallax', *SO*, 68: 40–68.

Fishwick, D. (1992) 'A temple of Vesta on the Palatine?', in *Mélanges T. Kotula*. Atlanta, GA: Scholars Press.

Flint-Hamilton, K. B. (1999) 'Legumes in ancient Greece and Rome', *Hesperia*, 68(3): 371–385.

Flory, M. B. (1984) '*Sic exempla parantur*: Livia's shrine to *Concordia* and the *Porticus Liviae*', *Historia*, 33: 309–330.

Flower, H. (2000) 'The tradition of the Spolia Opima: M. Claudius Marcellus and Augustus', *Classical Antiquity*, 19(1): 34–64.

Foley, H. P. (ed.) (1982) *Reflections of Women in Antiquity*. New York: Gordon & Breach.

Foucault, M. (1996) *The History of Sexuality. Volume I: An Introduction*. New York: Vintage.

Fox, M. (1996) *Roman Historical Myths: The Regal Period in Augustan Literature*. Oxford: Clarendon Press.

Foxhall, L. and Forbes, H. A. (1982) 'The role of grain as a staple food in classical antiquity', *Chiron*, 12: 41–90.

Fraschetti, A. (1981) 'Le sepolture rituali del Foro Boario', *CEFR*, 48: 51–116.

Fraschetti, A. (1984) 'Le sepoltura delle vestali e la citta', *CEFR*, 79: 97–129.

Fraschetti, A. (1988) 'Cognata numina. Culti della città e culti della casa del principe in epoca augustea', *StudStor*, 29: 941–996.

Fraschetti, A. (1999) 'Augusto e Vesta sul Palatino', *ARG*, 1(2): 174–183.

Frazel, T. D. (2003) 'Priapus's two rapes in Ovid's "Fasti"', *Arethusa*, 36: 61–97.

Frazer, J. G. (1931) *Publii Ovidi Nasonis Fastorum Liber Sex*, 5 vols. London: Heinemann.

Frazer, J. G. (1958 [1927]) *The Golden Bough*. New York: Macmillan.

Frei-Stolba, R. (1998) 'Flavia Publica, virgo Vestalis maxima. Zu den Inschriften des Atrium Vesta', in P. Kneissl and V. Losemann (eds) *Imperium Romanum. Studien zu Geschichte und Rezeption.* Stuttgart: Steiner.

Gabba, E. (1991) *Dionysius and the History of Archaic Rome.* Berkeley, CA: University of California Press.

Gagé, J. (1963) 'Matronalia: essai sur les devotions et les organisations culturelles des femmes dans l'ancienne Rome', *Coll. Latomus*, 60.

Gardner, J. (1986) *Women in Roman Law and Society.* Bloomington, IN: Indiana University Press.

Gersht, R. and Mucznik, S. (1988) 'Mars and Rhea Silvia', *Gerión*, 6: 115–167.

Gianelli, G. (1913) *Il sacerdozio delle Vestali romane.* Florence: Galletti e Cocci.

Giannecchini, G. (1980–1981) 'Seni crines', *AFLPer*, 18(1): 91–92.

Gowers, E. (1992) *The Loaded Table: Representations of Food in Roman Literature.* Oxford: Clarendon Press.

Graf, F. (1992) 'Römische Aitia und ihre Riten: das Beispiel von Saturnalia und Parilia', *MH*, 49: 13–25.

Graf, F. (2000) 'The rite of the Argei', *MH*, 57(2): 94–103.

Grimal, P. (1985) 'Matrona: les lois, les moeurs, le langage', *AFLNice*, 50: 195–203.

Gruen, E. (1968) 'M. Antonio and the trial of the Vestal Virgins', *RhM*, 111: 59–63.

Gruen, E. (1992) *Culture and National Identity in Republican Rome.* London: Duckworth.

Guarducci, M. (1964) 'Vesta sul Palatino', *RM*, 71: 158–169.

Guarducci, M. (1971) 'Enea e Vesta', *Röm. Mitt*, 78: 73–118.

Guarino, A. (1967) 'Manus e potestas', *Labe*, 13: 389–391.

Guizzi, F. (1968) *Aspetti Giuridici del Sacerdozio Romano: Il Sacerdozio di Vesta.* Naples: E. Jovene.

Gutzwiller, K. J. and Michelini, A. N. (1991) 'Women and other strangers: feminist perspectives in classical literature', in J. Hartman and E. Messer Davidow (eds) *(En)Gendering Knowledge.* Knoxville, TN: University of Tennessee Press.

Haastrup, K. (1978) 'The semantics of biology: virginity', in S. Ardner (ed.) *Defining Females.* Oxford: Berg.

Hallett, J. P. (1984) *Fathers and Daughters in Roman Society: Women and the Elite Family.* Princeton, NJ: Princeton University Press.

Hallett, J. P. (1990) 'Perspectives on Roman women', in R. Mellor (ed.) *From Augustus to Nero: The First Dynasty of Imperial Rome.* East Lansing, MI: Michigan State University Press.

Hallett, J. P. (1992) 'Heeding our native informants: the uses of Latin literary texts in recovering elite Roman attitudes toward age, gender and social status', *Classical Views*, NS 36(1): 333–355.

Hampl, F. (1983) 'Zum Ritus des lebendigbegrabens von Vestilinnen', in *Innsbrücker Beiträge zur Kulturwissenschaft*, 12.

Harmon, D. (1978) 'The public festivals of Rome', *ANRW*, 2.16.2: 1440–68.

Harmon, D. (1986) 'Religion in the Latin elegists', *ANRW*, 2.16.3. 1909–1973.

Harries, B. (1989) 'Causation and the authority of the poet in Ovid's *Fasti*', *CQ*, 39: 164–185.

Hawley, R. and Levick, B. (eds) (1995) *Women in Antiquity: New Assessments.* London: Routledge.

Hemker, J. (1985) 'Rape and the foundation of Rome', *Helios*, 12: 41–47.

Hickson, F. (1991) *Roman Prayer Language: Livy and the Aeneid of Virgil.* Stuttgart: B. G. Teubner.

Hill, H. (1961) 'Dionysius of Halicarnassus and the origins of Rome', *JRS*, 51: 88–93.

Hillen, H. J. (2003) *Von Aeneas zu Romulus. Die Legenden von der Gründung Roms; mit einer lateinisch-deutschen Ausgabe der Origo gentis Romanae*. Düsseldorf: Artemis & Winkler.

Hillner, J. (2003) '"Domus", family, and inheritance', *JRS*, 93: 129–145.

Holland, L. (1961) 'Janus and the bridge', *PMAAR*, 21: 313–331.

Holtheide, B. (1980) 'Matrona stolata: femina stolata', *ZPE*, 38: 127–134.

Hommel, H. (1972) 'Vesta und die frührömische religion', *ANRW*, 1: 2.

Hooker, E. M. (1963) 'The significance of Numa's religious reforms', *Numen*, 10: 87–132.

Hopkins, K. (1983) *Death and Renewal: Sociological Studies in Roman History*, vol. 2. Cambridge: Cambridge University Press.

Hug, A. (1933) 'Muria', *RE*, 31: 661–662.

Huth, O. (1946) *Vesta: Untersuchungen zum Indogermanischen Feuercult*. Leipzig: B. G. Teubner.

Jed, S. H. (1989) *Chaste Thinking*. Bloomington, IN: Indiana University Press.

Jehne, M. (1989) 'Die Dictatur optima lege', *ZRG*, 106: 557–572.

Johnson, J. R. (1976) *Augustan Propaganda: The Battle of Actium, Marc Antony's Will, the Fasti Capitolini Consulares, and Early Imperial Historiography*. Los Angeles, CA: University of California Press.

Johnson, J. R. (1978) 'The authenticity and validity of Antony's will', *AC*, 47: 494–503.

Jordan, H. (1886) *Der Tempel der Vesta und das Haus der Vestalinnen*. Berlin: Weidmannsche.

Kehne, P. (1998) 'Augustus und die spolia opima', in T. Hantos and G. A. Lehmann (eds) *Althistorisches Kolloquium aus Anlaß des 70. Geburtstags von Jochen Bleicken, 29–30 November 1996*. Stuttgart: Steiner.

King, U. (1995) *Religion and Gender*. Oxford: Blackwell.

Kleiner, D. E. (1996) *I, Claudia: Women in Ancient Rome*. New Haven, CT: Yale University Press.

Koch, C. (1932) 'Mola Salsa', *RE*, 30: 2516–2517.

Koch, C. (1958) 'Vesta', *RE*, 8 A: 1717–1776.

Koch, C. (1960) *Religio: Studien zu Kult und Glauben der Römer*. Nuremberg: H. Carl.

Kolbe, H. G. (1966–1967) 'Noch einmal Vesta auf dem Palatin', *RM*, 73–74: 74–104.

Korten, C. (1992) *Ovid, Augustus und der Kult der Vestalinnen*. Frankfurt am Main: Peter Lang.

Kraemer, R. (1992) *Her Share of the Blessings*. New York: Oxford University Press.

Lacey, W. K. (1992) 'Patria Potestas', in B. Rawson (ed.) *The Family in Ancient Rome: New Perspectives*. Ithaca, NY: Cornell University Press.

Lacey, W. K. (1996) *Augustus and the Principate*. Leeds: Francis Cairns.

LaFollette, L. (1994) 'The costume of the Roman bride', in J. L. Sebesta and L. Bonfante (eds) *The World of Roman Costume*. Madison, WI: University of Wisconsin Press.

LaFollette, L. and Wallace, R. (1993) 'Latin *seni crines* and the hair style of Roman brides', *SyllClass*, 4: 43–48.

Lambrechts, P. (1946) 'Vesta', *Latomus*, 5: 321–329.

Landi, C. (1950) *P. Ovidi Nasonis Fastorum Liber IV*. Aug. Taurinorum: I. B. Paravia.

Latte, K. (1960) *Römische Religionsgeschichte*. Munich: Beck.

Le Bonniec, H. (1958) 'Le culte de Céres a Rome, des origines a la fin de la République', *Études et Commentaires*, 27: 66–67.

Le Bonniec, H. (1965) *Ovidi Nasonis Fastorum Liber Primus*. Paris: Presses Universitaires de France.

Le Bonniec, H. (1969–1970) *Ovide Les Fastes*, 2 vols. Paris: Presses Universitaires de France.

Lefkowitz, M. and Fant, M. (1992) *Women's Life in Greece and Rome*. Baltimore, MD: Johns Hopkins University Press.

Levene, D. S. (1993) *Religion in Livy*. Leiden: E. J. Brill.

Lewis, R. G. (2001) 'Catilina and the Vestal', *CQ*, NS 51(1): 141–149.

Liddell, H. G. and Scott, R. (1925–) *Greek–English Lexicon*. Oxford: Clarendon Press.

Liebeschuetz, J. H. W. G. (1976) *Continuity and Change in Roman Religion*. Oxford: Clarendon Press.

Lindner, M. M. M. (1995) 'The Vestal Virgins and their imperial patrons: sculptures and inscriptions from the Atrium Vestae in the Roman Forum', PhD thesis, University of Michigan, MI.

Liou-Gille, B. (2002) 'Ops', *PP*, 57(324): 161–195.

Littlewood, R. J. (1980) 'Ovid and the Ides of March (*Fasti* 3.523–710): a further study in the artistry of the *Fasti*', *Studies in Roman Literature and History*, 2: 301–321.

López, F. A. (1991) 'Ilia/Rea Silvia: la leyenda de la madre del fundador de Roma', *EClás*, 33(100): 43–54.

Lovisi, C. (1998) 'Vestale, *incestus* et juridiction pontificale sous la République romaine', *MEFR*, 110: 699–735.

MacBain, B. (1982) *Prodigy and Expiation: A Study in Religion and Politics in Republican Rome*. Brussels: Latomus Revue D'Études Latines.

McClain, T. D. (2004) 'You're going to wear that?: *Innocentia*, behavior, and clothing in the trials of Postumia and Gaius Sempronius in Livy's *Ab Urbe Condita*', (CAMWS, 17 April 2004). Online. Available http://www.loyno.edu/%7Emcclain/tdmcv.htm#p (accessed 19 October 2005).

McDaniel, J. (1995) 'Augustus, the Vestals, and the *signum imperii*', PhD dissertation, University of North Carolina, Chapel Hill, NC.

McDougall, J. (1992a) 'Cassius Ravilla and the trial of the Vestals', *AHB*, 6(1): 10–17.

McDougall, J. (1992b) 'The reputation of Appius Claudius Pulcher, Cos. 143 BC', *Hermes*, 120: 452–460.

McGovern, P. E., Fleming, S. J. and Katz, S. H. (1995) *The Origins and Ancient History of Wine*. Amsterdam: Gordon & Breach.

McKeown, J. C. (1984) 'Fabula proposito nulla tegenda meo: Ovid's *Fasti* and Augustan politics', in A. J. Woodman and D. West (eds) *Poetry and Politics in the Age of Augustus*. Cambridge: Cambridge University Press.

Manthe, U. (2002) 'Testamente', in *RE* 12.1: 182–187.

Marquardt, K. J. and Mommsen, T. (1871–1888) *Handbuch der römischen Alterthümer*. Leipzig: S. Hirzel.

Marshall, A. (1989) 'Ladies at law: the role of women in the Roman civil courts', in C. Deroux (ed.) *Studies in Latin Literature and Roman History*. Brussels: Latomus.

Marshall, B. A. (1985) *A Historical Commentary on Asconius*. Columbia, MO: University of Missouri Press.

Martini, M. C. (1997a) 'Carattere e struttura del sacerdozio delle Vestali: un approccio storico-religioso: Primo parte', *Latomus*, 56(2): 245–263.

Martini, M. C. (1997b) 'Carattere e struttura del sacerdozio delle Vestali: un approccio storico-religioso: Due parte', *Latomus*, 56(3): 477–503.

Martini, M. C. (2004) *Le vestali: Un sacerdozio delle funzionale al 'cosmo' romano*. Brussels: Latomus.

Mattingly, H. *et al.* (eds) (1923–1984) *The Roman Imperial Coinage*, 9 vols. London: Spink.

May, G. (1905) 'Le Flamen Dialis et la Virgo Vestalis', *RE*, 7: 21.

Michels, A. K. (1967) *The Calendar of the Roman Republic*. Princeton, NJ: Princeton University Press.

Middleton, J. H. (1886) 'The Temple and Atrium of Vesta and the Regia', *Archaeologia*, 49: 391–423.

Miles, G. B. (1995) *Livy: Reconstructing Early Rome*. Ithaca, NY: Cornell University Press.

Miller, J. F. (1991) *Ovid's Elegaic Festivals*. Frankfurt am Main: Peter Lang.

Mommsen, T. (1952 [1887]) *Römische Staatsrecht*, 3rd edn. Basel: Schwabe.

Mommsen, T. (1955 [1899]) *Römische Strafrecht*. Graz: Akademische Druck- u. Verlagsanstalt.

Morani, M. (1981) 'Lat. "sacer" e il rapporto uomo-dio nel lessico religioso latino', *Aevum*, 50.

Moreau, P. (1982) *Clodiana Religio: Un proces politique en 61 avant J.C.*. Paris: Les Belles lettres.

Morgan, M. G. (1974) 'Priests and physical fitness', *CQ*, 24: 137–141.

Moyle, J. B. (1912) *Imperatoris Iustiniani Institutionum libri quattor*. Oxford: Clarendon Press.

Mueller, H.-F. (2002) *Roman Religion in Valerius Maximus*. London: Routledge.

Mulroy D. (1988) 'The early career of P. Clodius Pulcher. a re-examination of the charges of mutiny and sacrilege', *TAPhA*, 118: 155–178.

Münzer, F. (1920) *Römische Adelsparteien und Adelsfamilien*. Stuttgart: Metzler.

Münzer, F. (1937–1938) 'Die Römischen Vestalinnen bis zur Kaiserzeit', *Philologus*, 92: 47–67, 199–222.

Murgatroyd, P. (2002) 'The rape attempts on Lotis and Vesta', *CQ*, NS 52(2): 622–624.

Mustakallio, K. (1992) 'The "crimen incesti" of the Vestal Virgins and the Prodigious Pestilence', in T. Viljamaa, A. Timonen and C. Kritzel (eds) *Crudelitas: The Politics of Cruelty in the Ancient and Medieval World*. Krems: Medium Aevum Quotidianum.

Mustakallio, K. (1997) '*Sex Vestae Sacerdotes*: what did they represent?', *Annales Universitatis Turkuensis*, B.219: 73–80.

Nagy, B. (1985) 'The Argei puzzle', *AJAH*, 10: 1–27.

Nagy, G. (1974) 'Six studies of sacral vocabulary relating to the fireplace', *HSPh*, 78: 71–105.

Nash, E. (1968) *Pictorial Dictionary of Ancient Rome*, 2 vols. New York: Praeger.

Nesselrath, H. (1990) 'Die Gens Iulia und Romulus bei Livius (Liv. I, 1–16)', *WJA*, 16: 153–172.

Newlands, C. (1995) *Playing with Time: Ovid and the Fasti*. Ithaca, NY: Cornell University Press.

Nicholas, B. (1962) *An Introduction to Roman Law*. Oxford: Clarendon Press.

Nielsen, I. and Sigismund Nielsen, H. (eds) (1998) *Meals in a Social Context*. Aarhus: Aarhus University Press.

Nock, A. D. and Stewart, Z. (1934) 'Religious developments from the close of the republic to the death of Nero', *CAH*, 10: 465–511.

Nock, A. D. and Stewart, Z. (eds) (1972) *Essays on the Ancient World*. Oxford: Clarendon Press.

Noonan, J. D. (1983) '*Sacra . . . canam:* ritual in the love-elegies of Propertius 4', *CBul*, 59: 43–47.

North, J. (1976) 'Conservatism and change in Roman religion', *PBSR*, 44: 1–12.

North, J. (1989) 'Religion in republican Rome', *CAH*, 7(2): 573–624.

Oakley, S. P. (1998) *A Commentary on Livy, Books VI–X*. Oxford: Clarendon Press.

Ogilvie, R. M. (1970) *A Commentary on Livy: Books 1–5*. Oxford: Clarendon Press.

Pailler, J. M. (1994) 'L'honneur perdu de la Vestale et la garde de Rome', in Y. Le Bohec (ed.) *L'Afrique, la Gaule, la religion à l'époque romaine*. Brussels: Latomus.

Pailler, J. M. (1997) 'Vulcain et les "quasi-vestales"', *Pallas*, 46: 341–346.

Palmer, R. E. A. (1974) 'Roman shrines of female chastity from the caste struggle to the papacy of Innocent I', *RSA*, 4: 112–159.

Parker, H. N. (2004) 'Why were the Vestals Virgins? Or the chastity of women and the safety of the Roman state', *AJP*, 125: 563–601.

Pascal, C. B. (1981) 'October horse', *HSPh*, 85: 261–291.

Paschalis, M. (2001) 'Semina ignis', *AJPh*, 122(2): 201–222.

Pauly, A. *et al.* (eds) (1894–1978) *Real-Encyclopädie der klassischen Altertumswissenschaft*. Stuttgart: Metzler.

Phillips, C. R. (1992) 'Roman religion and literary studies of Ovid's *Fasti*', *Arethusa*, 25: 55–80.

Piganiol, A. (1973) *Scripta Varia*. Brussels: Latomus.

Pigon, J. (1999) 'The identity of the chief Vestal Cornelia (PIR2 C 1481)', *Mnemosyne*, ser. 4, 52(2): 206–213.

Platner, S. and Ashby, T. (1929) *A Topographical Dictionary of Ancient Rome*. London: Oxford University Press.

Pomeroy, S. (1975) *Goddesses, Whores, Wives and Slaves*. New York: Schocken.

Pomeroy, S. (ed.) (1991) *Women's History and Ancient History*. Chapel Hill, NC: University of North Carolina Press.

Porte, D. (1984) 'Les enterrements expiatores à Rome', *Revue de Philologie*, 63: 233–243.

Porte, D. (1985) *L'Etiologie religieuse dans les Fastes d'Ovide*. Paris: Les Belles Lettres.

Porte, D. (2003) 'La "oucherie sacrée" du 15 avril', *Latomus*, 62(4): 773–788.

Pötscher, W. (1998–1999) 'Die Funktion der "Argei"', *ACD*, 34–35: 225–234.

Poucet, J. (1985) *Les Origines de Rome: tradition et histoire*. Brussels: Facultés Universitaires Saint-Louis.

Pouthier, P. (1981) *Ops et la conception divine de l'abondance dans la religion romaine jusqu'à la mort d'Auguste*. Rome: Ecole française de Rome.

Preuner, A. (1864) *Hestia-Vestia*. Tübingen: Lauppschen.

Prosdocimi, A. L. (1991) 'Mola salsa', *ArchClass*, 43(2): 1297–1315.

Prowse, K. (1967) 'The Vestal circle', *G & R*, 14: 174–187.

Purcell, N. (2003) 'The way we used to eat: diet, community, and history at Rome', *AJPh*, 124(3): 329–358.

Radke, G. (1981) 'Die Dei Penates und Vesta in Rom', *ANRW*, 2.17.1: 343–373.

Radke, G. (1986) 'L'enfant de la vierge', in P. M. Martin and C. M Ternes (eds) *Hommage à R. Chevallier*. Tours: Centre de recherches A. Piganiol.

Radke, G. (1993) 'Römische Feste im Monat März', *Tyche*, 8: 129–142.

Rawson, B. (1986, repr. 1992) *The Family in Ancient Rome: New Perspectives*. Ithaca, NY: Cornell University Press.

Rawson, E. (1974) 'Religion and politics in the late second century BC at Rome', *Phoenix* 28: 193 ff.

Richlin, A. (1981) 'Approaches to the sources on adultery at Rome', in H. P. Foley (ed.) *Reflections of Women in Antiquity*. New York: Gordon & Breach.

Richlin, A. (1983) *The Garden of Priapus: Sexuality and Aggression in Roman Humour*. New Haven, CT: Yale University Press.

Richlin, A. (1997) 'Carrying water in a sieve: class and the body in Roman women's religion', in K. L. King (ed.) *Women and Goddess Traditions*. Minneapolis, MN: Fortress Press.

Rosaldo, M. and Lamphere, L. (1974) *Woman, Culture and Society*. Stanford, CA: Stanford University Press.

Roscher W. H. (ed.) (1965 [1884]) *Ausführliches Lexikon der Greichishen und Römischen Mythologie*. Hildesheim: Olms.

Rose, H. J. (1926) 'De Virginibus Vestalibus', *Mnemosyne*, 54: 440–448.

Rose, H. J. (1960) 'Roman religion 1910–1960', *JRS*, 50: 161–72.

Roussel, M. (1982) 'La semence de feu: mythe, institution, cosmobiologie', *Melanges Gareau*. Ottawa: Editions de l'université d'Ottawa, Cahiers des Études anciennes 14.

Rüpke, J. (1994) 'Ovids Kalendarkommentar: zur Gattung der libri fastorum', *A&A*, 40: 125–136.

Rüpke, J. and Glock, A. (2005) *Fasti sacerdotum*, 3 vols. Stuttgart: Steiner.

Ryberg, I. S. (1955) *Rites of the State Religion in Roman Art. MAAR*, 22.

Saller, R. (1986) 'Patria Potestas and the stereotype of the Roman family', *Continuity and Change*, 1: 7–22.

Saller, R. (1994) *Patriarchy, Property and Death in the Roman Family*. Cambridge: Cambridge University Press.

Samter, E. (1894) 'Vestalinnenopfer', *RM*, 9: 25–133.

Santinelli, I. (1904) 'Alcune questioni attinenti ai riti delle vergini Vestali: "Vesta aperit"', *Riv. Fil*, 30: 255–262.

Santinelli, I. (1906) 'La condizione giuridica delle Vestal', *Rivista di Filologia*, 32: 63–82.

Saquete, J. C. (2000) *Las Vírgines Vestales*. Madrid: Consejo Superior de Investigaciones Científicas.

Sawyer, D. F. (1996) *Women and Religion in the First Christian Centuries*. London: Routledge.

Scardigli, B. (1997) 'Servi privati delle Vestali', in M. Moggi and G. Cordiano (eds) *Schiavi e dipendenti nell'ambito dell' 'oikos' e della 'familia'*. Pisa: ETS.

Scardigli, B. (2003) 'Vestali integrante nella società romana', *SHHA*, 21: 97–104.

Scheid, J. (1978) 'Les prêtres officiels sous les empereurs julio-claudiens', *ANRW*, 2.16.1: 610–654.

Scheid, J. (1986) 'Le flamine de Jupiter, les Vestales et le général triomphant: variations romaines sur le thème de la figuration des dieux', *TR*, 7: 213–230.

Scheid, J. (1992a) 'Myth, cult and reality in Ovid's *Fasti*', *PCPhS*, 38: 118–131.

Scheid, J. (1992b) 'The religious roles of Roman women', in P. Schmitt-Pantel (ed.) *A History of Women in the West*. Cambridge, MA: Belknap Press of Harvard University Press.

Scheidel, W. (1996) *Measuring Sex, Age and Death in the Roman Empire: Explorations in Ancient Demography*, *JRA*, SS 21. Ann Arbor, MI: University of Michigan Press.

Schmittlein, R. (1965) 'Matra et Matruona', *RIO*, 17: 190.

Scholz, U. W. (1993) 'Consus und Consualia', in *Fest-Schrift für Walter Pötscher*. Horn: Berger.

Schwarz, K. (1941) 'Der Vestakult und seine Herkunft', PhD dissertation, Heidelberg University, Germany.

Scullard, H. H. (1980) *History of the Roman World from 753 to 146 BC*. London: Routledge.

Scullard, H. H. (1981) *Festivals and Ceremonies of the Roman Republic*. Ithaca, NY: Cornell University Press.

Shaw, B. (1987) 'The age of Roman girls at marriage: some reconsiderations', *JRS*, 77: 30–46.

Sherwin-White, A. N. (1966) *The Letters of Pliny: A Historical and Social Commentary*. Oxford: Clarendon Press.

Shotter, D. (1989) *Tacitus Annals IV*. Warminster: Aris & Phillips.

Siebert, A. V. (1995) 'Quellenanalytische Bemerkungen zu Haartracht und Kopf- schmuck römischer Priesterinnen', *Boreas*, 18: 77–92.

Siekveking, R. (1924) 'Palladion', in *Ausfürliches Lexicon der Griechischen und Römischen Mythologie*. Hildesheim: Olms.

Simon, E. (1990) *Die Götter der Römer*. Munich: Hirmer Verlag.

Sirianni, F. A. (1984) 'Was Antony's will partially forged?', *AC*, 53: 236–241.

Sissa, G. (1990) 'La verginità materiale: Evanescenza di un oggetto', *Quaderni Storici*, 75: 740–756.

Spaeth, B. (1996) *The Roman Goddess Ceres*. Austin, TX: University of Texas Press.

Staples, A. (1998) *From Good Goddess to Vestal Virgin*. London: Routledge.

Stehle, E. (1989) 'Venus, Cybele and the Sabine women: the Roman construction of female sexuality', *Helios*, 16(2): 143–164.

Stehouwer, P. G. (1956) *Etude sur Ops et Consus*. Groningen: J. B. Wolters.

Stein, A. and Petersen, L. (eds) (1952–1966) *Prosopographia Imperii Romani*. Berlin: Walter de Gruyter.

Storchi Marino, A. (1991–1994) 'Il rituale degli Argei tra annalistica e antiquaria', *AIIS*, 12: 263–308.

Strack, P. (1931) *Untersuchungen zur römischen Reichsprägung des zweiten Jahrhunderts*, 1: 72–75, 185–190, Stuttgart: W. Kohlhammer.

Syme, R. (1958) *Tacitus*, 2 vols. Oxford: Clarendon Press.

Szemler, G. J. (1986) 'Priesthoods and priestly careers in Ancient Rome', *ANRW*, 2.16.3: 2314–2331.

Tatum, W. J. (1990) 'Cicero and the *Bona Dea* scandal', *C. Phil*, 85: 202–208.

Temporini, H. and Haase, W. (eds) (1972–) *Aufstieg und Niedergang der römischen Welt*. Berlin: Gruyter.

Thomas, J. C. (1961) 'Accusatio Adulterii', *Iura*, 12(5): 65–80.

Thulin, C. O. (1906) *Die etruskische Disciplin*. Darmstadt: Wissenschaftliche Buchgesellschaft.

Torelli, M. (1995) 'Il pane di Roma arcaica', *in Nel nome del pane*. Bolzano: Associazione Homo Edens.

Toynbee, J. M. C. (1971) *Death and Burial in the Roman World*. London: Thames & Hudson.

Treggiari, S. (1991) *Roman Marriage*. Oxford: Clarendon Press.

Van Deman, E. B. (1908) 'The value of the Vestal statues as originals', *AJA*, 12: 324–342.

Van Deman, E. B. (1909) *The Atrium Vestae*. Washington, DC: The Carnegie Institute.

Vanggaard, J. (1971) 'On Parilia', *Temenos*, 7: 90–103.

Vanggaard, J. (1979) 'The October Horse', *Temenos*, 15: 81–95.

Vanggaard, J. (1988) *The Flamen: A Study in the History and Sociology of Roman Religion*. Copenhagen: Copenhagen Museum Tusculum Press.

Versnel, H. (1992) 'The festival for *Bona Dea* and the Thesmophoria', *G & R*, 39: 31–55.

Versnel, H. (1993) *Inconsistencies in Greek and Roman Religion 2. Transition and Reversal in Myth and Ritual*. Leiden: E. J. Brill.

Vidén, G. (1993) *Women in Roman Literature: Attitudes of Authors under the Early Empire*. Göteborg: Acta Universitatis Gothoburgensis.

von Blumenthal, A. (1938) 'Zur römischen Religion der archaischen Zeit–i. Zur *captio* der Vestalinnen', *RhM*, 87: 268–269.

Wagenwoort, H. (1966) 'Auguste et Vesta', in M. M. J. Heurgon, G. Picard and W. Seston (eds) *Mélanges d'archaeologie, d'épigraphie, et d'histoire offerts à Jérôme Carcopino*. Paris: Hachette.

Wallace-Hadrill, A. (1987) 'Time for Augustus: Ovid, Augustus and the *Fasti*', in M. Whitby, P. Hardie and M. Whitby (eds) *Homo Viator: Classical Essays for John Bramble*. Bristol: Bristol Classical.

Wardman, A. (1982) *Religion and Statecraft among the Romans*. London: Granada.

Watson, P. (1983) 'Puella and Virgo', *Glotta*, 61: 119–143.

White, K. D. (1995) 'Cereals, bread and milling in the Roman world', in J. Wilkins, D. Harvey and M. Dobson (eds) *Food in Antiquity*. Exeter: Exeter University Press.

Wildfang, R. S. L. (1999) 'The Vestal Virgins' ritual function in Roman religion', *C & M*, 50: 227–234.

Wildfang, R. S. L. (2001) 'The Vestal Virgins and annual public rites', *C & M*, 52: 223–255.

Wildfang, R. S. L. (2003) 'Why were the Vestals Virgin?', *Hommages à Carl Deroux (Collection Latomus)*, 4: 557–564.

Wilkins, J., Harvey, D. and Dobson, M. (eds) (1995) *Food in Antiquity: A Survey of the Diet of Early Peoples*. Exeter: Exeter University Press.

Williams, G. (1991) 'Vocal variations and narrative complexity in Ovid's Vestalia: *Fasti* 6.249–468', *Ramus*, 20: 183–204.

Wiseman, T. P. (1989) 'Roman legend and oral tradition', *JRS*, 79: 129–137.

Wissowa, G. (1924) 'Vesta', in *Ausfürliches Lexicon der Griechischen und Römischen Mythologie*, 6. Hildesheim: Olms.

Wissowa, G. (1958) *RE*, vol. 8A.2.

Wissowa, G. (1971 [1912]) *Religion und Kultus der Römer*. Munich: Beck.

Worsfold, T. C. (1932) *The History of the Vestal Virgins of Rome*. London: Rider.

Wright, R. (1995) 'Vesta: a study on the origin of a goddess and her cultus', PhD dissertation, University of Washington, WA.

York, M. (1986) *The Roman Festival Calendar of Numa Pompilius*. Frankfurt am Main: Peter Lang.

Zhuravlev, D. (ed.) (2002) *Fire, Light and Light Equipment in the Graeco-Roman World*. Oxford: Archaeopress.

Ziolkowski, A. (1998–1999) 'Ritual cleaning-up of the city', *AncSoc*, 29: 191–218.

Index

Related titles from Routledge

Girls and Women in
Classical Greek Religion
Matthew Dillon

'Highly recommended ... no collection of classical, religious or gender studies would be complete without it.' – *Choice*

'A work of considerable scholarship, and one on which the author is to be congratulated.' – *Minerva*

'It makes accessible a substantial body of disparate material.' – *JACT Review*

'Wisely, this important contribution to understanding the female dimension of ancient religion does not make the worship of goddesses a central concern.' – *International Review of Biblical Studies*

It has often been thought that participation in fertility rituals was women's most important religious activity in classical Greece. Matthew Dillon's wide-ranging study makes it clear that women engaged in numerous other rites and cults, and that their role in Greek religion was actually more important than that of men. Women invoked the gods' help in becoming pregnant, venerated the god of wine, worshipped new and exotic deities, used magic for both erotic and pain-relieving purposes, and far more besides.

Clear and comprehensive, this volume challenges many stereotypes of Greek women and offers unexpected insights into their experience of religion. With more than fifty illustrations, and translated extracts from contemporary texts, this is an essential resource for the study of women and religion in classical Greece.

ISBN10: 0–415–20272–8 (hbk)
ISBN10: 0–415–31916–1 (pbk)

ISBN13: 978–0–415–20272–5 (hbk)
ISBN13: 978–0–415–31916–4 (pbk)

Available at all good bookshops
For ordering and further information please visit:
www.routledge.com

Related titles from Routledge

Women and Religion in the First Christian Centuries

Deborah F. Sawyer

Women and Religion in the First Christian Centuries focuses on religion during the period of Roman imperial rule and its significance in women's lives. It discusses the rich variety of religious expression, from pagan cults and classical mythology to ancient Judaism and early Christianity, and the wide array of religious functions fulfilled by women. The author analyses key examples from each context, creating a vivid image of this crucial period which laid the foundations of western civilization.

ISBN10: 0–415–10748–2 (hbk)
ISBN10: 0–415–10749–0 (pbk)

ISBN13: 978–0–415–10748–8 (hbk)
ISBN13: 978–0–415–10749–5 (pbk)

Available at all good bookshops
For ordering and further information please visit:
www.routledge.com